D0659326

CIVIL RESISTANCE

WHAT EVERYONE NEEDS TO KNOW®

CIVIL RESISTANCE

WHAT EVERYONE NEEDS TO KNOW®

ERICA CHENOWETH

OXFORD
UNIVERSITY PRESS

OXFORD
UNIVERSITY PRESS

Oxford University Press is a department of the University of Oxford. It furthers
the University's objective of excellence in research, scholarship, and education
by publishing worldwide. Oxford is a registered trade mark of Oxford University
Press in the UK and certain other countries.

"What Everyone Needs to Know" is a registered trademark of
Oxford University Press.

Published in the United States of America by Oxford University Press
198 Madison Avenue, New York, NY 10016, United States of America.

© Oxford University Press 2021

All rights reserved. No part of this publication may be reproduced, stored in
a retrieval system, or transmitted, in any form or by any means, without the
prior permission in writing of Oxford University Press, or as expressly permitted
by law, by license, or under terms agreed with the appropriate reproduction
rights organization. Inquiries concerning reproduction outside the scope of the
above should be sent to the Rights Department, Oxford University Press, at the
address above.

You must not circulate this work in any other form
and you must impose this same condition on any acquirer.

Library of Congress Cataloging-in-Publication Data
Names: Chenoweth, Erica, 1980– author.
Title: Civil resistance : what everyone needs to know / Erica Chenoweth.
Description: New York, NY: Oxford University Press, 2021. |
Includes bibliographical references and index.
Identifiers: LCCN 2020050583 (print) | LCCN 2020050584 (ebook) |
ISBN 9780190244392 (hardback) | ISBN 9780190244408 (paperback) |
ISBN 9780190244422 (epub)
Subjects: LCSH: Civil disobedience. | Nonviolence.
Classification: LCC JC328.3 .C4739 2021 (print) |
LCC JC328.3 (ebook) | DDC 303.6/1—dc23
LC record available at https://lccn.loc.gov/2020050583
LC ebook record available at https://lccn.loc.gov/2020050584

3 5 7 9 8 6 4 2
Paperback printed by LSC Communications, United States of America
Hardback printed by Bridgeport National Bindery, Inc., United States of America

To the States or any one of them, or any city of the States,
   Resist much, obey little,
   Once unquestioning obedience, once fully enslaved,
   Once fully enslaved, no nation, state, city of this earth,
   ever afterward resumes its liberty.

                  —Walt Whitman, *Leaves of Grass*

TABLE OF CONTENTS

3. Civil Resistance and Violence from within the Movement   **142**

LIST OF FIGURES AND TABLES

ACKNOWLEDGMENTS

This book was long in the making, and I express my deepest thanks to all those who helped me to get it over the finish line. I thank David McBride and Oxford University Press for the motivation to set some thoughts to paper in this volume, as well as Holly Mitchell, Leslie Johnson, Liz Davey, and Bob Land for their editorial assistance.

I thank my colleagues and friends for their continual encouragement—and supportive critiques—of my work. Particular thanks go to my colleagues at Harvard—especially Archon Fung, Iris Bohnet, and Dean Doug Elmendorf for providing me the time to complete this manuscript during my first two years in Cambridge. My Kennedy School colleagues Cornell Brooks, Dara Cohen, Marshall Ganz, Nancy Gibbs, Douglas Johnson, Jennifer Lerner, Samantha Power, Sushma Rahman, Hannah Riley-Bowles, Mathias Risse, Dani Rodrik, Eric Rosenbach, Maya Sen, Wendy Sherman, Kathryn Sikkink, Stephen Walt, and Jay Ulfelder are constant sources of encouragement and food for thought. I am also deeply grateful to all of the students in my course, Civil Resistance: How It Works, which I taught during the Spring and Fall semesters in 2020. Our stimulating and lively discussions helped me to sharpen the ideas presented in this book. I especially thank Zesean Ali for his careful review of the completed manuscript, as well as the five 2020 HKS Topol Fellows—Anikó Bakonyi, Enrique Gasteazoro, Niku Jafarnia, Morgan Pratt, and Inayat Sabhikhi—who provided incisive and constructive comments on each chapter.

I am grateful to Richard Jackson and the University of Otago's National Centre for Peace and Conflict Studies, which provided me with a William Evans Fellowship for writing, engagement, and reflection during New Zealand's summer of 2016. I am also grateful for the chance to have presented these ideas at many different fora over the years, which has allowed me to understand "what everyone wants to know" about civil resistance. I appreciate opportunities to discuss this work among scholars at Uppsala University, University of Oslo, Harvard University, Columbia University, University of Massachusetts–Amherst, and Wellesley College. I also appreciate many productive conversations and debates with activists at numerous community-centered events in Denver, Little Rock, London, Berkeley, Oakland, Nashville, Cambridge, Santa Fe, The Hague, Nairobi, Portland, Memphis, Boston, New York, and beyond.

When I started the book, I was a professor at the Josef Korbel School of International Studies at the University of Denver. I thank my colleagues there, especially Debbi Avant, Marie Berry, Rachel Epstein, Cullen Hendrix, Oliver Kaplan, Julia Macdonald, Tricia Olsen, and Timothy Sisk, for their support. I also thank Cassy Dorff and Evan Perkoski for numerous enriching conversations that helped me think through this book while they were fellows there. And I thank my Korbel School students, particularly Joel Day, Sooyeon Kang, Maria Lotito, Pauline Moore, Jonathan Pinckney, and Christopher Shay, for engaging so eagerly with the topic of civil resistance—as well as for their assistance in developing the data used to support this and other projects. I am also grateful to Allyson Hodges and Mohammed Otaru for their help assembling references and summaries of cases.

I also wish to convey special thanks to the International Center on Nonviolent Conflict (ICNC), which in the past has provided me resources for data collection, access to scholars and activists interested in civil resistance, and exceedingly fertile ground for a lifetime of learning and discovery on this topic. I am especially grateful for numerous exchanges with and support from Hardy Merriman, Maciej Bartkowski, and Peter Ackerman. I am also grateful for the opportunity to learn from scholar-practitioner specialists like Howard Barrell, Shaazka Beyerle, Victoria Bin-Hui, Steve Chase, Howard Clark, Veronique Dudouet, John Gould, Tom Hastings, Mary Elizabeth King, George Lakey, Rev. James Lawson, Jason Macleod, Ivan Marović, Michael Nagler, Sharon Nepstad, Jamila Raqib, Chaiwat Satha-Anand, Janjira Sombatpoonsiri, Gene Sharp, Maria Stephan, Stellan Vinthagen, Stephen Zunes, and many others. I truly stand on the shoulders of giants.

I am immensely grateful for the keen editorial skills of E. J. Graff, who graciously stepped in as an editor at the end of the drafting process. E. J.'s professionalism, substantive expertise on the topic, penchant for accessible writing, and encouragement were essential to finishing the project. Thanks as ever to Charlie Porter, who helped pull the references into shape in the final hour. John Ahlquist organized a group to read and comment on the final manuscript, and I thank him along with Sarah Barr, Martin Epson, Hunter Gatewood, Mike Uy, and Sherry Wong for their helpful suggestions on the draft.

Next, I thank the millions of activists around the world whose tireless and dedicated work provides the inspiration for my own. There are many organizers and activists who have shared with me vital lessons and continually motivated my work in this area with a sense of humanity and urgency. This has taught me more than I ever could have learned from books, articles, films, and music about historical cases. They are too numerous to count, but they know who they are. I am particularly indebted to Farida, Viri, Jeannette, Max, Carlos, Paulina, Isabella, Nelini, Eli, Erin, Rachel, Paul, David, D.J., Katrina, Cybelle, Austin, Anthony, Dominique, Kazu, Kifah, Marium, Ankur, Daniel, George, LaTosha, Evan, Julie, Nada, Srdja, Rivera, Jamie, Victor, Dana, Jessica, Adam, Edna, Roger, Kathy, Alice, Greg, Stephen, Kai, and countless others who have humbled, challenged, and encouraged me over the past few years. I'm in awe of you, and I thank you for your unwavering insistence on justice. I will forward any royalties generated from this book to the activist organizations and communities who are on the frontlines and have taught me so much in the struggle for a better world.

And, as always, I am most grateful for my loving family and the countless ways that they have supported me throughout my life and career. To Kathe and Courtney—thanks for always being there, no matter what. To Spring, Richard, and Julia—thanks for being such curious, enthusiastic, and loving supporters. To Andrea and Bo— thanks for supporting me and always helping me to not take myself too seriously. To Grammy—thank you for your unconditional love and for nurturing my passions for learning, service, and justice. To my parents, Richard and Marianne, to whom I owe everything—thank you for your constant encouragement, love, and faith in me. And to Zoe, love of my life, intellectual heroine, partner in all things, and perpetual inspiration for my moral imagination—thank you for giving me the courage, motivation, clear-eyed and incisive feedback, time, and support to follow through on this modest contribution to justice.

As I finished drafting this manuscript, the global COVID-19 pandemic claimed the life of my beloved grandfather, Alan Abel. Throughout his life he was motivated by a commitment to justice, fairness, and service to others. His spirit was with me as I completed the manuscript, even as I remained constantly aware of the profound loss his passing created for my grandmother, my family, and the many lives he touched. This book is my tribute to his memory. I hope the result would have made him proud.

PREFACE

In June 2006, I stumbled into the study of nonviolent resistance as a skeptic.[1] Like many others in my field of international relations, I was concerned primarily with questions about why people pursue political violence—terrorism, communal violence, civil war, and insurgency—and how to contain it. Most of us start from the assumption that people turn to violence because it works. Numerous examples from history suggest that violence is the only way to seriously contest power—and that violence often pays. The French Revolution, the Algerian Revolution, the Chinese Revolution, the Vietnam War, the Soviet-Afghan War, and many other examples suggest that armed insurrection by militarily inferior forces has often defeated powerful states.

But that summer I attended a workshop organized by the International Center on Nonviolent Conflict that introduced me to civil resistance, its theoretical and strategic dimensions, and the ways people power movements had accomplished in many cases what violent rebellion could not. The books and articles we read made the claim—sometimes implicit, other times explicit—that civil resistance was as effective or even more effective than armed struggle in achieving major political concessions. These arguments were largely based on cases like Serbia, where the Otpor movement had initiated the downfall of Slobodan Milošević; Poland, where the Solidarity movement had successfully challenged the entrenched Communist Party; the Philippines, where the People Power movement had removed Ferdinand Marcos from power; and the US civil rights movement, where lunch counter sit-ins, boycotts, and marches had initiated the desegregation of many southern cities and created the base for a broader campaign.

I thought these cases were probably exceptional. For every case like Serbia, Poland, or the Philippines, I could recall a case like Tiananmen Square, Hungary 1956, or Burma 1988 in which popular uprisings were crushed. After all, even Mohandas Gandhi's effort to expel the British from India had ushered in a period of violent turmoil, punctuated by India's bloody partition with Pakistan. Moreover, I suspected that successful cases could be explained by other factors—weak states incapable of suppressing unarmed actors; international actors willing to patronize nonviolent movements; moderately democratic institutions that accommodated them; social, economic, or demographic characteristics that predisposed some populations to embrace nonviolent action where others would turn to violence; or plain old government incompetence in shutting down a popular uprising.

Maria Stephan, who was at the workshop, challenged me to develop a research approach that could prove my skepticism. So she and I teamed up to design a study that could assess—systematically and empirically—the relative success rates of nonviolent and violent mass movements, as well as the underlying causes for these successes. Drawing on thousands of source materials—including encyclopedias, bibliographies, case studies, historical documents, news reports, and other scholars' published lists of popular revolutions—we developed a list of cases of nonviolent mass mobilization featuring at least one thousand observed participants seeking maximalist (country-level) goals from 1900 to 2006. We did not count smaller campaigns, or reform movements.

After two years of data collection and vetting with subject experts, I ran the numbers. I was shocked. More than half of the campaigns that had relied primarily on nonviolent resistance succeeded, whereas only about a quarter of the violent ones did. Moreover, when I ran a variety of regression models that included features of the regime as control variables, I could find no systematic statistical association between structural features of the country and the outcomes of the campaigns. Generally speaking, nonviolent campaigns were succeeding more often than violent campaigns *despite* a variety of structural factors—like geography, wealth, military power, or demographics—that we typically associate with predetermining such outcomes.

Stephan and I published our findings in 2011, which coincided with the height of the Arab Spring.[2] In the ten years since, many scholars have further developed research on how civil resistance campaigns develop, why they succeed or fail, and how they change the societies in which they emerge, producing important new debates and consensus about key questions. What's more, scores of new mass movements around the world have expanded the range of places where civil resistance is shaping history. This has refined our understandings of how nonviolent resistance works.

Although many cases don't make headline news, the past decade—2010 to 2020—has seen more revolutionary nonviolent uprisings around the world than in any other period in recorded history.[3] In fact, there have been more such campaigns in the first two decades of the twenty-first century than there were during the entire twentieth century. From Armenia to Sudan, from Belarus to India, from Chile to Hong Kong, from Thailand to Burkina Faso, large-scale movements have fundamentally reshaped the political landscapes of dozens of countries around the world.

The United States has been part of these trends as well. The past ten years has seen a dramatic increase in mass mobilizations in the US. From Occupy Wall Street to United We Dream, from Black Lives Matter to Standing Rock, from the Women's March to Families Belong Together, from #MeToo to Protect the Results, from Justice for Breonna Taylor to Joy to the Polls, people power has affected the past decade of American politics in unprecedented ways.

During this time—due in part to my research interests, but mostly to compelling moral crises—I have evolved from being a detached skeptic of civil resistance to becoming an invested participant in nonviolent movements. I now study the history and practice of resistance with much greater urgency, for the sake of my own democracy and in solidarity with human rights defenders around the world. In particular, crackdowns against recent movements have led me to study more intently the historical campaigns led by oppressed peoples all around the world, as well as the lessons of Black, Indigenous, and queer people leading ongoing campaigns for justice in the US. As a participant or ally in antiracism campaigns, the movement for immigrant rights, the sanctuary movement, the climate movement, the LGBTQ+ rights movement, and the democracy movement in the United States, I've learned a great many lessons from skilled activists and organizers. As a result, my own understanding has grown about the ways that people power campaigns develop, unfold, resolve, and transform. These lessons provide both inspiration and cautionary tales. This book may therefore read both like an appeal and a warning.

In particular, several emerging patterns are cause for concern for people invested in achieving social, political, and economic justice. The first is a disturbing global wave of rising authoritarianism, with countries like India, Poland, Hungary, Turkey, Brazil, Thailand, the Philippines, and the United States all backsliding toward autocracy over the past decade. In these and many other countries, aspiring demagogues have rolled back or eliminated civil rights protections for marginalized groups, assaulted judicial independence, threatened political opponents with imprisonment, bullied or persecuted journalists, carried out brazen attacks on elections and the voting process, and turned a blind eye to armed vigilantes attacking their domestic opponents. Indeed, this slide toward authoritarianism is exactly what has provoked so many mass movements around the world to rise up in defense of democracy and basic rights.

The emergence of digital authoritarianism itself is a cause for particular concern. The digital age has created the semblance of social connection, while empowering autocrats to better surveil, control, and disrupt perceived political opponents. China, Iran, Russia, and Saudi Arabia have used digital tools to silence opponents, spread propaganda and disinformation, and sow polarization and division among their rivals. So, too, have regimes in smaller countries, like Togo and Bahrain, relied on digital surveillance to curtail civil society.

Recent trends among mass movements also show some cause for concern. Even though nonviolent resistance is now ubiquitous as a leading strategy for creating change worldwide, the data also suggest that governments are defeating revolutionary nonviolent movements more often than in prior decades.

Data on these movements suggest that this apparent decline in movement effectiveness may be related to changes in the ways that these movements have developed and unfolded in the digital age. There are four key changes in particular, which I discuss in more depth in Chapter 5:

- Contemporary movements are smaller in size than their historical counterparts.
- Contemporary movements seem to rely more on street demonstrations than other methods of nonviolent action, such as mass noncooperation, like work stoppages, walkouts, rolling strikes, boycotts, or general strikes. Symbolic displays of resistance do not necessarily weaken the opponent's sources of power.
- Contemporary movements tend to embrace "leaderless resistance" instead of establishing accountable leadership structures that can assist with coordination and strategy.[4]
- Contemporary movements are increasingly characterized by less disciplined nonviolent action. This is important because fringe violence tends to alienate supporters, polarize societies, and increase harsh repression by the state rather than expanding the movement's bases of support and alliances or building transformative power.

Moreover, there are some persistent myths about whether and how civil resistance works, which also might undermine its general appeal and effectiveness. These myths include the ideas that:

- Nonviolent action is weak and passive.
- Violence is the quickest and most reliable path to liberation.
- Nonviolent resistance is impossible or ineffective against extreme injustice.
- Nonviolent resistance cannot produce genuine social, political, or economic transformation.
- People use nonviolent resistance—and promote it to others—when they have convenient access to power, and that this method of resistance is unavailable to marginalized communities.

- Movements win when their causes are righteous, regardless of which technique of struggle they use.

Despite these common myths and critiques about nonviolence, civil resistance is an idea whose time, again, has come. This book engages directly with questions that observers, colleagues, students, activists, friends, journalists and the general public have asked me about civil resistance over the years I've spent studying it. I try to lend a perspective grounded in synthesizing the best evidence available to help further dispel myths and misconceptions about the empirical record of nonviolent resistance, and to reveal its potential power.

How to Read This Book

I hope this book can be a continuing conversation. The question and answer format is dictated by the What Everyone Needs to Know® series itself, but this format has a few key benefits. First, the Table of Contents reflects the pressing questions people have asked me regarding what civil resistance is, how it works, and why it's so important for everyone to understand. I've done my best in each section to address what we know—and what we don't know—about them. Second, the book unfolds in a fairly sequential way, with each chapter picking up where the last one left off. This means that you may encounter concepts and historical examples in multiple parts of the book when they are relevant to multiple questions. However, you can also jump around to different sections that address your most pressing questions without necessarily missing out on vital background.

This book is a basic empirical introduction to what I think everyone should know about civil resistance, discussing patterns of civil resistance in fairly general terms. The book focuses on global trends, patterns, and dynamics rather than in-depth accounts of specific historical examples of nonviolent resistance. Although I use examples of civil resistance campaigns to illustrate different points from time to time, I defer to other experts for those interested in specific knowledge about in-depth theoretical and conceptual discussions, as well as detailed knowledge about the workings of particular campaigns. The book is not a chronicling of everything that *is known* about civil resistance—many in-depth studies are available that parse various findings, nuances, and controversies, and I point readers in the direction of these resources throughout the book. I urge serious students to avail themselves of the full bibliography; those who want a few additional citations will find the "Selected Resources" section sufficient. The book is designed to serve those who are curious about people power but have never studied it, and to offer some novel insights for seasoned veterans of nonviolent movements as well.

Second, this book is not intended to be the last word on the subject. Civil resistance is an emergent phenomenon, and the world is changing rapidly. Ten years from now, one might write an entirely different book on the subject, revising many of the tables, charts, and substantive conclusions I've drawn from them. The book focuses on what practical implications we can draw from historical cases and global trends. The best way to read this book, then, is to see whether the text resonates with your own observations, intuitions, and experiences; to take what is useful and leave the rest.

Third, many of the ideas I offer in this book have been published in different articles, op-eds, blog posts, and other formats. I note that in endnotes where it applies. Much of my knowledge emerges from my repeated interactions with frontline activists and intellectual giants in the field, some of whom I name in the acknowledgments. But this is the first time I've put my thoughts together in one place, and in a format intended to reach a large audience. I am grateful to those whose knowledge and contributions to the field have cultivated my own, and those who have encouraged me to synthesize and communicate these insights more broadly.

And fourth, despite the Q&A format, I don't necessarily intend for anyone to read this book as a prescriptive manual on how to *do* civil resistance. People who are waging nonviolent struggle are always in the best position to decide for themselves the best course of action to take. There is no generalizable recipe for effective resistance anyway. But there are distinct lessons from the past that could inform the present and the future. Therefore, although I don't give advice, I do tell readers what I make of the available evidence, with caveats appropriate to each instance. Where there are low levels of confidence about certain findings, I try to articulate that clearly. Where there is fairly robust agreement in the field about certain findings, I likewise express degrees of consensus.

The book has a progressive political orientation, which is deliberate. My hope is that readers will come away feeling more informed about civil resistance—its role in human history, its role in our world today, its controversies, and the empirical realities of its strengths and limits. My goal is to serve those seeking broader understanding about the realistic alternatives to violence in our world, to counter those whose view of civil resistance is shaped more by polemic than by real-world evidence, and to make people who read this book feel more equipped, prepared, and empowered to make a difference in the global fight for justice.

CIVIL RESISTANCE

WHAT EVERYONE NEEDS TO KNOW®

CIVIL RESISTANCE

A BRIEF INTRODUCTION

Ring the bells that still can ring
Forget your perfect offering
There is a crack, a crack in everything
That's how the light gets in.

—Leonard Cohen

Civil resistance is a form of collective action that seeks to affect the political, social, or economic status quo without using violence or the threat of violence against people to do so. It is organized, public, and explicitly nonviolent in its means and ends. This book summarizes some of the main takeaways from history about the ways that civil resistance campaigns have formed, strategized, organized, and mobilized.

This chapter introduces you to the impressive history of civil resistance over the millennia, but it also grapples with some of the key controversies that persist regarding how to define civil resistance and how to understand its impact on the world around us. But before we discuss this technique's development over the centuries, let's define our terms.

Why call it "civil resistance" and not something else?

I've titled the book *Civil Resistance* because that term best captures the historical legacy out of which people have developed and refined the technique. The term itself has only been in use for about 100 years. Mohandas Gandhi coined the term while struggling against British colonialism in India. Over the years, many academics and practitioners—from Gene Sharp to Rev. James Lawson—came to adopt the term to describe this emergent phenomenon.

Civil resistance is a method of active conflict in which unarmed people use a variety of coordinated, noninstitutional methods—strikes, protests, demonstrations, boycotts, alternative institution-building, and many other tactics—to promote change without harming or threatening to harm an opponent. In English, the term "civil" derives from the Latin *civis*, meaning "citizen." In contemporary usage, the term "civil" conjures a sense of public responsibility, in which people collectively assert their rights and needs on behalf of their communities. The term "resistance" derives from the Latin *resistere*. *Sistere* is a strong form of the verb stare, "to stand." The prefix *re* adds intensity to the word.[1] Through civil resistance, people from all walks of life come together to take a stand, with great intensity and strength, and demand justice and accountability of others.

Some civil resistance methods can be, and often are, incredibly disruptive and confrontational—like gluing oneself to a major thoroughfare, deliberately overcrowding jail cells, or refusing to vacate an official's office. People or institutions targeted by nonviolent mobilization often feel deeply threatened; such resistance jeopardizes their power, status, and comfort without giving them many straightforward options for resolving the conflict. They respond accordingly, with attempts to suppress nonviolent dissidents using arrests, imprisonment, targeted killings, torture, and other forms of coercion. Those using nonviolent resistance often expect and prepare for violence by their opponents. But nonviolent dissidents avoid using violence themselves, because violence is less effective than these other tactics against entrenched armed power. Not all proponents of civil resistance believe in or endorse pacifism, though some do. And not all pacifists use civil resistance, though some do.

Because this approach is so often misunderstood, it's worth examining each element of the definition a little more closely.

First, civil resistance is a *method of conflict*—an active, confrontational technique that people or movements use to assert political, social, economic, or moral claims. Civil resistance actively promotes conflict, creating disruption and amassing power to affect, alter, or transform the status quo. It is about fighting back when people believe they have been mistreated by powerful individuals, organizations, governments, or political systems, and building up new systems that address underlying injustices. Civil resistance is an antidote to passivity and apathy.

Second, civil resistance is waged by *unarmed civilians without directly harming the opponent*. The people who are making changes are ordinary people equipped with their own creativity and ingenuity—along with their various sources of social, economic, cultural, and political leverage—with the goal of influencing their communities and societies. Also civil resistance undertakes actions that are not violent. For most scholars and practitioners, the "civil" part of "civil resistance" explicitly means rejecting armed or violent actions in this mode of conflict. Of course, definitions of "nonviolent" and "violent action" are themselves controversial. For our purposes, people waging civil resistance do not use weapons or physical attacks like punching, trampling, assaulting, or killing while they are directly confronting their opponents. But the term "civil" does not necessarily mean "friendly," "respectful," or "polite." On the contrary, scholars typically classify interruption, rude gestures, turning one's back, heckling, shaming, stigmatizing, and ostracizing opponents as nonviolent behaviors that, when used in combination with other methods, can impose costs on their opponents and their supporters.

Third, civil resistance involves *coordinating a diverse set of methods*. This approach to struggle is deliberate and premeditated, and purposefully uses a variety of methods—like strikes, protests, go-slows, stay-aways, occupations, noncooperation, and/or the development of alternative economic, political, and social institutions, among others—to build power and leverage from below. Just because people are protesting in the streets does not mean they are engaging in civil resistance. Spontaneous, improvised street actions that are not coordinated across various civic groups as part of a broader strategy rarely have staying power or capacity for long-term transformation. Nor does organizing a one-off protest or strike qualify a group as part of a civil resistance movement. Civil resistance is neither spontaneous nor purely symbolic, but rather involves a protracted struggle with the same coordinated groups—civic associations, youth groups, unions, religious institutions, and other civil society groups—working together over time toward the same goal.

Fourth, civil resistance involves *noninstitutional actions*. In other words, civil resistance is deliberately disobedient, acting outside of existing institutions, laws, and larger systems that have become widely viewed as unjust or illegitimate. Civil resistance often works to openly challenge, contest, undermine, subvert, divide, or replace such institutions. Voting, holding campaign rallies, writing and collecting petitions, lobbying, calling one's member of Congress, and organizing legal advocacy campaigns are typically not considered civil resistance—since all of these actions occur within the system. Some tactics that *are* considered civil resistance, because they take place outside official channels, include the following: holding an unauthorized or illegal march, violating "unjust laws," holding strikes and work stoppages, tax refusals, and direct actions such as blockading banks, boycotting products, or occupying a politician's office. All are typically considered extra-institutional. There are hundreds—if not thousands—more examples.

Of course, in practice, many civil resistance campaigns combine both institutional and unauthorized action. The US civil rights movement, for instance, involved various forms of civil resistance—marches, bus boycotts, lunch counter sit-ins, consumer boycotts, silent processions, public prayer and worship, mass demonstrations, the deliberate overloading of jails, and many other methods—alongside more traditional political methods like issuing public statements, legal advocacy, lobbying the White House and congressional elites, and supporting antiracist candidates for public office. However, movements that rely *only* on institutional action, like rallying for political candidates or writing letters to public officials, are typically not considered civil resistance movements.

Finally, the goal of civil resistance is to *affect the status quo*. Civil resistance tends to seek change—often revolutionary change—within a broader society. Civil resistance tends to have a popular or civic quality, involving groups or coalitions working together to make collective claims about political, economic, social, religious, or moral practices and concerns—on behalf of a larger group. For instance, Black activists during the civil rights movement did not act to secure rights for movement participants alone; rather, they sought to eliminate the entire system of segregation, racism, and white supremacy in the United States, for everyone. The Sudanese Revolution, which toppled the dictatorship of Omar al-Bashir in April 2019, eliminated a brutal regime to bring democratic change to all Sudanese people.

In reviewing what civil resistance is, understanding what it isn't can be useful. First, civil resistance is not the use of a single technique, like protest. Recall that civil resistance tends to involve many different nonviolent techniques—like demonstrations, strikes, stay-aways, blockades, the creation of alternative institutions, and other forms of noncooperation—sequenced intentionally to dislodge entrenched power. The technique implies organization and coordination. Civil resistance campaigns often have individuals or coalitions in leadership roles, helping to coordinate and guide the campaign's strategy. Protest can be part of civil resistance, but protest can also happen spontaneously, without significant organization, and without a civil resistance campaign's shared goals, strategies, or organizing committees. People who take to the streets to respond to a particular instance of brutality or an offensive and newly announced policy are voicing their rage. But they are not necessarily engaged in civil resistance, which implies continual, coordinated, collective action using a mix of techniques toward a decisive outcome. In fact, as we see later in this volume, isolated protests' effects are typically quite different than the effects of protests that are associated with broader civil resistance campaigns.

Second, civil resistance is not necessarily about peaceful conflict resolution. In a very real sense, civil resistance constructively *promotes* conflict. That said, conflict resolution has a role in many civil resistance campaigns—either as a way for movements to deal with their own internal disputes and conflicts, or as a way for them to prepare for bargaining once they bring their opponents to the negotiation table. After the Zapatista movement in Chiapas, Mexico, moved away from armed struggle and embraced political resistance in 1994, for example, members have developed a number of internal processes for handling conflict related to and within the movement, including its own autonomous judicial processes. And in Poland in 1989, one of the ways that the Solidarity movement dislodged the Communist government was the movement's historic Round Table Talks with Communist Party elites. In these, between February and April 1989, over thirty Solidarity and opposition movement leaders succeeded in persuading the government to allow free and independent trade unions, to establish a presidency instead of rule by the Communist Party's general secretary, and to establish an elected senate. Several months later, Solidarity swept the national elections, deposing the Communist Party from its authoritarian rule over Poland. It was the beginning of the end of Soviet-aligned Communist control over Eastern Europe. And Solidarity managed to bring the government to the table only because it had run such a successful civil resistance campaign over nine years, including strikes, factory shutdowns, protests, establishing underground universities, and printing and circulating an illegal newspaper called *Solidarność* (*Solidarity*), from which the movement got its name.

Third, civil resistance is not necessarily equivalent to nonviolence, although it might use that approach. Commitment to the concept of nonviolence, rather than civil resistance, grows from moral arguments about how nonviolent action is the most righteous approach to political action—both its means and its ends. Principled nonviolence prohibits the use of violence on moral grounds. Similarly, pacifism is a principled position that unconditionally rejects the use of violence, seeing violence as immoral. While many pacifists are convinced that nonviolent alternatives work better than violent ones, their primary commitment is to the moral righteousness of the means and the justice of the ends.

That's not quite true for those committed to civil resistance; they may be primarily concerned with strategy, not morality. Most proponents of civil resistance see this technique as a functional alternative to violence, and therefore they tend to be interested in when and whether civil resistance works—remaining agnostic about whether it is morally superior to violence. That said, many people who study or advocate strategic nonviolent action are themselves pacifists, even though they frame their discussion of civil resistance in utilitarian terms—hoping to convince nonpacifists of its viability.

However, many related terms could have made a decent alternate title for this book, including nonviolent mobilization, nonviolent action, nonviolent struggle, people power, unarmed insurrection, "war without weapons," strategic nonviolence, nonviolent struggle, political defiance, Satyagraha, positive action, nonviolent revolution, or mass uprisings. Many people use these terms somewhat synonymously, although others see crucial differences between these concepts. Although I do use these terms largely synonymously through this book, I've avoided the word "nonviolent" in the title because many people tend to interpret that term as equivalent to words like "passive," "submissive," "inactive," "peaceful," or "resigned."

Doing so conjures in many readers' minds such possibilities as resignation, submission, passivity, or playing nice in the face of profound injustice. That's not what this book is about.

How has civil resistance developed?

Civil resistance techniques have been recorded as long as humans have been keeping histories—from ancient Egypt to ancient Greece to the early Roman Empire. For instance, the first recorded strike in human history happened in around 1170 BC, when Egyptian laborers building burial chambers for King Ramses III refused to work until they received stable food rations.[2] Many early Christians refused Roman imperial military conscription, usually paying for this objection with their lives.[3] The first known feminist rebellion in North America was a sixteenth-century civil resistance campaign by Iroquois tribal women to end unregulated warfare within the Iroquois nation. Men exclusively controlled declarations of war, along with other political powers. Iroquois women coordinated a sex and childbearing strike, refused to harvest and prepare crops, and refused to produce moccasins necessary for war-making. Ultimately Iroquois women won the power to veto war declarations.

Even though people have used civil resistance methods throughout history, the technique did not have a name until Mohandas Gandhi popularized the term "civil resistance" a century ago.

Yet the root of civil resistance entered the lexicon in 1848 when writer and philosopher Henry David Thoreau delivered a lecture in Concord, Massachusetts, called "Resistance to Civil Government." The lecture was published as a pamphlet in 1849, which came to be known as *On the Duty of Civil Disobedience*. In that tract, Thoreau argued that citizens ought to disobey government laws or policies that violated their own moral conscience—to avoid becoming agents of injustice themselves. He also began to theorize about transgressive, noninstitutional action he believed to be occasionally necessary to restore basic freedoms, liberties, and justice.

Thoreau was writing in opposition to slavery and to the Mexican-American War of 1846–1848, which abolitionists and anti-imperialists generally perceived to be an immoral conquest. But Thoreau's writings inspired several generations of dissidents and philosophers who followed him—not least among them was Gandhi, who read Thoreau during his first time in jail.

When he encountered Thoreau's writings, Gandhi was already a skilled practitioner and scholar of resistance, having been inspired by numerous worker and anti-colonial rebellions taking place around the world. But he was really the innovator of civil resistance as a way to prosecute organized, civilian-led conflicts against militarily superior opponents. From 1893 to 1914, Gandhi worked as an attorney in South Africa, where he was troubled by discrimination, segregation, and other racist policies that applied to nonwhite inhabitants of South Africa under the colonial system. At various points, he was kicked off a train for trying to board in first class, pushed off a footpath reserved for whites, and ordered to remove his turban—and he also witnessed many other forms of discrimination against migrant laborers. He wanted to end these injustices and developed a series of practices he called *satyagraha* (truth-force or soul-force) as a method of refusing to cooperate with injustice while developing just alternatives. Gandhi had also been impressed by the anti-tsarist rebellion of 1905 in Russia, during which hundreds of thousands of Russians in the city and country alike had revolted against Tsar Nicholas II through a nonviolent general strike and various other demonstrations, leading the tsar to establish some democratic reforms. Gandhi was also deeply affected by the writings of Russian novelist and pacifist Leo Tolstoy, with whom he carried out a multiyear correspondence about the morality and necessity of renouncing violence in all its forms.

In 1907 Gandhi began his first official satyagraha to demand the repeal of the racist Asiatic Registration Laws (the Black Act), which required all Indians in South Africa to register and be fingerprinted by colonial authorities and to carry registration papers at all times. Gandhi organized migrant Indian workers to disobey the law, picket colonial offices, travel without registration papers, and refuse to work. In doing so, he experimented with what he called "passive resistance"—popular refusal to cooperate with unjust laws without using violence against the opponent—to lead communities to advocate for dignity and rights. Over the course of seven years, thousands of striking Indians were imprisoned, including Gandhi himself. But the laws were repealed in 1914, proving to Gandhi that nonviolent collective dissent could be an effective method even for people living under colonial rule.

By 1915, having achieved the repeal of the Black Act, Gandhi returned to India and began to imagine a new movement against British colonial rule there. It was there that Gandhi gave the technique the names many now use to describe it—civil resistance, nonviolence, nonviolent action, and nonviolent struggle. Organizing numerous satyagrahas against British colonialism in the 1920s, Gandhi built a mass following and a national leadership for noncooperation, civil disobedience, and self-determination. This culminated in the 1930 Salt March, during which Gandhi and tens of thousands of Indians marched 240 miles from his Ahmedabad retreat to the Arabian Sea to resist a monopolistic colonial law that prevented Indians from making and consuming their own salt. When the entourage arrived at the sea, Gandhi encouraged his followers to deliberately violate the law by boiling their own salt as a method to both resist colonial rule and claim self-sufficiency in producing the commodity. The movement escalated to include strikes, mass protests, mass noncooperation with various colonial laws, and a campaign to develop economic self-sufficiency so that Indians could free themselves from dependency on colonial products. Although Gandhi's movement against British colonial rule in India had many shortcomings, it showed millions of people worldwide that unarmed civilians engaged in collective noncooperation could wield enormous power.

Many people today have limited understandings of what Gandhi achieved, remembering only his strict moral positions against violence or meat-eating. Gandhi's messages still appear on bumper stickers, posters, and T-shirts—leaving skeptics to see his work as noble but naïve, inspiring but ineffective, laudable but futile.

Such cynics might be right if Gandhi's moral commitments were the only reasons he favored the use of civil resistance against the British Raj. But in reality, Gandhi was a fierce pragmatist. He abandoned the term "passive resistance" after realizing the term conveyed a sense of resignation and acquiescence, rather than active struggle and defiance. He also wanted to dissociate the technique from woman suffragists in England, who had begun to use the term "passive resistance" to describe militant tactics, including protestor violence, that Gandhi did not recognize as consistent with the path of satyagraha. Gandhi began to use the term "civil resistance" as a sort of mashup between "civil disobedience" and "passive resistance."

Although many people before Gandhi had used techniques of civil resistance sporadically, they had rarely done so in full consideration of its long-term potential as a political strategy for liberation. Gandhi's singular contribution to the theory and practice of nonviolent action was his self-consciousness about producing a comprehensive technique that combined noncooperation against oppression with the creation of alternative institutions that would alleviate poverty, discrimination, and injustice.

Other groups struggling against oppressive systems took notice of Gandhi's work. In the early twentieth century, Black activists and clergy from the United States began a decades-long interchange between the United States and India, hoping to draw inspiration and know-how from the Indian experience.[4] These activists were themselves experienced in building capacity for mass mobilization to confront injustice, but they were eager to learn from the experiences and successes of others struggling for equality. And so numerous Black pacifist activists traveled to India to learn from Gandhi and his successors. Martin Luther King Jr. had been exposed to Thoreau's *Civil Disobedience* while a college student at Morehouse, and he had learned about Gandhi's Salt March during a sermon by Howard University president Rev. Dr. Mordecai Johnson while King was a student at Crozer Theological Seminary. Several other prominent civil rights leaders also educated themselves as to the potential applications of civil resistance to destroy systems of racism in the United States.

Among these was James Lawson, a Methodist minister from Berea, Ohio, who visited Gandhi's old ashram in the 1950s to learn and develop new strategies for resisting injustice in the US. As a conscientious objector during the Korean War, Lawson had spent eighteen months in federal prison, reading, praying, and reflecting on Gandhi's practices. He studied Gandhi's autobiography and developed his own understanding of the steps necessary to prepare, provoke, and shepherd a successful liberation movement among ordinary Black people who lived their lives under constant threat of lynching and police brutality, discrimination, and the Jim Crow laws that enforced segregation across the American South. Gandhi's Salt March inspired Lawson and others to hold workshops on the theory and practice of nonviolent resistance in Nashville starting in 1958. Many local university and high school students attended these workshops and began planning and organizing a campaign to desegregate downtown Nashville. In late 1959 and early 1960, students—including John Lewis, C. T. Vivian, Marion Barry, James Bevel, Diane Nash, and Bernard Lafayette, and other key figures of the civil rights movement—launched a campaign that combined lunch counter sit-ins, marches, strikes, boycotts of downtown businesses, and voluntary imprisonment to overwhelm Nashville's jails and courtrooms. Their campaign ended enforced segregation in Nashville within six months. Ella Baker, Fannie Lou Hamer, Bayard Rustin, Vincent Harding, and others also drew from these experiences to catalyze people power and organized resistance against legalized segregation, racist voter suppression, economic injustice, sexism, militarism, and other social ills in the United States.

These experiments with civil resistance techniques likewise inspired many other anticolonial and antiracism struggles around the world, in spite of evidence that Gandhi himself harbored racial prejudice and discriminatory views.[5] Although many African anticolonial movements in the nineteenth and mid-twentieth century used both unarmed and armed struggle to fight for independence, people power movements in Ghana, Zambia, and elsewhere won independence largely through civil resistance.[6] Similarly, through an unrelenting combination of protests, civilian-led boycotts, strikes, and other methods of nonviolent action, Black South Africans successfully confronted and ended legal apartheid in that country. Moreover, many observers argue that the most effective period of the Palestinian National Movement was during the first eighteen months of the First Intifada (1987–1993), a struggle waged by a broad-based coalition of Palestinian civic groups that coordinated various nonviolent methods to push for Palestinian self-determination and independence from Israel.[7]

While the technique of nonviolent action has diffused globally, intellectuals and scholar-practitioners took notice. Pacifist thinkers from the 1920s and 1930s traveled to India to learn from Gandhi's experience. Upon return from India, the American philosopher and peace activist Richard B. Gregg wrote the first book outlining a systematic theory of nonviolent resistance. Called *The Power of Non-Violence*, it was published in 1934. The book influenced numerous peace activists throughout the 1930s and 1940s, including

A. J. Muste, a leading pacifist thinker in the United States; and Aldous Huxley, then leader of the United Kingdom's Peace Union. It also influenced many other academics in the aftermath of World War II, who saw the global arms race and advent of the nuclear age as major justifications to theorize realistic alternatives to violence.[8] This included feminist thinkers, like Barbara Deming, who wrote numerous books on the power of nonviolent action to both resist oppression and create a just and inclusive future.[9]

Gene Sharp, whom many consider to be the father of the field of civil resistance studies, served nine months in prison for protesting the draft during the Korean War. After working with various pacifists and researchers, he received his Ph.D. from Oxford University. From his work there, he wrote a three-volume opus, *Theory of Nonviolent Action*, published in 1973. The book articulated his own theory of how well-organized and well-prepared civilians could successfully build power, mobilize, and wage unarmed struggle—a topic we return to in Chapter 2. He identified commonalities across historical cases—such as Gandhi's movement, Dutch and Norwegian resistance to Nazi occupation, and the Russian Revolution—and generated a list of 198 methods of nonviolent action. That list—and Sharp's theories on nonviolent action—remain a prominent resource for many students and practitioners of nonviolent action today.[10]

Many of Sharp's writings were subsequently translated and disseminated around the world. Numerous organizations—such as the Albert Einstein Institution, the International Center on Nonviolent Conflict, Nonviolence International, and others— emerged during the 1990s and 2000s to systematize the theory and practice of nonviolent action. These developments jump-started an era in which activists and organizers around the world could access a proliferation of training manuals, documentaries, oral histories, and web resources about how nonviolent resistance works.

Today, a quick Google search of trainings, organizations, toolkits, manuals, and online bibliographies about civil resistance would turn up hundreds or thousands of relevant entries. Organizations like the International Center on Nonviolent Conflict have supported scholarly research on nonviolent resistance, held workshops for activists to meet with scholars, designed online courses, and amassed huge resource libraries for those interested in the topic. In the United States alone, groups like the BLACKOut Collective, Beautiful

Trouble, Training for Change, and the Sunrise Movement offer trainings, field guides, and collective wisdom for people learning how to wage struggle and organize their communities to build power.[11] More broadly, groups like Nonviolence International and CANVAS offer trainings and workshops for people learning how to organize for change and wage nonviolent struggle.

How successful is civil resistance?

The answer to this question might surprise you: compared with the alternatives, nonviolent resistance is a stunningly successful method of creating change.[12] Let's first look at the aggregate success rates of 627 revolutionary campaigns—violent and nonviolent—over the past 120 years. Revolutionary campaigns involve large-scale mobilizations seeking to topple governments or create new nation-states. In other words, these are hard to achieve. Violent revolutions are those in which the revolutionaries relied on armed insurgency, urban guerilla attacks, assassination campaigns, and other forms of armed struggle to achieve their goals—like the Russian Revolution of 1917, North Vietnamese insurgents' opposition to US military forces from 1960 to 1975, and the Cuban Revolution of 1959. Nonviolent revolutions are those in which the revolutionaries are unarmed, and relied primarily on methods like protests, demonstrations, strikes, nonviolent sit-ins and occupations, and mass noncooperation—like the Honduran pro-democracy movement of 1944, the Danish Resistance against Nazi occupation of 1940–1943, and South Korea's April Revolution of 1960. You can see a list of all 627 revolutionary campaigns in the Appendix of this book. For our purposes, I define "success" as the overthrow of a government or territorial independence achieved decisively because of the campaign within a year of its peak.[13] Applying this standard definition of success to both types of revolutions, over 50% of the nonviolent revolutions from 1900 to 2019 have succeeded outright—while only about 26% of the violent ones did (Figure 0-1).

That's a staggering figure that undercuts a widespread view that nonviolent action is weak and ineffectual while violent action is strong and effective. In Chapter 2, I explain why campaigns of civil resistance have succeeded more often than their violent counterparts—often overcoming incredibly difficult barriers to do so. And if you're wondering about the fates of such countries after their revolutions

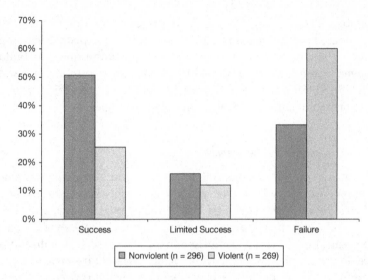

Figure 0-1 Success Rates of Revolutions, 1900–2019

end—like popular well-being, stability, or transformative political change—stay tuned for that discussion in Chapter 5.

What are some foundational examples of civil resistance?

Civil resistance has been used for centuries, in many situations, and toward many goals. Table 0-1 provides a brief summary of some highlights in the development of civil resistance as an approach. This list is not comprehensive by any means. But it should give you the impression that civil resistance has played an important part in world history—even if it can be difficult to conjure examples off the top of one's head.

American Revolution

American colonists waged a civil resistance campaign against British imperial rule from 1763 to 1775, before the Revolutionary War. While many people associate the American Revolution with the armed insurrection of George Washington's Colonial Army against King George's British regulars, this armed revolt didn't happen until after an extended period of effective civil resistance that made it all but impossible for the British government to govern

Table 0-1 A Partial List of Significant Examples of Nonviolent Resistance

Period	Locations	Description	Iconic Figures (where applicable)
1700s BC	Egypt	Midwives resist genocide	Shiphrah and Puah
1170s BC	Egypt	Laborers strike against Ramses III for food rations	
750s BC	Rome	Antiwar intervention by Sabine women against two warring factions of Rome	Sabine women
494 & 449 BC	Rome	Commoners in Rome engage in a general strikes and mass noncooperation (including secession) to win the right to elections and civil law	Plebians
AD 200s–300s	Roman Empire, including Numidia (contemporary Algeria)	Anti-Roman military conscription	Early Christians, Tertullian, Origen, Maximilianus, Martin of Tours
1100s–1309	Southern France	Anti–Roman Catholic Church	Cathars
1200s–1600s	Europe	Protestant Reformation	Waldensians, Taborites, Anabaptists, Mennonites, German Baptist Brethren, Quakers, Diggers
1500s	France	Antityranny	Étienne de la Boétie
1540s–1615	Americas	Anticolonialism	Bartolomé de las Casas, Guaman Poma de Ayala
Early 1600s	Iroquois Nation	Antiwar	Iroquois women
1765–1775	American colonies	American Revolution	John Adams, Benjamin Franklin, James Madison, Thomas Jefferson, Quakers

(continued)

Table 0.1 Continued

Period	Locations	Description	Iconic Figures (where applicable)
1832	Jamaica	Christmas Day Rebellion	Samuel Sharpe
1700s–1861	United States	Abolition movement	Harriet Tubman, Frederick Douglass, Sojourner Truth, William Wells Brown, Maria Stewart, Harriet Beecher Stowe, William Lloyd Garrison, Frances Ellen Watkins Harper
1815–1860s	United States / Europe	Peace movement	David Low Dodge, Noah Worcester, Henry Holcombe, Charles Whipple, Julia Ward Howe, Jean-Jacques de Sellon, Alexis de Tocqueville, Victor Hugo, Leo Tolstoy, Bertha von Suttner, Frédéric Passy
1871–1912	United States / United Kingdom	Labor movement	Eugene Debs, Helen Keller, A.J. Muste
1848–1929	United States / United Kingdom	Woman suffrage	Frances Ellen Watkins Harper, Mary Ann Shadd Cary, Mary Church Terrell, Nannie Helen Burroughs, Ida B. Wells, Sojourner Truth, Elizabeth Cady Stanton, Susan B. Anthony, Emma Goldman, Jane Addams, Emmeline Pankhurst, Sylvia Pankhurst
1867–1880	New Zealand	Anticolonialism	Te Whiti-o-Rongomai
1905	Russia	Revolution of 1905	Leo Tolstoy
1905–1911	Iran	Persian Constitutional Revolution	Mohammed Mossadeq

Table 0.1 Continued

Period	Locations	Description	Iconic Figures (where applicable)
1870s–1916	Ireland	Independence movement	Ladies Land League, Arthur Griffith
1909–1968	United States	Civil rights movement	Ida B. Wells, W. E. B. Du Bois, James Farmer, George Houser, Andrew Johnson, Rosa Parks, Martin Luther King Jr., Bayard Rustin, Fannie Lou Hamer, Ella Baker, Thurgood Marshall, John Lewis, Barbara Johns, James Lawson, Harry Belafonte
1914–1919	Global	Anti–World War I movement	Helen Keller, A. J. Muste, Bertrand Russell, Clive Bell, Wilfred Owen, Siegfried Sassoon
1919–1922	Egypt	Egyptian independence movement	
1919–1949	India	Indian independence movement	Mahatma Gandhi
1919–1940	United States	Workers' rights movement	W. E. B. Du Bois, A. J. Muste, A. Philip Randolph, United Auto Workers
1929–1930	Nigeria	Igbo Women's War	Madame Nwanyeruwa, Madam Mary Okezi, Ikonnia Nwannedia Nwugo
1920s–1940s	Ghana, Nigeria, Zambia	African independence movements	Kwame Nkrumah, Jaja Wachuku, Obafemi Jeremiah Oyeniyi Awolowo, Kenneth Kaunda
1930–1934	Northwest Frontier of India (contemporary Khyber Pakhtunkhwa in Pakistan)	Khudai Khidmatgar / Muslim Pashtun movement	Badshah Khan

(continued)

Table 0.1 Continued

Period	Locations	Description	Iconic Figures (where applicable)
1941–1945	Worldwide	Anti–World War II movement	Richard Gregg, A. Philip Randolph, Dorothy Day, Women's International League for Peace and Freedom, Ralph DiGia
1942	Norway	Anti-Nazi movement	Norwegian teachers
1943	Germany	Rosenstraße protests	German wives of Jewish men
1945–1980s	United States, worldwide	Antinuclear movement	Robert Oppenheimer, Albert Einstein, Andrei Sahkarov, Plowshares movement, Clamshell Alliance, György Konrád
1948–1994	South Africa	Anti-apartheid	Nelson Mandela, Desmond Tutu, Mkhuseli Jack
1965–1970	United States	California grape workers' strike and boycott	César Chávez, Dolores Huerta
1965–1973	United States	Anti–Vietnam War movement	Women Strike for Peace, Daniel Berrigan, David Dellinger, Students for a Democratic Society
1968	Worldwide	Student-led protests against imperialism, economic inequality, and authoritarianism	
1977–1980s	Argentina, Brazil, Chile, Uruguay	Latin American pro-democracy movements	Mothers of the Plaza De Mayo
1980–1989	Poland	Solidarity	Lech Walesa, Adam Michnik
1983–1986	Philippines	People Power Revolution	Cory Aquino
1988–1990	Burma	Pro-democracy movement	Aung San Suu Kyi
1989	China	Tiananmen Square	Student protesters

Table 0.1 Continued

Period	Locations	Description	Iconic Figures (where applicable)
1989	Czechoslovakia	Velvet Revolution	Václav Havel
1991	Latvia, Estonia, and Lithuania	Singing Revolution	Pro-democracy, pro-independence groups
1991	Soviet Union	Defense against a military coup	Boris Yeltsin
2000–2010	Serbia, Georgia, Ukraine, Kyrgyzstan, Belarus	Color Revolutions	Srdja Popović, Ivan Marović
2010–2013	Tunisia, Egypt, Yemen, Bahrain, Libya, Syria	Arab uprisings	April 6 Movement, Tawwakkol Karman, Ouided Bouchamaoui
2011	Worldwide	Occupy Wall Street	
2014–present	United States	Movement for Black Lives / Black Lives Matter	Alicia Garza, Patrice Cullors, Opal Tometi
2016–2020	United States	Resistance against Donald Trump	Women's March; Protect the Results; Choose Democracy; Hold the Line
2019–present	Hong Kong	Pro-democracy movement	
2019–2020	Lebanon, Chile, Iraq, Bolivia, India, Pakistan, Kashmir	October Revolutions	

Sources: Global Nonviolent Action Database; various others (see appendix).

the American colonies. Methods included boycotts of British goods; refusal to consume British-made goods; noncooperation laws requiring colonists to export raw materials from the American colonies to Britain; colonists' mass refusals to serve on juries under Crown-appointed judges; destruction of Crown property, as in the Boston Tea Party, and the creation of parallel economic, judicial, and political institutions—including the Continental Congress itself. In fact, after all this resistance, by the time the Second Continental Congress approved the Declaration of Independence and authorized a Continental Army, the colonies were already de facto independent.[14] As John Adams wrote in a letter to Thomas Jefferson, "What do we mean by the revolution? The war? That was no part of the revolution; it was only an effect and a consequence of it. The revolution was in the minds of the people, and this was effected from 1760 to 1775, in the course of fifteen years, before a drop of blood was shed at Lexington."[15]

Abolitionists

Abolitionists used civil resistance techniques against slavery throughout the nineteenth century in Britain, the Caribbean, and the United States. Coordinated work stoppages were a common form of unarmed collective action among people who were enslaved in Haiti, the Dominican Republic, and Jamaica, who used the withholding of their labor to secure more humane conditions from plantation owners. For instance, in Jamaica in 1831–1832, enslaved people organized a massive strike—a coordinated refusal to work— to press their demands that exploitative plantation owners begin paying wages and allowing greater freedoms, an action that became the Christmas Rebellion, also known as the Baptist War. Ultimately sixty thousand of Jamaica's three hundred thousand enslaved people joined in, making it the largest such uprising in the British West Indies. Although the organizers intended to use peaceful strikes, some groups armed themselves and began fighting British Dragoons and paramilitary groups. The uprising collapsed after eleven days, after which the last living rebels surrendered. In horrific reprisals, plantation owners killed at least five thousand enslaved people during the rebellion and its aftermath. And yet the rebellion—along with the plantocracy's disproportionate response—inspired and horrified people throughout Great Britain and intensified support for the abolitionist cause. Within two years, the British government passed a partial emancipation law; four years later, it fully abolished chattel slavery in all of its colonies. The Jamaican uprising was neither the first nor the last campaign in which people collectively withheld labor to win powerful concessions.

Nationalist and anti-colonial movements

People on every continent have undertaken struggles to reclaim their rights and autonomy from colonial authorities. For instance, during the Indian independence movement of 1919–1947, civil resistance techniques were used by both Indian Hindus like Gandhi and lesser-known Pashtun Muslims like Badshah Khan. Khan recruited a hundred thousand members to a "nonviolent army," who swore an oath to wage nonviolent struggle against British rule in contemporary Pakistan.

Indeed, history is full of notable anticolonial resistance during which people in Asia and Africa embraced civil resistance by refusing to purchase products imported from colonizing countries, pay imperial taxes, or mine local resources for export—including the Nigerian independence movement (1945–1950), the East Timorese independence movement (1974–1999), and the Ghanaian independence movement (1890s–1950s). In the last example, national independence leader Kwame Nkrumah followed Gandhi's example by experimenting with what he called "positive action."[16]

More recent self-determination movements have often relied heavily on techniques of civil resistance. That's true for the Palestinian national movement during the First Intifada (1987–1989), the Kosovo Albanian self-determination movement (1989–1999), and the ongoing movement against Indian occupation in Kashmir.[17] Civil resistance campaigns against military occupation have occurred in places as diverse as Nazi-occupied Denmark (1940–1943), Soviet-occupied Czechoslovakia (1967–1968), and Morocco-occupied Western Sahara (1999–present).[18] And many secession movements have embraced civil resistance techniques, including the ongoing Southern Yemen secession movement (2007–present) and the Catalan movement in Spain (2014–present).

Labor movement

One of the most potent methods of civil resistance is the refusal to work in unjust conditions. The global labor movement has long used civil resistance, among other techniques, to demand fair working conditions. Beginning in the nineteenth century, organized labor action worldwide effectively established minimum wages, pressed for laws against exploitation of child workers, established two-day weekends, capped daily work hours, demanded paid benefits and paid holidays, and more. Civil resistance has been one of labor's powerful tools for promoting and expanding labor rights, particularly as strikes or work stoppages became popular. A recent study suggests that the repeated use of general strikes in Europe led to Western European governments' concessions on issues like pensions.[19] There are many more recent examples. For instance, in 2018, hotel workers in the Unite Here Local 26 union in Boston won historic concessions from Marriott International. Enduring rain, wind, and snow on the picket line for forty-six days, they successfully used their collective power to win greater wages, better benefits, and job security protections. In 2018 and 2019, teachers across nine US states used strikes, walkouts, and protests to demand higher wages, increased support for staff, smaller classrooms, and other essential work protections. In West Virginia, Virginia, Colorado, California, and Arizona, these "#RedforEd" strikes and walkouts resulted in pay increases for teachers and staff, as well as a variety of other concessions. And during the global pandemic of 2020, medical staff, grocery store workers, and public servants walked out of their jobs to effectively demand more concerted government action on COVID-19; personal protective equipment like masks, gloves, and gowns; hazard pay; and paid sick leave.

Peace, antiwar, and anti-nuclear movements

In the 1960s and 1980s, the US peace movement and the US and European antinuclear movements used civil resistance methods. For instance, in the late 1970s and 1980s, the Clamshell Alliance, a coalition of peace and antinuclear groups in the United States, routinely undertook civil disobedience actions like members chaining themselves to nuclear installations' fences, setting up human blockades around nuclear power plants, holding mass demonstrations, and even occasionally dismantling or destroying equipment at nuclear facilities.

Racial justice movements

Movements for racial justice have emerged and grown in many different political, economic, and social systems, using civil resistance methods. As I mentioned earlier, Black students, clergy, workers, and civic groups relied on the technique during the US civil rights movement (1953–1968) and in South Africa by Black organizers and allies in their struggle against apartheid (1990–1994).[20] More recently, in the United States, the Black Lives Matter movement has used civil resistance techniques to demand an end to police or vigilante killings of Black people, to protest and the criminal justice system's failure to prosecute the perpetrators and to demand justice to Black communities affected by police brutality. Since it emerged in 2013 after the acquittal of Trayvon Martin's killer, Black Lives Matter and the Movement for Black Lives have deployed innovative civil resistance techniques and strategies against racism, police brutality, and structural violence against Black life in the United States. During the summer of 2020, after the killings of Ahmaud Arbery, Breonna Taylor, and George Floyd, tens of millions of Americans mobilized in what was the largest and broadest mass mobilization in recorded US history.[21]

Feminist movements

Beginning in the mid-nineteenth century and continuing to today, women's rights movements have used civil resistance in nearly every country in the world. In India over the past decade, antiviolence groups demand accountability and justice for victims of rape and femicide, organizing massive marches, pressuring police to investigate sexual assault allegations, and confronting alleged perpetrators with sit-ins and rallies. Started in the United States by organizer Tarana Burke in 2006, the worldwide #MeToo movement has encouraged survivors of sexual violence to speak up and identify their perpetrators, using such methods as coming out as a survivor of sexual abuse, naming perpetrators, organizing legal support funds for survivors, and engaging in rallies, protests, and vigils to fight patriarchal and sexist norms of silence and complicity in many different social settings.

Environmental justice movements

People increasingly use civil resistance to demand environmental justice. Indigenous communities across the world—from Brazil to West Papua to Standing Rock—have taken powerful stands against corporate exploitation of land, the privatization of natural resources, pollution, and the violation of autonomy and land rights. For instance, in 1999–2000 activist Oscar Olivera led a successful campaign in Bolivia against attempts to privatize rainwater in Amazon rainforests populated by Indigenous communities, a campaign called the Cochabomba Water Wars. And in 2016 in the United States, tens of thousands of people descended on the Standing Rock Indian Reservation in North Dakota and South Dakota to support the Standing Rock Sioux and help them to defend their territory against a planned Keystone XL Pipeline project, which was expected to destroy the natural ecosystem and poison their local water sources. Organizations like Greenpeace regularly deploy nonviolent direct action and civil disobedience to insist on environmentally sustainable approaches and to disrupt and prevent big corporations from extracting minerals and fossil fuels without regard for the climate or the local communities affected by hazardous by-products. The transnational Extinction Rebellion movement has challenged global inaction on climate change, bursting onto the scene on November 16, 2019, with a series of rallies, bridge and highway blockades, and acts of civil disobedience in London. Similarly, Greta Thunberg and countless other youth activists have faithfully refused to attend school on Fridays, engaging in a series of #FridaysForFuture strikes worldwide. In the United States, the Sunrise Movement uses various forms of creative nonviolent resistance to build a broader youth constituency to wage nonviolent struggle for environmental justice.

Movements for safety and security

Further, a number of different movements around the world have used civil resistance to demand civil stability, safety, and security in places where states, armed guerrillas, or organized criminal groups used systemic violence against some or all of the population. For instance, in the Colombian Civil War from 1964 to 2016, citizens established "peace villages" where residents refused to cooperate with either armed groups or the state. Mexico's Movement for Peace with Justice and Dignity, which mobilized from 2011 to 2013, was a response to the violence of Mexico's drug wars, committed by drug lords, gangs, and federal troops alike.[22] Between 2004 and 2011, in at least one Sicilian city, a mass refusal to pay protection money effectively ended the mafia's grip over that city's businesses.[23] And in the

Syrian and Iraqi civil wars, people in Raqqa and Mosul organized courageous resistance campaigns against various armed groups, including the Islamic State, by combining overt acts of defiance with everyday forms of resistance.

Anticapitalist movements

Movements have demanded revolutionary change to the ways in which capitalism has led to the concentration of wealth in the hands of a few at the expense of the many. Over the course of the twentieth century, numerous student, worker, and poor peoples' movements have demanded that their governments protect workers from exploitative corporate practices, harsh effects of globalization, and unfair workplace practices, while also demanding reforms to market capitalism.[24] Biennial convenings of the World Trade Organization have been disrupted by movements protesting globalization and demanding just economic practices, perhaps most notably in Seattle in 1999. In 2011, the Occupy Wall Street movement went global, inspiring hundreds of marches, work stoppages, citizens' assemblies, and tent-city encampments around the world. After months of mobilization, this movement had called renewed attention to economic inequality, corporate injustice, and excessive corporate influence on politics worldwide.

Prodemocracy movements

In the past century, hundreds of civil resistance campaigns have worked to depose authoritarian, antidemocratic, or corrupt regimes—at times struggling against counter-movements aiming to reinstate them. Such campaigns have ranged from Portugal (1974) to Poland (1980–1989), from East Germany (1989) to Egypt (2011), from Serbia (2000) to Swaziland (2011), from Tunisia (2010) to Togo (2013), from Georgia (2003) to Guatemala (2015), and from Brazil (1984–1985) to Burkina Faso (2014). In all of these cases—and hundreds of others—people power movements have tried to topple dictatorial regimes or defend democracies against authoritarian power-grabs. Over the past decade alone, powerful movements have erupted in countries as diverse as Turkey, Kenya, South Korea, Iceland, and the United States challenging government corruption and financial mismanagement with mass demonstrations, citizen investigations, information-sharing, and naming and shaming of corrupt activities.

A Note on antidemocratic movements

Some movements have emerged with more sinister aims—including restoring authoritarian politics after a democratic transition. In Egypt in 2013, for instance, the Tamarod (Rebellion) movement encouraged the Egyptian army to depose democratically elected Mohammed Morsi and remove the Muslim Brotherhood from power, under the pretext that Morsi's government was both too Islamist and too incompetent. Similarly in Thailand in 2014, a popularly backed military coup overthrew democratically elected prime minister Yingluck Shinawatra and installed a military junta in her place. During the Iranian Revolution, a broad-based coalition that unified leftists and Islamists to overthrow Shah Reza Pahlavi was overtaken by well-organized fundamentalist groups led by Ayatollah Khomenei, imposing an authoritarian and fundamentalist religious regime that dramatically restricted individual rights.[25] And since 2016, far-right and neo-Nazi groups in Germany have been relying on the work of nonviolent resistance scholar Gene Sharp to better understand how to build and wield people power to pursue their racist and exclusionary aims.[26]

That such antidemocratic groups are trying to misappropriate these techniques should motivate those of us who are fighting for liberation, justice, equality, and democracy to learn how to use them more effectively.

Where this book is headed

Today, we know much more about civil resistance than we did even a decade ago. Developments in research and the practice of civil resistance itself have made it all the more important—and potentially powerful—to inform people around the world with answers to their urgent questions about how to wage nonviolent struggle effectively and ethically. This book aims to offer those answers whenever possible, while noting current debates and controversies when we just don't have clear answers yet.

In Chapter 1 we dive deeper into the basics of civil resistance—core concepts, which methods count as civil resistance and which methods do not, and how pragmatic uses of civil resistance intersect with moral claims.

Chapter 2 addresses the question of how people build social and political power from below, how civil resistance succeeds, and whether there are conditions under which civil resistance is impossible. Here, the crucial point is that civil resistance campaigns succeed when they become large and diverse enough to reflect a serious challenge to the status quo—and when they begin to create defections from their opponent's side.

Chapter 3 takes on the complicated question of violence from within a movement. Here we review recent research findings that address how fringe violence from within a movement affects the political situation for those pushing for change.

In Chapter 4 we look at myths and realities of civil resistance against brutal opponents. We look at the ways in which civil resistance campaigns have succeeded in spite of episodes of extreme brutality—including against genocidal opponents—and the options available to movements fighting against racist regimes in particular.

Finally, Chapter 5 concludes with a discussion of the long-term effects of civil resistance on different societies—whether successful civil resistance campaigns tend to leave societies better or worse off. We also explore how civil resistance campaigns have changed over the past decade—particularly with the emergence of digital activism—and how movements have persisted in the face of rising authoritarianism, global economic crises, and the global coronavirus pandemic.

Throughout the book I return to a core point: that civil resistance provides immense possibilities for people to organize collectively against injustice, in almost every circumstance. Civil resistance does not always succeed. In fact, nonviolent resistance fails as often as it succeeds. But civil resistance is an increasingly common political approach, succeeding far more often than its detractors would have you believe. In fact, it's hard to find an example of progressive political change that occurred without it.

1

THE BASICS

Power concedes nothing without a demand. It never did and it never will.
—Frederick Douglass

In the Introduction, we defined civil resistance as a form of struggle in which unarmed people coordinate a variety of actions—such as strikes, protests, sit-ins, boycotts, stay-away demonstrations, noncooperation, and lots of other tactics—to build power and force change. Using civil resistance, people show their collective power. Across the millennia, in every part of the world, people have confronted oppression using a wide range of civil resistance approaches and techniques. They have succeeded not because they melted the hearts of their opponents, but because the resisters outnumbered the opposition and therefore changed the political and social balance of power.

This chapter addresses some common misconceptions about civil resistance. They include the ideas that civil resistance requires passively accepting suffering, that civil resistance means being civil and respectful, that protest is the primary form of civil resistance, that civil resistance is only available to people in privileged positions, and that the methods of civil resistance cannot be abused for unjustified or immoral aims.[1] None of these are necessarily true, as you'll see.

How does civil resistance create change?

To understand the logic of civil resistance, you have to first appreciate a particular mental model about how people make change in the world. There are two primary theories of how to make social or political change; depending upon which one you subscribe to, you'll either be more skeptical or optimistic about civil resistance as a way for people to transform society.

Let's start with the skeptics. Many popular myths about political power can obscure or underestimate civil resistance's potential to succeed.[2] This is because a common theory of change, which we might call the *control approach*, focuses on the near-invincibility of entrenched power and implies that only militant and violent action can challenge the system and upset power.[3] The theory underlies justifications for armed insurrection that include that of the Chinese revolutionary Mao Zedong, who famously argued that "power flows from the barrel of a gun"; Algerian revolutionaries against French occupation in 1954–1962, who argued that violence was the only way through which a colonized people could free themselves from an internalized sense of inferiority;[4] some current defenders of the US Constitution's Second Amendment, who argue that the right to own and bear guns is a safeguard against a tyrannical government; eighteenth-century French revolutionaries who believed that the aristocracy could only be truly destroyed in France by executing or terrorizing its remaining members; and Marxist-Leninist groups during the early-twentieth-century Russian Revolution, who argued that violence would be required to seize the means of production from the bourgeois class. Still others see power as the ability to maintain status quo social, political, racial, or economic hierarchies, such as white supremacy. This theory of change accepts militarism as a necessary evil in defending or transforming an unjust society. And its notion of power, which privileges elite politics and the ability to wield overpowering violence, is often taken for granted in the popular imagination. If you subscribe to this theory of change, you will have a tough time believing that civil resistance can create a real or substantive difference in society.

But this theory of change is often wrong. Oppressive systems tend to be much more fragile than they appear. Despite their most earnest efforts, those tyrants who have publicly claimed their invincibility usually admit in private that they are far more vulnerable than their public image projects. Most of the armed revolutions that have succeeded over the past hundred years—from the Russian Revolution to Mao's Chinese Revolution to the Algerian Revolution to that led by the North Vietnamese Liberation Army—were not victorious because they outmatched their opponents militarily. Rather, they succeeded because they had comprehensive strategies that defeated their opponents politically.

Moreover, the control approach cannot explain why so many nonviolent struggles have succeeded over the past two centuries against militarily superior opponents. As we saw in the Introduction, nonviolent revolutions succeeded in overthrowing regimes or creating territorial independence in twice as many cases as violent revolutions did. What's more, the control approach considers those holding power to be essentially a monolithic group. It conflates dictatorships and dictators, forgetting that the latter must be supported by a pyramid of people. It conflates systems and individuals—the people in the pyramid who have their own minds and decisions to make. Theorists of civil resistance argue that there is no such thing as a monolithic regime. Oppressive systems are different from the people operating within them. Dictators are entirely separate from those who must cooperate to hold up the status quo: the militaries, intelligence services, economic and political leaders, and civil workers. Few standard notions of power recognize that governments pay a high political cost if they use violence to restore order. Even if they win through brutalizing their civilian opponents, very few dictators enjoy a stable and prosperous legitimacy after committing atrocities.

So, what theory of change can help us make sense of these historical patterns? A second theory of change—which I refer to as the *legitimacy approach*[5]—starts from an idea of power that focuses on the ability to influence what happens to whom, where, and how. Three fundamental assumptions motivate this approach: (1) power is based on legitimacy rather than coercion; (2) power is never permanent; and (3) no system is monolithic. Let's look at each of these in turn.

First, political power comes from the ability to get other people to cooperate and obey authority voluntarily. They do this when they consider obedience to be in their own interests, or when they see whoever or whatever is wielding that power to be doing so legitimately. Once a population comes to feel that a leader or government doesn't deserve that power and large numbers of people stop voluntarily complying with its directives, that power is very difficult to restore. Leaders or governments that respond by using violence are not demonstrating strength or power. Instead, they are paradoxically demonstrating their weakness, because they have lost the population's voluntary cooperation, obedience, or consent to be governed. Governments that have to use violence to compel cooperation and obedience reveal the fact that citizens wouldn't choose to obey of their own volition. Seen this way, Syrian president Bashar al-Assad's use of death squads, sniper fire, and shelling of entire neighborhoods during the 2011 Syrian uprising did not showcase his power. Instead, it revealed that his legitimacy was hollow and vulnerable—and that he couldn't win back popular cooperation through popular appeals, reforms, concessions, or other ways of responding to the people who had mobilized to confront his regime.

Second, no oppressive system is monolithic. Whether it is a dictatorship, a foreign military occupation, or an unjust economic system, every oppressive system leans on the cooperation and acquiescence of the people involved in what activist and intellectual George Lakey calls its "pillars of support." Those include:

- Security forces, such as the military's various branches; intelligence services; police forces; any regional or local military or policing organizations, like a national guard; semiofficial militias or paramilitaries; and so on.
- Economic elites, such as bankers, wealthy business owners, small business owners, trade associations, lobbyists, and companies.
- Bureaucrats who make sure the government's various functions run, including legislative, executive, and judicial staff; civil servants in diplomatic posts; and public sector workers in sanitation, utilities, postal services, public health services, and other public institutions.
- Independent media and government-run or -influenced media, including TV and radio stations, newspapers, websites, and so on.
- Religious authorities, from top leaders like bishops, imams, or rabbis to those who serve in local congregations.
- Educational institutions, like universities and other academic institutions; student organizations; academic professional associations; and scientific labs for research and development.

- Cultural figures, like television, film, or social media personalities, musicians, athletes, and other celebrities.
- Organized labor, like teachers', nurses', and custodial staff unions; workers' rights groups, like those that advocate on behalf of nonunionized workers; and professional associations, like doctors' or lawyers' associations.
- Civil society organizations, such as civil rights groups, educational foundations, and various advocacy organizations.

Governments rely on civil servants, military and intelligence officials, taxpayers, foreign allies or patrons, and ardent supporters. But governments aren't the only organizations that can't function without daily cooperation from their supporters. Companies rely on their employees, managers, executives, trustees, shareholders, and consumers. Universities rely on custodial staff, security guards, students, administrators, donors, alumni, faculty, staff, and often state legislatures. Broader systems of oppression—like white supremacy, patriarchy, homophobia, xenophobia, transphobia, and ethnic chauvinism—rely on ideological beliefs or justifications, people who perpetuate these ideas, institutions that cooperate with and enshrine these systems into public life, and people who continually cooperate with (and often benefit from) these institutions.

Numerous practitioners and philosophers of resistance have recognized that when people collectively refuse to consent to or obey status quo systems, they can make radical demands of those with institutional power—including scrapping the existing system and replacing it with something else. This is particularly true if they are able to build coalitions and alliances with other groups that expand their bases of power. In other words, it is not only up to tyrants to decide how long they get to maintain the status quo. To a significant degree, it is also up to the people they rely upon to carry out their wishes, as well as the much larger population of people whom they claim to govern and represent.

Masses of people change systems when, through popular collective action, they pull those pillars of support away from the power holder—the government, the university administration, the church—so as to disrupt or collapse an oppressive system. That could lead to:

- Workers refusing to work until safe and fair workplace standards are met.
- Shareholders ousting poor corporate leadership.
- State legislators refusing to carry out the wishes of a corrupt governor.
- A nation's police or security services abandoning a dictator.
- Prominent business owners and bankers pushing politicians for reform.

People power movements win primarily by building enough power from below to separate those in charge from their existing sources of control—or to transform institutions and practices so drastically that existing structures become obsolete. As Frederick Douglass famously said in 1857,

Power concedes nothing without a demand. It never did and it never will. Find out just what any people will submit to, and you have found out the exact amount of injustice and wrong which will be imposed upon them; and these will continue till they are resisted with either words or blows, or with both. The limits of tyrants are prescribed by the endurance of those whom they oppress.

The people who make up these pillars of support—civilian bureaucrats, state media, military and police officers, business owners and bankers, popular public figures, important international allies—aren't necessarily converted to the cause through a genuine change of heart. They often stop cooperating with the status quo because they come to believe that doing so serves their own interests.

In apartheid South Africa, for instance, white business owners' fortunes were fading under the pressure of Black-led[6] boycotts and international sanctions. Few of these white business owners became converts to the African National Congress's (ANC's) vision of ridding the country of racial, political, and economic inequality. But they knew they wouldn't prosper unless they pressured the government to acquiesce to what one trade association member described as "legitimate claims" for racial equality for Black South Africans.

So they put pressure on the ruling party to reform, and they got their opportunity to do so when pro-apartheid leader P. W. Botha suffered a mild stroke and resigned in 1989. National Party leaders appointed reformist Education Minister F. W. de Klerk to lead their party. De Klerk was later elected state president, and, in a speech to Parliament in February 1990, he announced that he would remove the ban on the ANC and release Nelson Mandela from prison after twenty-seven years. These steps led to historic negotiations with the ANC, resulting in a 1992 referendum where a large majority of white South Africans voted to end legal apartheid. Newly able to vote, in 1994, millions of Black South African voters put the ANC in power in a landslide electoral victory. This vignette shows how civil resistance campaigns can put both direct and indirect pressure on economic and political pillars of support, forcing them to accommodate the movement's demands.

The legitimacy approach's third major assumption is that power is never permanent. All power holders must constantly replenish their power: by fulfilling an implicit or explicit social contract, through good performance, or through moral righteousness. They must continually demonstrate their legitimacy both to their own pillars of support and to the broader public. Civil resistance visibly questions the legitimacy of the status quo; large-scale civil resistance reveals that this legitimacy is in crisis.

Here's what's crucial: the legitimacy approach does not assume that the opponent possesses even a baseline level of morality. Power holders may be extremely brutal, arrogant, self-concerned, and petty. In fact, a legitimacy approach to power assumes that there is no such thing as a benevolent dictator; if incumbents think they can kill with impunity, they will.[7] As John Adams wrote to Thomas Jefferson in 1816, "Power always thinks it has a great Soul, and vast Views, beyond the Comprehension of the Weak; and that it is doing God Service, when it is violating all his Laws."[8] But the adversary's lack of morality or empathy does not matter nearly as much as the organized resistance movement's ability to use a broad range of co-ordinated, cleverly devised methods to shake up, overextend, and outmaneuver the opponent while eroding its political, economic, social, and military sources of power.

How do you define nonviolent action?

In some ways, "nonviolent action" is intuitive and obvious: it means taking action without hurting anyone. Civil resistance movements that undertake nonviolent actions do not physically harm or threaten to physically harm any person. People involved in such actions are unarmed; they do not carry weapons, throw Molotov cocktails, and so on.

But the term "nonviolent action" is often misunderstood as passive or submissive. In fact, some people engaged in creative forms of resistance are insulted by the adjective "nonviolent," because their actions are often defiant, disruptive, and confrontational, with a plan of action intended to antagonize the opponent. While civil resistance movements do not hurt others physically, they nevertheless behave in ways that are forceful and coercive, blocking their opponents from achieving their goals or pushing them to act against their wishes. Nonviolent resistance as a strategy involves creating an active conflict with the opponent—one fought with different tools than are used in a violent or militarized approach.

The term "nonviolent action" can also be misunderstood as nonviolent *interaction*—an exchange between two groups that is totally free of violence. In fact, those using nonviolent action stick to nonviolent action themselves, but their adversaries often use violence toward them—before, during, and after a confrontation. When people power movements use nonviolent methods like protests, it is often precisely because police or military troops have brutalized them—and police or military sometimes assault people using nonviolent action with tear gas, rubber bullets, live ammunition, beatings with clubs, arrests, imprisonment, torture, and disappearances.[9] When I refer to "nonviolent action," then, I mean nonviolent action by dissidents—regardless of how authorities respond. But there is often a lot of violence involved in civil resistance campaigns, particularly among those that adopt revolutionary goals.

You may have heard the term "nonviolent direct action." That usually implies more confrontational and riskier forms of action than the average symbolic demonstration or vigil might entail. People using direct action have chained themselves to bulldozers, trespassed onto high-security sites and poured blood on office files, glued themselves to the pavement at a busy intersection, or occupied a runway at an airport. Consider these real-life examples:

- During 1999's disruptions of the World Trade Organization's meeting in Seattle, where activists were protesting globalization's effects on poverty, inequality, and the environment, the Ruckus Society used PVC pipes to bind activists' arms together to block traffic.
- In 2013, Sister Megan Rice, who as of this writing is a ninety-year-old peace activist who has been arrested over three dozen times, was convicted of destroying federal property as part of a direct action to protest the global threat of nuclear weapons. In 2012, she and several others associated with the Plowshares movement cut through several fences at the Oak Ridge, Tennessee, Y-12 national security complex to reach the uranium storage bunker. Once there, she and two fellow Catholic peace activists hung banners, prayed, and hammered on the outside wall of the bunker.
- During Donald Trump's inauguration as US president in January 2017, Black Lives Matter activists protested his promised policies by sitting down and forming a human blockade outside the entrance of the National Mall, where the inauguration was taking place.
- Between 2018 and this writing, the group Extinction Rebellion, which demands immediate and aggressive action on climate change, has used a number of direct actions, including flying drones at London Heathrow Airport to ground airplanes, thus keeping them from emitting carbon, and gluing themselves to major thoroughfares in UK cities including London and Edinburgh to stop traffic—again, preventing carbon emissions, however temporarily—and awakening people to the climate threat.

All of these methods are disruptive, often illegal, and often controversial. They inconvenienced and angered other people, from ordinary travelers to political authorities. Those involved risked arrest and physical harm. But in no way did any of these methods physically harm or threaten to harm anyone else.

Nonviolent actions may involve people using their own bodies to dramatize an injustice, protect others from harm, or disrupt the status quo. Such actions can sometimes have unintended consequences. For example, during a wave of protests associated with the Occupy Wall Street movement in 2011, some activists blockaded major roadways. Critics complained that this nonviolent action could unintentionally bring physical harm to others— especially if ambulances, fire trucks, and similar emergency vehicles were stuck in the traffic jam. But a road blockade is a nonviolent method; the possibility of unintended, incidental harm does not make a road blockade a violent activity.

What are common nonviolent actions?

When people think of nonviolent action, protests and mass demonstrations often come to mind. But that's just the beginning. Civil resistance movements have used hundreds, if not thousands, of actions to change their political situations. Some scholars have attempted to catalogue and classify these. For instance, scholar Gene Sharp famously identified "198 methods of nonviolent action" while writing his doctoral dissertation at Oxford University in the 1960s. He grouped these into three categories, as shown in Table 1-1: protest and persuasion, noncooperation, and nonviolent intervention.

Some people may be tempted to see Sharp's list as a "menu" for civil resistance. But actually, Sharp suspected that there were far more than 198 methods. The number he chose to publish in 1973 was arbitrary, and after that he stopped counting. Why? The nonviolent resistance scholar and practitioner Mary Elizabeth King reports, "He told me that he realized that every nonviolent struggle might create its own new nonviolent method."[10] Some technology-savvy scholars have updated Sharp's list to include tactics activated through cellular phones, digital platforms, social media, and even drones. But people involved in movements or researching them haven't had the time to track down and categorize all of the tactical innovations that occur every day around the world.

Table 1-1 Nonviolent Methods and Examples

| Protest and Persuasion | Noncooperation | | | Nonviolent Intervention |
	Social Noncooperation	Economic Noncooperation	Political Noncooperation	
Making public statements; mass petitions; leaflets; underground newspapers; mock elections; displays of portraits; protest disrobings; rude gestures; vigils; singing; marches; motorcades; teach-ins; turning one's back; walk-outs; silence	Lysistratic nonaction (sex strike); student strikes; boycott of social events; suspension of sports activities; stay-at-home; sanctuary; protest emigration (*hijrat*)	Consumer boycotts; consumption of forbidden goods; suppliers' and handlers' boycott; lockout; general strike; tax refusal; withdrawal of bank deposits; lightning walkout; reporting in "sick"; economic shutdown; go-slow	Withholding allegiance to authority; speech calling for resistance; election boycott; noncooperation with conscription; civil disobedience	Fast; hunger strike; sit-in; nonviolent obstruction; speak-in; guerrilla theater; alternative institutions; stay-in strike; nonviolent land seizure; defiance of blockade; overloading of administrative systems; seeking imprisonment; dual sovereignty

Source: Sharp 2005; Swarthmore Nonviolent Action Database

Sharp's analyses leave out some kinds of political activity that aren't generally considered techniques of civil resistance: negotiation, dispute resolution, and community organizing. Negotiation and dispute resolution involve ways that a civil resistance campaign can bargain and compromise with its opponents, while also resolving conflicts that arise within a movement. "Community organizing" refers to working with people to encourage them to stand up for their concerns, rights, and interests, to build their power for longer-term transformation, and perhaps to lead or join a movement someday. While these important efforts often complement civil resistance, civil resistance refers to active mobilization and direct confrontation with the opponent.

Table 1-2 Categorizing Nonviolent Actions

	Commission	Omission
Dispersion	Coordinated and dispersed flash mobs, development of worker cooperatives, political boycotts, stay-at-home demonstrations, divestments, embargos, alternative schools and education systems, singing illegal songs, overloading administrative systems, etc.	Coordinated electricity shut-offs, reporting in sick, stay-at-home strikes, etc.
Concentration	Sit-in, nonviolent occupation, march, demonstration, rally, teach-in, reverse strike, seeking imprisonment, turning one's back, etc.	Collective silence, go-slow demonstration, walkouts, etc.

Within civil resistance, Sharp distinguishes between acts of commission—in which unarmed people take an action that the opponent does not want them to—and acts of omission—in which people stop doing something they are expected to do.[11] Following on the work of political scientist Robert Burrowes, political sociologist Kurt Schock also distinguishes between methods of concentration, in which people gather in a particular space, and methods of dispersion, in which people stay away from a particular space (see Table 1-2).[12]

In what order should a movement try these various tactics? That entirely depends on the movement's particular circumstances and context. So far, no one has found a clear and successful formula that works everywhere, every time. However, most experienced activists agree that extensive planning and strategizing are ideal before mobilization begins.

What is the difference between civil resistance and protest?

Protest is one method of civil resistance—and not necessarily the most effective kind. Protest is typically a symbolic action intended to raise public awareness of an issue and demand change. Because protests and demonstrations—especially very large ones—can bring a lot of attention, many people conflate protests with civil resistance. But an effective civil resistance campaign typically involves many nonviolent methods above and beyond protest, like those described in Table 1-1. Few if any civil resistance campaigns have succeeded using protest alone.[13]

What roles do art and music play in civil resistance?

Artists and musicians are often important in civil resistance—both by getting involved directly and by documenting and memorializing what happened during revolutionary times.

For example, street art—which is visual art created in public locations—typically flourishes during civil resistance campaigns. Amateur and professional artists create and display such things as graffiti, tagging, wall and street murals, posters, stickers, street installations, video projections, and sculpture. More recently, movements' artists have created digital street art, like holograms and video projections on the sides of buildings. Street art is different from public art more broadly because it is usually created and displayed without any official sanction, deliberately circumventing and subverting mainstream, legal channels of public expression. Street art often conveys a strong social or political message in a way that comes across as transgressive and rebellious.

As a result, street art can powerfully communicate a movement's claims, its legitimacy, and its opponents' inability to silence dissent. The slogans, symbols, and street performances performed by people living with HIV and AIDS in the 1980s are a case in point. Activists used street banners, popularizing the slogan "Silence = Death." They reappropriated the pink triangle used to designate gay people in Nazi concentration camps, wearing it as a symbol of their struggle against homophobia and government inaction on AIDS and HIV research and treatment. Activists from the associated group ACT UP adopted numerous guerrilla art tactics, including surrounding Republican senator Jesse Helms' home in a giant, inflated 15-foot condom to protest his stigmatization of people with AIDS in September of 1991.

Street art has also featured prominently in antiauthoritarian campaigns. During the 2011 Egyptian Revolution, artists used graffiti to spread slogans calling for President Hosni Mubarak to step down. Some artists moved beyond walls and used their bodies as canvases; one protester in Tahrir Square wrote, "Leave, I miss my wife," across his chest. Many street artists used noms de plume to avoid detection. In situations where being publicly identified is dangerous, street art may be an especially useful way to anonymize resistance. As the pseudonymous British artist Banksy said, "Graffiti is one of the few tools you have if you have almost nothing."

Sometimes, even anonymously painting graffiti or slogans that criticize the regime can be incredibly dangerous. In March 2011 in Deraa, Syria, a group of teenage boys painted "The people want the fall of the regime" on a city wall. They'd been inspired by the recent wave of uprisings in Tunisia, Egypt, and Libya. In response, President Bashar al-Assad's brutal security services arrested and tortured fifteen boys, murdering a thirteen-year-old. The teens' transgressive act—and the government's horrific overreaction to it—is widely considered to be the spark that ignited the Syrian uprising, which led to the country's nine-year-long civil war and earned Deraa's popular designation as the "cradle of the revolution."

Some street artists create work capturing a movement's zeitgeist, during and after a revolution. For instance, during the Cold War, the Soviet Union erected the Berlin Wall between East Germany and West Germany. Street artists covered its miles-long concrete in graffiti. After the wall fell, in perhaps the most famous mural depicting the Cold War era, artist Dmitri Vrubel painted a larger-than-life image of Leonid Brezhnev, the Soviet Union's general secretary, kissing Erich Honecker, the East German Socialist Party's general secretary from 1971 until October 1989. The two men had kissed during the 1979 celebration of the anniversary of the Soviet Union establishing East Germany as the German Democratic Republic in 1949. Vrubel painted the mural on the eastern side of the Berlin Wall in 1990, captioning it in German and in Russian: "My God, help me to survive this deadly love."

In May 2016, artists Dominykas Čečkauskas and Mindaugas Bonanu painted a similar mural in Vilnius, Lithuania—but this time, depicting Russian president Vladimir Putin kissing then–US presidential candidate Donald Trump, captioned, "Make Everything Great Again."

In another iconic piece of street art, Banksy spray-painted and stenciled numerous pieces on the concrete wall that the Israeli government had built between Jerusalem and the West Bank, all of them challenging both the wall and Israel's military occupation of Palestinian territories. His memorable 2003 image, called *Love Is in the Air* (*Flower Thrower*), depicts a masked activist preparing to throw a bouquet of colorful flowers at an unseen opponent. The image aims to replace the Israeli government's common depiction of Palestinian activists as Molotov-cocktail-throwing vandals by picturing dissent as beautifully courageous.

We often see street theater, which is closely related to street art, during civil resistance campaigns as well. For example, in Tahrir Square during the 2011 Egyptian Revolution, protesters would dramatize nonviolently confronting the police, Hosni Mubarak, and other regime authorities. In Serbia during 2000, the Otpor movement—which aimed to remove Milošević from power—held mock funerals depicting the death of democracy in Serbia. In Syria in November 2012, four women staged a rare antiwar protest in the main souk, or open air market, in Damascus; dressed in bridal gowns, they portrayed "Brides of Syria" who objected to the killing. For fifteen minutes they marched through the souk, holding signs demanding that Syrians stop killing one another and singing wedding songs before security forces arrested them. One of the four, Lubna Zaour, told *The New York Times*, "It was a strange sight, brides in a police car."[14] She and her sister were detained, beaten, and then released after two months. Their landlords evicted them, their father lost his business, and their family fled to southern Turkey. Their act of defiance struck a nerve, though; calling for peaceful revolution at a time when government forces are organizing mass detentions and dissidents are beginning to arm themselves for civil war is a dangerous act indeed.

Further, during revolutionary times many people use their creativity to carefully document, record, and publicize various elements of revolutionary processes. As Egyptian muralist Ammar Abo Bakr put it, "What we did in Egypt in recent years was not about presenting art, at least it wasn't to me: We used walls as a newspaper. We learned to do so out of a need: The TV presenter and satirist Bassem Youssef was a doctor, but then he learned to use YouTube. Mosab El-Shamy Rassd was studying medicine, but then he took his camera and took to the streets. Me, I was a fine arts assistant professor. I left the faculty to report on the revolution on the city's walls."[15]

Musicians have written evocative pieces to tell stories about ongoing struggles, often rooting their songs in folk traditions to convey the unity and civic quality of action. Some of the most enduring songs of the classic rock and folk scenes in the United States—by Joan Baez to Bob Dylan to Neil Young—emerged out of protest against US-led wars and imperialism. American activist and political scientist Mary Elizabeth King writes that during the US civil rights movement, songs like "We Shall Overcome" raised courage, declared commitment, united participants, and targeted specific opponents like police chiefs:

> As a contemporary expression of spirituals, freedom songs derived from the black choral tradition that developed from the African and American experiences, matured in the fires of southern slavery. They addressed frustrations, forged bonds of personal loyalty, assuaged fear and dread, and fortified a people under stress. A strong tradition of composing during performance, in response to need, meant that new phrases would be added or a stanza changed to take up a specific issue, such as deciding whether to go to jail the next day. Song leading became an organizing tool.[16]

In the 1960s, soul artists like Nina Simone, Sam Cooke, and Aretha Franklin composed, performed, and popularized music centered in Black liberation. In the late 1970s and early 1980s, rap and hip-hop emerged from neighborhood block parties in the Bronx, where Black artists and dancers mixed influences from soul, R&B, and Caribbean culture to articulate political autonomy and cultural resistance through defiant lyrics and popular beats. Many contemporary Black hip-hop, R&B, and soul artists like Public Enemy, Kendrick Lamar, Beyoncé, and Janelle Monaé continue to popularize music centered in Black liberation in ways that can create a sense of solidarity, urgency, and inspiration among listeners.

Estonia's revolution for independence from the Soviet Union was literally called the Singing Revolution. During the Baltic uprising against Soviet domination in 1987–1991, two million people formed a human chain, joining hands and singing songs based in local traditions, recovering a sense of national unity. In Mali's 1990–1991 uprising against the Traoré dictatorship, a traditional group of what Malians called "songsayers" would travel from village to village to convey news of the ongoing protests. Because large numbers of people were unable to read, oral histories—especially those conveyed by folk music—were a powerful way of communicating the demands of the Alliance for Democracy in Mali (ADEMA) in its struggle against dictatorship.

Live music performances also provide convenient gathering spaces through which movements can recruit and mobilize others. In Serbia on New Year's Eve in 1999, student activists organized a rock concert in Belgrade. That may not sound revolutionary. But it was a rare display of defiance in a one-party state that discouraged rock music because of its rebellious undercurrents. Just months before, Serbian autocrat Slobodan Milošević's militias had massacred Kosovo's Albanians—and in response, NATO had bombed Belgrade. Thousands turned out for the concert, which featured rock musicians and comedians poking fun at Milošević's regime and calling for people to rally behind opposition politicians. As the clock turned to midnight, organizers stilled the festive mood to display pictures and read the names of Serbian soldiers killed during the Balkan Wars—openly rebuking Milošević and his regime for their lack of accountability. Student leader Srdja Popović explained that the purpose of the evening was to tell people, "Go home and think what to do so the next Orthodox New Year we have a reason to celebrate. . . . This is the year life finally must win in Serbia."[17]

Singing can also reduce fear among protesters, bystanders, or striking workers who fear they're about to be attacked or will face reprisals later. For example, in Lebanon's October Revolution of 2019, among the many songs and chants was a spontaneous rendition of "Baby Shark," sung by demonstrators to comfort a fifteen-month-old baby and his mother who were stuck in traffic because of the massive gathering.

And of course, many artists' creations reflect on and recall revolutions that fell short of their goals. The avant-garde Egyptian artist Laila Soliman, for instance, created and directed plays about the January 25, 2011, uprising that lasted eighteen days in Tahrir Square—showing its feminist revolutionary organizing, its unprecedented coalition crossing social boundaries, and the military regime's incarceration and torture of dissidents afterward. The musical *We Live in Cairo*, commissioned by the Art Repertory Theater in Cambridge, Massachusetts, similarly depicted the dashed hopes of Egypt's young revolutionaries. In this production, playwrights Daniel and Patrick Lazour explore the Tahrir Square street art, showing its slogans, posters, banners, and social media as a canvas, and composing songs about the revolution and counterrevolution.

Of course, music and art can play a role in expressing loyalty and reverence for autocratic leaders as well. Nationalistic music, poetry, and portraiture often feature heavily in stoking sentiments of fealty to ruling elites. Musicologist Nomi Dave, for instance, writes about how musicians and artists in Guinea took pleasure in writing songs of praise for dictator Sékou Touré—even after he died.[18] Much like any technique, then, art and music can play a role in both dissent and loyalty.

But as with journalism, precisely because of the cultural power of telling the truth through music, literature, and visual arts, most authoritarian regimes monitor cultural figures and censor their output. In Iran, for example, Supreme Leader Ali Khamenei has banned independent poetry and books and jailed artists, claiming, "Poetry must be the vanguard of the caravan of the revolution."[19]

Of course, few would expect street art, dissident art, or protest songs to create change on their own. But such art can create a common cache of knowledge and reinforce transgressive narratives, complementing and emboldening the work of other activists. As American leftist historian Howard Zinn is often quoted as saying, "They have the guns, we have the poets. Therefore, we will win."

What is the role of humor in civil resistance?

One way to show that an adversary can't control all of the people all of the time is to joke about him. In her book *Humor and Nonviolent Struggle in Serbia*, political scientist Janjira Sombatpoonsiri argues that humor can serve very specific functions in the waging of nonviolent conflict.[20]

First, humor—especially satire and parody—can directly challenge regimes' propaganda by undermining its original purpose and creating levity and clarity about the truth. Czech thinker, activist, and eventually president Václav Havel's foundational insight about building power from below is the necessity of "living in the truth"—that is, refusing to capitulate to the opponent's self-serving and false narrative of events.[21]

Second, humor can bring levity, cheerfulness, and a carnivalesque mood to an otherwise antagonistic, grim, or grave situation. This shift in feeling can be especially important when the regime has started to use force against dissenters. Festive events can attract large numbers of people seeking refuge from monotony, hopelessness, and betrayal. During a protest against Syrian dictator Bashar al-Assad in September 2011, for example, unarmed activists brought fireworks and video cameras to confront security forces armed with tanks and mortars. The videos captured the absurd disjunction between that display of military might being mocked by protesters shooting fireworks into the sky—and powerfully showed the Syrian government's disproportionate response to an unarmed civilian uprising.

Third, humorous actions can often allow people to imagine new ways to challenge the status quo. In fact, humor is so threatening that it can be deadly. In totalitarian systems, telling a joke that criticizes those in power can be a capital offense. That's because totalitarianism is based on completely controlling the social and historical narrative, what's considered "the truth," and the flow of information more broadly. In Stalin's Soviet Union, hundreds of people were convicted of telling jokes that defied the regime and were sentenced to gulags or death. Between 1942 and 1944 the People's Court of Berlin issued 4,933 death sentences for people telling "defeatist jokes" against the Nazi Party. In 1944, one Berlin munitions worker named Marianne Elise K. was executed for undermining the war effort "through spiteful remarks." Her crime? Telling this joke to her fellow munitions factory workers:

Hitler and Göring are standing on top of Berlin's radio tower. Hitler says he wants to do something to cheer up the people of Berlin. "Why don't you just jump?" suggests Göring.[22]

A coworker who overheard the joke reported it to local authorities, leading to Marianne Elise's execution.

Despite these attempts at total control, jokes satirizing Nazi officials and Stalin's regime were common during those authoritarian periods. They were typically whispered in barrooms among trusted friends and confidantes as a way to blow off steam, and they were not necessarily intended as active resistance. But the ubiquity of criticism and satire even under totalitarian regimes shows that no system can achieve complete control over all of the people all of the time. And once many people start telling jokes, they might begin to believe that the emperor has no clothes. That makes humor especially transgressive and subversive in oppressive systems. As the Iraqi writer Khalid Kishtainy writes,

> Humor is more required in a nation's darkest hours, for it is at such times that people begin to lose faith in themselves, submit to despair, and descend into melancholy and depression. Life appears to be meaningless, and the homeland feels like a spider's web. People lose contact with fellow citizens and eventually come to accept their solitude. The will to stand together and resist is thus destroyed. Humor is the best remedy for such ills. Laughter lifts one from melancholy and lethargy; a political joke told by another reconnects citizen with citizen. Both are no longer alone. There are others who have shared my thoughts; we have shared suffering and hopes. Laughter is a collective fraternity. One doesn't laugh alone.[23]

This is why, Kishtainy argues, the development and widespread use of political humor and satirical literature are essential to any successful civil resistance strategy.[24]

What are "parallel institutions"?

"Parallel institutions" are unofficial social, cultural, economic, and governance systems and practices that circumvent—and perhaps ultimately supplant—the regime's structures. They succeed when they can meet community needs that the existing system does not. They're "parallel" because they're working alongside but separate from existing oppressive institutions. Movements develop such institutions—and build legitimacy and authority—before they have fully "won."

We can find many examples throughout history. For instance, in the introduction, we discussed how important such institutions

were in freeing the thirteen American colonies from British imperial rule. During the twentieth century, many self-determination
and independence movements succeeded in part by building such
parallel institutions.

The Irish independence movement is an instructive case. The
movement began in the 1870s, during which Irish nationalists
demanded autonomy from Great Britain. Arthur Griffiths was
the chief architect of Sinn Fein (meaning "Ourselves"), which was
established in 1905 as a political group committed to Irish self-
government. Griffiths believed that total self-reliance would create
true independence. In 1918, as thousands of British soldiers were
dying in World War I, Sinn Fein helped to organize a massive civil
disobedience campaign in which two million Irishmen refused military conscription. Griffiths then used British elections in 1918 to run
Sinn Fein candidates, who swept the elections in all Irish areas except for Unionist strongholds. The newly elected Sinn Fein ministers
refused to sit in the British Parliament, instead meeting at Mansion
House in Dublin and declaring themselves the Dáil Éireann, an
independent Assembly of Ireland, which still exists today. This
shadow government, although labeled a terrorist organization
by the British government, established authority in Irish towns,
created new courts, encouraged local companies to purchase only
Irish-made products and not import from Britain, refused to pay
British taxes, and closed British-backed workhouses. Nevertheless,
the conflict escalated, culminating in the Irish War of Independence
between 1919 and 1922, after which most of Ireland seceded from
the United Kingdom and formed the Irish Free State. But while the
bloody events of the Irish War of Independence are often given as
the only narrative for Irish independence, historian David Carrol
Cochran writes that the movement ultimately succeeded because it
had paved the way by creating alternative institutions and entirely
severing the Irish from any political and economic cooperation with
Britain. As Cochran writes, "The historical evidence is clear that the
Dáil's campaign of noncooperation and parallel government did just
as much or more to make Ireland ungovernable and force the British
into negotiations."[25]

In fact, the Dáil reportedly inspired India's Jawaharlal Nehru and
Mohandas Gandhi to similarly break free from British colonial domination by developing parallel institutions. They were impressed

by Sinn Fein's unarmed strategy—and were deeply skeptical of the Irish Republican Army's armed revolt.

Gandhi was convinced that successful civil resistance required more than just confronting the opponent with mass noncooperation. His approach—which he called *satyagraha*—therefore had two branches, equal in importance. In one branch, people would engage in obstructive programs, or civil disobedience and civil resistance. In the other branch, Indian communities would live independently from colonial rule by building new structures, systems, processes, and resources. For instance, Gandhi urged Indians to spin their own yarn using the "charkha," or spinning wheel, so that they would not depend on imported British thread to make clothing. Similarly, rather than cooperating with a restrictive Salt Law that prohibited Indians from harvesting and using salt themselves, Gandhi led hundreds of thousands of Indians to the shoreline to harvest salt as a tangible sign of India's independence. In doing so, Gandhi sought to break the colonial monopoly on goods produced in India and to replace it with an entirely self-sufficient Indian economy—freeing India from colonial authorities' commodities.

These lessons were compelling to other leaders struggling against colonial rule. In the 1940s, Ghanaian independence leader Kwame Nkrumah was reportedly so convinced by Gandhi's emphasis on self-sufficiency that he promoted what he called "positive action" to rebuild Ghana's economic, social, and political institutions to be by and for Africans.[26] Nkrumah advocated pan-African identity to build solidarity among people fighting for liberation across the continent, while also attempting to build Ghanaian independence before it was legally realized in 1957. While Nkrumah later endorsed armed struggle in liberation movements across Africa, Ghana's independence was largely won through what we would now call civil resistance.

Another example of a movement developing alternative institutions is the prison abolition movement in the United States. This movement has the ambitious goal of eliminating the carceral system, including prisons—or, at least, drastically reducing the numbers of people who are in them. While that's a dramatic goal, part of what the movement is aiming to achieve is to transform the practice of criminal justice to focus on rehabilitation rather than punishment. Along the way, groups rooted in abolitionist principles have developed many parallel institutions to support communities that have been harmed by mass incarceration and the criminalization of poverty. For instance, in honor of Mother's Day in 2018, a Black-centered, Black-led group called the National Bail Out Collective developed an annual fundraiser to bail out Black mothers who had been charged but not convicted of crimes, and were behind bars simply because they couldn't pay bail. Such efforts thereby collectively subvert an oppressive system and support communities affected by it.

Many movements develop co-ops and other alternative economic systems, which are particularly useful in providing basic necessities. For instance, during the late 1960s and early 1970s, the Black Panther Party's Free Breakfast Program responded to institutionalized racism and inadequate government solutions to poverty by cooking and serving meals to over ten thousand children a day in poor urban neighborhoods. Such activities can be particularly impactful during long-lasting general strikes. In apartheid-era South Africa, Black townships were able to successfully boycott white-owned businesses to protest apartheid in large part because Black shopkeepers in the townships had stockpiled food, water, clothing, and other essentials. Buying and selling within the Black townships built long-term organizational capacity and economic power while withholding revenue from businesses that benefited from apartheid.

In systems where the state owns or controls news sources, movements can create alternative media outlets. Poland's Solidarity movement was named after its newspaper, called *Solidarność* (*Solidarity*), which had millions of subscribers—despite the fact that the communist regime had banned it. And in Nazi-occupied Europe, resistance newsletters and newspapers were ubiquitous, challenging the image of total control the Nazis and their local collaborators attempted to project.

Some civil resistance movements have developed or embraced parallel governments. The Catalan independence movement in Spain has its own national assembly, with its own government, that operates in parallel to the Spanish government. In 2016, the Catalan government organized an illegal referendum in Catalonia to gauge public support for independence, violating a Spanish order. Although many of its leaders are now in prison, the national assembly used to hold direct negotiations with the Spanish govern-ment on expanding autonomy and independence for Catalonia.

Similarly, in Venezuela in January 2019, Juan Guaidó become the president of the National Assembly, the country's legislature, and was recognized as the de facto President of Venezuela—even though Nicolás Maduro had manipulated the constitution to remain in of-fice and refused to step down from power. Guaidó later appointed politician Leopoldo López to establish a shadow cabinet, staffing such positions as foreign minister, defense minister, and finance minister, so that if Maduro's government fell, Guaidó and his fellow ministers could make the transition into government as seamlessly as possible.

In some cases, groups or movements have completely withdrawn from all political, social, and economic systems and tried to rebuild them from scratch. For instance, in Chiapas, Mexico, in 1994, the Zapatista movement rose up against the Mexican government to de-velop a totally autonomous society, building new economic, govern-mental, social, and even military institutions that would put justice and equity for marginalized groups first. After a few days of armed attacks to drive out police and federal forces, the Zapatistas declared an autonomous zone that they maintain to this day. Many Egyptians involved in the 2011 Tahrir Square encampments described a sim-ilar (if more ephemeral) experimental atmosphere, where people gathered in different tent areas like "the library" to discuss ways to reform Egypt's constitution and law, or the "media tent" to upload images and develop new narratives about the revolution and the state's response.

Organizers and strategists disagree about when it is most ef-fective to build alternative institutions. Gandhi thought building a constructive program was an essential first step in a nonviolent campaign, because it was from these institutions that Indians could claim true independence from British colonial rule—whether or not the British acquiesced. However, theorist Gene Sharp believed that campaign leaders should establish parallel institutions at the end of a campaign, once a revolutionary coalition has gathered enough mo-mentum and backing to ensure that these newly created institutions would include all those invested in the movement.

In practice, movements often emerge and take on lives of their own before strategists can debate and settle these issues. As a result, many movements attempt to prefigure the new society from within. In 2011, participants in Occupy Wall Street gathered in Zuccotti Park to hold people's assemblies and open debates to reinforce the movement's attempts at leaderless, deliberative democracy. Tent encampments featured various teach-ins, debates, and study groups where people worked to debate and design more equitable systems of democracy and economy. None of these were fully planned ahead, but movement organizers and activists attempted to build the type of society within the encampment that they wanted to create in the world at large.

Regardless of when a movement develops them, the nonviolent resistance scholar and practitioner Michael Nagler argues that parallel institutions can help a fairly disorganized nonviolent campaign coalesce around common objectives. Parallel institutions can also help movements to survive when crackdowns become too severe and dissidents must go underground. Nagler argues that parallel institutions can give dissidents less risky options than direct and overt forms of resistance that might get them arrested, attacked, or killed.[27]

For instance, when people can still find the movement's news and literature even though leaders are underground and no public protests are underway, they can be reassured that opportunities for the movement may arise again. As the Soviet Union's influence began to wane in Eastern Europe during the 1980s, pro-democracy intellectuals and activists realized that they couldn't yet directly challenge the ruling Communist Party with street protests, lest their governments imprison or massacre those brave enough to participate at the outset. Instead, activists emphasized building communities that could care for each other's basic needs no matter what their governments tried to do to them. In Poland, communities built Workers' Defense Committees that supported families of workers who were in trouble with Communist Party authorities. Dissidents published underground newspapers and newsletters, and communities developed "flying universities" that convened in people's homes and provided uncensored content. Václav Havel, a political philosopher living in Czechoslovakia and future Czech president, wrote,

Defending the aims of life, defending humanity is not only a more realistic approach, since it can begin right now and is potentially

more popular because it concerns people's everyday lives; at the same time (and perhaps precisely because of this) it is also an incomparably more consistent approach because it aims at the very essence of things.[28]

They were right. Building parallel institutions behind the "Iron Curtain," the colloquial name for countries controlled by the Soviet Union, helped these movements to win in the end. Before masses of people toppled the Berlin Wall in 1989, these movements had almost rendered their oppressive governments obsolete to day-to-day life.

Is rioting considered civil resistance?

It depends somewhat on the purpose and the scope of the activity. A riot is simply a disturbance by a crowd. Spontaneous riots with no broader civic objective—for instance, when sports fans riot after a game—are definitely not civil resistance. But for riots with a broader civic message attached to them, the answer can be complicated—and it depends upon whether the riots cause harm to people.

Sociologist Ben Case[29] argues that riots are ubiquitous in civil resistance campaigns around the globe—and that such riots are morally and strategically appropriate. Riots do sometimes erupt in the midst of a broader, and overwhelmingly peaceful, civil resistance campaign. People who riot are often unarmed, although they may vandalize property, loot stores, set fires, damage power lines, and so on. Other times, people bring weapons to riots and attack other people; such cases would not count as civil resistance. Regardless, as riots persist, it is often the case that people get hurt or killed by fires, accidents caused by the downing of traffic lights or power outages, police violence, or people seeking to exploit the chaos to settle scores. For example, in 1992, a jury acquitted four Los Angeles police officers who had been videotaped brutally beating a man named Rodney King—and South Central Los Angeles erupted into riots that lasted for days, leaving over 60 people dead, thousands of buildings burned, extensive properties looted, and over $1 billion in damage. Many other solidarity demonstrations against the acquittals around the US did not escalate to this extent.

But riots can escalate into longer-lasting violent episodes as well, in part because authorities typically crack down on riots much more harshly—assaulting people and firing tear gas, rubber bullets, and even live ammunition. And some scholars find that riots produce political backlash, even beyond what prejudice or disdain already existed. Political scientist Omar Wasow, who documented nonviolent and violent protests by Black activists during the civil rights movement, compared the reaction to riots with the reaction to nonviolent protests. He found that riots tended to undermine public support for civil rights and to increase votes for Republican political candidates who promised to restore law and order, whereas nonviolent protests tended to increase support for civil rights and supports for Democratic political candidates.[30] Beyond the US context, economist Emiliano Huet-Vaughn studied the impacts of nonviolent and violent strikes and labor protests among French workers. Ultimately, he found that when workers engaged in rioting, they achieved fewer concessions.[31] And in research that covers data across countries in Africa from 1990 to 2014, political scientist Margherita Belgioioso and I found that riots do not significantly increase a movement's probability of success. That research focuses on all kinds of social protest (such as protests for democracy, human rights, and workers' rights), and we looked at the momentum of protest on the departure of the country's national leader.[32]

Regardless of their efficacy, some strategists of civil resistance see riots as understandable combustions of popular energy after tragedies or injustices—and that the real violence lies in the systems that lead to such catastrophes. Dr. Martin Luther King Jr. made this case in a 1968 speech at Stanford University called "The Other America":

> I think America must see that riots do not develop out of thin air. Certain conditions continue to exist in our society which must be condemned as vigorously as we condemn riots. But in the final analysis, a riot is the language of the unheard. And what is it that America has failed to hear? It has failed to hear that the plight of the Negro poor has worsened over the last few years. It has failed to hear that the promises of freedom and justice have not been met. And it has failed to hear that large segments of white society are more concerned about tranquility and the status quo than about justice, equality, and humanity. And so in a real sense our nation's summers

of riots are caused by our nation's winters of delay. And as long as America postpones justice, we stand in the position of having these recurrences of violence and riots over and over again. Social justice and progress are the absolute guarantors of riot prevention.[33]

Here, King isn't necessarily condoning riots or protester violence, even if they are fighting for racial justice. But he does insist that the way to end those riots is to tackle the overwhelming poverty and racial injustice that provoked riots in the first place. Similarly, King had little tolerance for those who criticized rioters for inciting white backlash, reportedly saying, "It may well be that shouts of Black Power and riots in Watts and the Harlems and the other areas are the consequences of the white backlash rather than the cause of them."[34]

Crucially, though, the term "riot" itself is pejorative. Authorities, officials, and their sympathizers may use the term "riot" to demean and delegitimize social movements using peaceful if confrontational approaches, like a silent march, a protest, or a strike. During the 2020 Black-led antiracism uprisings in the United States, for example, President Trump and administration officials routinely referred to mass protests as "riots," even though reports showed that protestors remained strictly nonviolent in over 97 percent of the events, despite the fact that police beat, tear-gassed, and assaulted hundreds of protestors and arrested thousands more.[35] Having cast their opponents as "rioters," authorities then try to arrest and imprison them, deflect attention away from the movement's goals, tarnish activists' reputations, and undermine popular sympathy for them. We should therefore always ask which side of the conflict—the authorities or the protesters—are the ones labeling the event as a riot. And we should always be skeptical when officials, or journalists reporting official statements, call an action a "riot."

Mislabeling rebellions for political purposes has an extensive history. Political scientist Zoe Marks once brought to my attention a case that illustrates this perfectly: the 1929 Igbo Women's War, a mass nonviolent campaign in Nigeria, which British colonial documents referred to as the "Aba Women's Riots." In the run-up to the campaign, the British colonial administration attempted to tax Nigerian households and restrict the traditional political, social, and economic roles that had given Nigerian women considerable decision-making power in their homes and villages. Ultimately, thousands of Igbo women throughout British Nigeria collectively refused to allow officials to appraise their properties and withheld their taxes. They also organized large demonstrations outside the offices and residences of colonial authorities, while also surrounding (and sometimes destroying) the huts of local Igbo leaders who had been appointed by the British to govern (called "warrant chiefs"), whom they saw as complicit in the new colonial rules. Women drew on taboos regarding female nudity and publicly undressed, shaming men for cooperating with the colonial system. The women also released political prisoners. While their actions were nonviolent, the women proudly called all this "warfare" to make clear that they were fearlessly confronting colonial authorities. Although the women involved in the Igbo Women's War used peaceful methods, colonial troops killed several of them. As the campaign went on, the British government replaced numerous warrant chiefs, and several commissions of inquiry came and went. Because of their persistent inability to regain control, local British colonial recorders classified these events as "riots" in the official record, characterizing the women as unruly and hysterical. But eventually, the women succeeded in retaking power, with many women themselves becoming warrant chiefs and judges. The powerful women's collective action network that emerged from the Igbo Women's War continued to organize demonstrations and noncooperation against colonial power numerous times in subsequent decades, ultimately playing a key role in Nigeria's independence. Despite the official record, Nigerian scholars have recovered and reclaimed this episode as a story of nonviolent resistance.[36]

Yes, riots are complicated. Riots can be chaotic scenes, and participants can often lose track of who is part of the movement and who are provocateurs aiming to make a protest look chaotic, thereby undermining its legitimacy. When protesters begin physically attacking bystanders or police, such escalations can have unpredictable or negative political effects that extend well beyond the events themselves. But movements that are well organized can often return the public narrative to its core claims and demands, undermining authorities' attempts to paint the movement as thuggish or threatening and returning attention to the state violence that often provokes such events in the first place.

Does property destruction count as civil resistance?

Opinions vary. Most scholars consider nonviolent action to be action waged by unarmed people that does not physically harm or threaten to harm a person. When it is disciplined and discriminating, and sends a clear message, property destruction can be considered a nonviolent method of sabotage. But when it's undisciplined or indiscriminate, or sends an ambiguous message about whether its perpetrators intend to harm people, property destruction can be a gray area for many, even if it's not technically violent.

In one famous example, in December 1773, about sixty pro-independence American dissidents dressed as Mohawk Indians boarded three ships in Boston Harbor and dumped 342 chests of tea into the sea. They were meticulously careful not to destroy property unnecessarily; they reportedly even replaced one iron padlock they had broken when opening the tea chests.[37] This act clearly hurt no one physically. However, it sent a clear message to the British imperial authorities that colonists had the ability to do economic damage—in this case, £10,000 of damage in a single night (which would be more than £1.5 million today). The perpetrators were widely celebrated as patriots by other revolutionaries—and also avoided being denounced by other pro-independence leaders who favored a more gradual, negotiated exit from Great Britain. Two centuries later, during the 1960s in the United States, some antiwar activists burned and destroyed draft cards—federal property—to protest the Vietnam War. And other antiwar activities have tried to destroy weapons or munitions in an attempt to prevent or end violence. In all of these cases, property damage avoided harming others, had discriminate targets, and projected a clear message of nonviolent intent.

But property damage can send more mixed signals when it appears to be indiscriminate, such as lighting buildings on fire or smashing the windows of passenger cars, especially when it unintentionally harms people, including passersby. Smashing windows, burning cars, and vandalizing homes often draws widespread public criticism—suggesting, to many, lawlessness rather than a desire to build a more just system. Historical and cultural context can play a role in how a broader society interprets such tactics, too. For instance, in countries that have recently emerged from war or pogroms targeting property, the destruction of property may trigger collective trauma rather than curiosity or sympathy. Many observers are confused about the message of these actions. Spectators may wonder: Are the demonstrators just burning off steam? Defying authority? Carelessly destroying local businesses? Targeting specific business owners for retribution? Or sending a broader message about the need to destroy capitalism and its economic inequalities? If they are out to destroy capitalism, what are they proposing to build in its place? Will the world that they are trying to build also involve smashing windows or burning police cars? What world are they inviting us to? Who will be allowed, and who will be excluded from the new society?

Such questions consciously or subconsciously preoccupy many who observe large-scale property destruction during protests—even if such actions are not technically violent. That provides an important reminder that just because an action is classified as nonviolent does not necessarily mean it is tactically or strategically wise. The same could be said of any nonviolent method.

Are hunger strikes, self-immolation, and other forms of self-harm considered civil resistance?

Hunger strikes, self-immolation, and the like are nonviolent techniques because the protagonist does not physically harm or threaten to harm others. Those involved are working to send a clear message: remove the reason for my suffering, and we can begin to resolve our conflict.

Many movement activists and leaders have held hunger strikes in prison, including suffragists fighting for the right to vote and equal pay for women in the United Kingdom from 1909 to 1914. American suffragists, like Alice Paul, followed suit. The suffragists' hunger strikes allowed them to continue waging nonviolent struggle from within prison. As women began to endure torturous forced feeding—a wildly unpopular technique of repression—suffragists outside of prison wrote newsletters and printed posters detailing the grim events. As the general public heard and read about women willingly suffering for a higher cause, the hunger strikers gained the moral high ground. Hunger strikes continually put British and American government authorities in a tactical dilemma. Jailers could either subject prisoners to forced feeding, bringing them increased sympathy and support—or prison authorities could release hunger strikers from detention, allowing them to organize more action on behalf of their cause.

Decades later, a similar dilemma faced the authorities in Northern Ireland in 1981 after they captured members of the Provisional Irish Republican Army (PIRA) in connection to several bombings. Bobby Sands, a PIRA member, led a widely publicized hunger strike in prison in opposition to dehumanizing conditions. He died of starvation after sixty-seven days along with nine others. Sands was widely seen as a martyr of the movement, galvanizing recruitment for the PIRA in the aftermath.

César Chávez, Mahatma Gandhi, and others have used hunger strikes and fasts to protest their own movements' lack of discipline. Chávez, a key organizer of the California Farm Workers Union, went on a hunger strike to shame union members who had attacked against farmers and their supporters during a protest. Gandhi frequently undertook hunger strikes to pressure different Indian nationalist organizations to cooperate with one another against British colonial rule, or to protest riots and anticolonial violence.

Hunger striking causes extreme suffering and carries the risk of serious injury, illness, or death. But setting oneself on fire has historically been a more lethal tactic of self-harm. Responding to extreme injustice by taking one's own life—and in such a visible and painful way—has powerful symbolic effects. The act may signal sacrificial commitment to a cause, appeal to the opponent's moral conscience, and convey that the movement wishes the opponent no harm. In South Vietnam in 1963, six Buddhist monks set themselves on fire in protest of anti-Buddhist massacres by the pro-Catholic South Vietnamese government. These acts became international symbols of justice, souring John F. Kennedy's relationship with the Vietnamese president Ngo Dinh Diem, and motivating deeper US engagement in the conflict between South Vietnam and North Vietnam once Diem was overthrown and assassinated in 1963. Between 1966 and 1974, dozens of Vietnamese people self-immolated in protest of US support for South Vietnam, the South Vietnamese government's repressive policies, and the war between North, South, and the US. Powerful symbolic acts like self-immolation sometimes lead to diffusion, with dissidents replicating such techniques in other countries or other contexts. For instance, once the United States entered the Vietnam War, nine Americans replicated the monks' tactics by burning themselves alive in the United States—this time, in protest of the nation's relentless escalation of aerial bombing, counterinsurgency, and boots on the ground. In India, numerous Tamil activists burned themselves alive in the mid-1960s to protest the imposition of Hindi in place of the Tamil language. And anticommunist dissidents in Poland, Czechoslovakia, Hungary, and Romania engaged in waves of self-immolation in the late 1960s and early 1970s as well.

More recently, in 2008, the Chinese government cracked down on a Tibetan movement demanding freedom, democracy, and self-determination and protesting China's occupation of Tibet, its ban on Buddhist practices, and its policy of resettling Han Chinese in the region to dilute its character. Since then, over 150 Tibetans—largely Buddhist monks, nuns, and youth—have set themselves on fire in protest. It's a controversial tactic in Tibet. Some critics suggest that the incidents have only increased Chinese repression, attempting to extinguish the practice by expanding surveillance in the region. But others argue that the technique shames the Chinese government and signals Tibetans' willingness to sacrifice their lives to improve their political situation—potentially bringing international sympathy and support. What's more, self-immolation gives people a sense of total control of their own lives. In deciding when and how to die, and to die on behalf of their community, these protesters resist and escape government control in a decidedly nonviolent way. As the Dalai Lama said, "I think the self-burning itself is practice of nonviolence. These people, you see, they easily use bomb explosive, more casualty people. But they didn't do that. Only sacrifice their own life. So this also is part of practice of nonviolence [sic]."[38]

Sometimes self-immolation can spark a broader movement for change. In Tunisia in December 2010, Mohammed Bouazizi set himself on fire after he was fined for selling fruit from his cart without a permit. His sacrifice—and the structural economic injustices that motivated it—so deeply resonated with hundreds of thousands of Tunisians that they mobilized a mass uprising and ousted Ben Ali, a dictator approaching his thirty-second year in power. That set off the Arab uprisings in 2010 and early 2011.

Self-immolation, then, lets individuals signal their independence from government control, dramatizes injustices inflicted on a community, and can set off broad-based mobilization. Sometimes self-harm does shame those who are its targets; sometimes it has little effect. Certainly, the wave of antiwar self-immolations in Vietnam and the United States eroded American popular support for involvement in the Vietnam War. But like any other tactic, self-immolation and hunger strikes accomplish little on their own. Unless such tactics are legible as part of a larger movement and can help that movement expand its support, they remain isolated acts that cannot create change on their own.

What is the difference between civil resistance and civil disobedience?

In civil disobedience, people deliberately break a law—nonviolently, believing that the law is immoral or unjust—while knowing that they'll go to prison as a result. Trying to get away with breaking the law doesn't count. The lawbreaking must be visible, committed publicly as a protest against what someone perceives as injustice. And the person who breaks the law must be fully willing to accept the punishment, serving a prison term if that's required. For instance, if someone's drafted into the armed forces but refuses to serve—often known as "conscientious objection"—going to prison instead counts as civil disobedience, but escaping to another country would not. Civil disobedience can be one method of civil resistance—but not all civil resistance includes civil disobedience. And an individual may commit an act of civil disobedience without being part of a civil resistance campaign.

In one of the more well-known acts of civil disobedience—indeed, the act that gave the technique its name—iconoclast Henry David Thoreau went to jail in 1846 after he refused to pay a local poll tax. Thoreau had believed the tax was levied to support the Mexican-American War, which he believed was illegal and immoral; moreover, he objected to paying a tax to what he believed was a racist and unjust federal government protecting slaveholders. He was disgusted that his fellow northerners appeared indifferent to slavery and racism. Legend has it that essayist and neighbor Ralph Waldo Emerson visited Thoreau during his night in jail and asked

Thoreau why he was there—to which Thoreau responded, "Why are you *not* here?"

Upon being released, Thoreau wrote to his fellow citizens to explain why they should violate unjust laws. His pamphlet "Resistance to Civil Government" explained why he was willing to serve time in prison rather than follow an unjust law that supported an unjust system.

Thoreau's writings have inspired numerous people around the world to use civil disobedience as part of their campaigns to protest injustices at home and abroad.

Is digital hacktivism ever considered civil resistance?

"Hacktivism"—both the term and the actions it describes—emerged in the mid-1990s. It means using digital technology to pursue collective political goals. Hacktivism takes many forms, as examined here.

To many people, hacktivism is controversial as political action because people can wage political struggle anonymously and individually, without accountability to a broader movement structure. Moreover, hacktivism often appears disconnected from political goals, instead appearing as online harassment or organized criminal activity rather than effective movement organizing.

Over twenty years ago, activist and author Naomi Klein suggested that hacktivism could be more legitimate and effective if those who practiced it were more thoroughly integrated into and coordinated with broader international human rights campaigns. In 1998, she wrote,

> *Imagine if computer hackers, the daredevils of the networked world, suddenly became principled political activists; if they had a mission besides breaking and entering; if they had more to prove than that they are smarter than whoever designed your computer system, if their targets were selected as part of well-organized, thoroughly researched, international human rights campaigns.*[39]

Certainly, activists could use the internet—as during the Sudanese Revolution, during which they turned their Facebook and Twitter profile pictures blue to project solidarity with Sudanese activists, or during the Egyptian Revolution of 2011 during which activists used Facebook to coordinate and organize events—as part of a movement for social change.

But hacktivism as it's been practiced over the past twenty years hasn't always had those effects. Let's look at three forms of hacktivism in particular: gaining access to and publishing private documents, distributed denial of service (DDoS) attacks, and doxxing.

Hacking and releasing private documents

Most civil resistance scholars would say that hacking a private server to expose information about government corruption could count as civil resistance, as long as two conditions were met. First, what was exposed would have to be relevant to the public interest; second, the release would have to be just one action in a campaign involving other methods aimed at achieving a particular outcome. More generally, leaking information in the public interest can be a powerful form of civil resistance. For instance, in 1971, military analyst Daniel Ellsberg leaked the Pentagon Papers to the *New York Times* and *Washington Post*, exposing the fact that for years, presidential advisers had known that the US war in Vietnam was disastrous and unwinnable—and kept sending troops anyway. As part of a broad movement opposing the war, that release transformed the discussion, helping Americans better understand what was actually happening. Ellsberg was charged under the Espionage Act in 1973 and released on bail. Although he admitted to leaking the data and was willing to go to prison, a federal judge later dismissed the charges because of illegal investigation practices against Ellsberg. His actions are easily classified as part of a broader civil resistance campaign: a robust antiwar movement already underway in the United States.

A one-time hack that exposes documents alleging corruption might count as civil resistance, too. For instance, in 2010, US army intelligence analyst Chelsea Manning released classified documents about the wars in Afghanistan and Iraq; she pled guilty to the main charges in 2013. Therefore, this act may fall under the category of civil disobedience. But it was not part of a broader civil resistance campaign, in which a movement infrastructure was ready to use this release as part of a broader strategy toward a particular goal.

If leaks put individuals in harm's way—for instance, by exposing intelligence operations' sources and methods, which could lead to people being killed—that's not civil resistance, as it threatens physical harm. That's the controversial accusation against former security analyst Edward Snowden, who in 2013 leaked thousands of pages of classified intelligence documents, which the US government claimed compromised the safety of its informants and operatives. Of course, governments often try to discredit or delegitimize whistleblowers.

DDoS (distributed denial of service) attacks

DDoS attacks disrupt a particular target's internet service by sending a flood of system traffic—so much that it overwhelms a server, network, or service. When DDoS attacks succeed, the targeted systems can't function temporarily. DDoS attacks can be part of a broader campaign. Consider the 2018–2019 Sudanese Revolution, when a broad-based coalition of pro-democracy activists rose up against dictator Omar al-Bashir, toppling him after three decades in power. During the campaign, several hacktivist groups—the Ghost Squad Hackers, the Sudan Cyber Army, and the Brazil-based group Pryzraky—aimed DDoS attacks at Sudanese government websites. For example, in February 2019, Ghost Squad Hackers used DDoS attacks against the Sudanese chamber of commerce, the ministry of petroleum and gas, the ministry of the interior, and the office of the presidency. In March, the group Anonymous aimed a DDoS attack on the Sudan president's office and left websites altered in insulting ways; Anonymous also aimed DDoS attacks against Sudan's ministry of labor, the central bureau of statistics, the ministry of agriculture, the Sudan national police, and several media and local government websites. On April 6 alone, hackers targeted over 250 Sudanese domains with DDoS attacks.[40] No one knows whether these activities had any independent effects on the revolution, nor is it clear whether the hacktivists coordinated with any of the groups mobilizing against al-Bashir. At the time, hundreds of thousands of Sudanese people were in the streets protesting al-Bashir's ongoing presidency, which they ultimately ended; that massive popular uprising probably would have succeeded with or without the DDoS attacks.

DDoS attacks can be carried out as the online equivalent of a method that civil resistance movements have often used: flooding administrative systems. During the early stages of the US civil rights movement, activists would sit in at lunch counters, asking to be served a cup of coffee from waitstaff who'd been told they could only serve white people. These activists would routinely volunteer to be arrested in such massive numbers that they would overwhelm the jail cells and court proceedings, costing local authorities time and money. In 2011, the Russian government's child welfare agency took one activist's children away, charging her with child negligence in retaliation for her political activism. In response, her movement's members overwhelmed the child protective services' administrative offices with phone calls and protests outside the building, demanding the children's return. The agency's administrator grew tired of the harassment and released the children back to their mother.

DDoS attacks can be used in similar ways. Generally speaking, as long as resisters don't target administrative systems whose interruption could result in someone's bodily harm or death—avoiding, for instance, bringing down emergency services, traffic grids, electric grids, healthcare systems, and so on—disrupting administrative systems can be carried out in a way that is consistent with civil resistance, as long as one is physically harmed as a result; and the action takes place as part of a broader movement's strategies. Thus, DDoS attacks could be one tool in the civil resistance box, perhaps used more often than other hacktivist techniques.

Of course, not all hacktivist collectives behave in ways consistent with civil resistance as a technique. Many are shadowy, only loosely affiliated (if at all) with a broader movement or local grassroots activism, and carry out their actions with little clear accountability to others. For instance, in 2013 Anonymous used a DDoS attack to overwhelm servers for thirty Philippines government websites, drawing attention to corruption there. Although this action drew some media attention, there is no indication that the group coordinated with people living in the Philippines who may have had their own story to tell.[41]

Doxxing, or releasing private information to shame, harass, or
punish individuals

The third hacktivist method that we're considering is doxxing,
a technique in which hackers publicly expose their target's private information, usually on the internet. The information shared
often includes bank account information; home addresses; private videos, photos, or emails; and employers' information. Many
people associate doxxing with personal vengeance—exposing
or harassing people to settle a personal score. But doxxing also
has some political variants, where activists use doxxing to expose corruption, scandalous romantic details, or contact information that allows activists to call, email, or stage protests at the
homes of their adversaries. Activists who doxx political leaders,
for instance, often say they are trying to expose wrongdoing—or
simply to inconvenience or shame their political adversaries into
changing their behaviors. Critics of doxxing call it harassment,
however, because publicly shaming an individual often looks pu-
nitive and retaliatory. With doxxing, because exposing someone's
home, job, and beliefs can prompt someone else to assault or kill
them, the line between nonviolent and violent resistance may be
blurred.

Doxxing is not on Gene Sharp's list of methods, although social
ostracism and "haunting" individuals are. Doxxing may be a digital
mashup of those two methods, since the person who's been doxxed
is often harassed and shamed publicly for months or longer, to the
point of having to go into hiding after getting threats of physical assault, sexual assault, or death. Once again, how and why activists dox
someone make all the difference in whether the action qualifies as civil
resistance. If activists dox someone so that they'll be ostracized for their
behavior—and if it leads to social ostracism only—then it may qualify
as civil resistance. But if someone doxxes an individual in order to harm
them—for instance, by publishing someone's home address along with
a hateful screed that might encourage violence against them—it cannot
be considered an act of nonviolent resistance. Even if a movement
intends no harm to a doxxed individual, the method can be volatile;
it's impossible to control how others act in response to such exposure.

Doxxing is the online equivalent of a tactic that has long been
in use: publishing posters and newsletters that contained private

information about movement opponents. In the 1980s and 1990s, for instance, US antiabortion activists published and widely circulated on conspicuous "WANTED" posters the names, addresses, and professional networks of doctors who performed abortions. As a result, several doctors were killed at their clinics or in their homes; numerous others endured attempted murders, bombings, and arson attacks against abortion clinics and staff. Many observers believed that those flyers, combined with widespread movement rhetoric arguing that abortion doctors were literally murdering children, incited the violence against these doctors. However, none of the publishers were charged with crimes.

More recently in the United States, antifascist activists have doxxed people whose association with neo-Nazi groups hadn't previously been public; this loosely coordinated effort aimed at bringing their affiliations into public view, in order to cost them both socially and economically. Some of those targeted in this way have lost their jobs and been ostracized by their friends, family, or communities. Antifascists argue that publicly exposing such associations ensures information transparency and puts legitimate social pressure on people with violent and reprehensible views. As a result, most antifascist activists consider doxxing to be the equivalent of the post-Holocaust Nazi hunting efforts, which nonviolently exposed people associated with fascism.[42] Antifascist doxxing is part of a broader effort to remove all venues through which fascists can organize or speak publicly. Tracking the whereabouts of alt-right and white nationalist groups, antifascists often engage in street fighting, blockades, and other ways to disrupt their platforms. Many antifascists believe that the goal of removing fascists from public discussion is so important that it justifies the means.

But doxxing is not limited to antifascist groups. Over the past few years, far-right groups such as the Proud Boys have begun to employ doxxing techniques against their perceived enemies, including antifacism and antiracism activists. People participating in racial justice protests in the US during the summer of 2020 had numerous disturbing and threatening encounters with doxxing. Far-right groups, which glorify violence, feel no constraints in using this tactic to harass and intimidate individuals associated with leftist groups.

Are most people involved in nonviolent campaigns pacifists?

Usually not. If the movement and its goals attract a vast number of people, few will be pacifists. Requiring everyone involved to become pacifists would virtually guarantee that the movement would stay small. But one of the reasons to use civil resistance rather than violence is that civil resistance movements spend less time and fewer resources persuading potential supporters that their actions are moral and just. People can be convinced that nonviolent resistance is more effective than violence—and agree to forgo violence for that reason. With skilled organizing and leadership, movements have maintained nonviolent discipline without having any strict pacifists involved at all.

Even Gandhi, the standard-bearer of civil resistance, was not a strict pacifist. He famously said that he believed that if the choice were between violence and submission to oppression, people should use violence. In 1927, he wrote in the newspaper *Young India*, "My creed of nonviolence is an extremely active force. It has no room for cowardice or even weakness. There is hope for a violent man to be some day non-violent, but there is none for a coward."[43] That said, Gandhi was committed to using nonviolent resistance—and saw as a failure his inability to convince every Indian of its spiritual and political power.

How is civil resistance related to "civility"?

These concepts are basically unrelated. "Civility" often connotes politeness, respectfulness, and tolerance for others' opinions and views. But civil resistance needn't involve any of those. Rather, the word "civil" here refers to a movement's collective, civic character— and to the limits it embraces.

Civil resistance is civic action—action involving other citizens, other members of a shared community. People collectively use this method to express their claims, shine a light on injustice, and make public demands. But they do so together, and they do so on behalf of many people. Civil resistance is effective when people use it collectively, making a claim about how that community or nation ought to treat its members. That distinguishes it from individual acts of resistance and defiance—which can inspire others, but rarely create change on their own.

Second, civil resistance is a method that embraces limits on its tactics, rejecting the use of violence. It is conducted with civilian, not military, methods. Civil resisters may be disruptive, as in shutting down highway traffic by blockading a highway. Or they may use more subtle approaches, as when someone feigns ignorance when a soldier from an occupying army asks for directions to the nearest store. But civil resistors are not violent. They don't carry weapons. They don't threaten others with violence. They defeat their opponents with skill and political maneuvering, not through terror or military might.

To keep the moral high ground and avoid being accused of igniting disorder or inciting violence, many civil resistance campaigns are careful to stay far away from any tactics that might look chaotic or illegitimate. Such movements emphasize that they wish their opponents no harm by using numerous nonviolent tactics, bringing in a large and diverse group of participants, and frequently insisting on their peacefulness. At the same time, their refusal to back down, even at a personal cost to many of those involved, also emphasizes their refusal to be misused, oppressed, or subjugated. Staying within these carefully drawn lines means that some observers or factions will accuse the movement of not being radical or transgressive enough to lead to change—or that whatever they do manage to change doesn't transform society fully enough.

But civil resistance can be highly transgressive and defiant even when obviously nonviolent. There was nothing polite or obedient or status quo about Black students occupying whites-only lunch counters at Woolworth's in Greensboro, North Carolina, in 1960, sparking similar acts of defiance throughout the South. Such visibly dangerous but determinedly peaceful acts brought enormous swelling momentum for the US civil rights movement, which in the end utterly transformed race relations in the US South. That transformation stalled in the mid-1960s; institutional and structural racism remains in place. But social transformation isn't a one-and-done effort; many generational iterations are required. And the fact that racial inequality hasn't been entirely eradicated cannot be blamed on the US civil rights movement's use of nonviolent rather than armed resistance to end Jim Crow.

Indeed, civil resistance—including in the mid-twentieth-century US South—has repeatedly won impressive changes, often in situations where armed uprisings failed, and with far less cost to human life.

What is the difference between a civil resistance campaign and a social movement?

A campaign mobilizes people for a limited time, using a series of coordinated methods to achieve a discrete goal. As we've discussed, these are disruptive methods like strikes, protests, sit-ins, boycotts, and other forms of noncooperation—outside the system's normal methods for political or economic engagement like joining a party, running for office, filing petitions, and so on. Social movements may conduct campaigns, but campaigns can happen outside of an organized social movement. For instance, the civil rights movement included a variety of campaigns, such as the Montgomery bus boycotts, the Nashville desegregation campaign, and the Freedom Rides. Alternately, civic groups make their demands, press for change, and then disband just as quickly as they came together. For instance, some have argued that the Tunisian Revolution of Dignity in 2010–2011 emerged as more of a campaign than a movement, with a variety of groups uniting to oust dictator Ben Ali from power.

Social movements differ from campaigns in that they are enduring phenomena that work over a long period of time; they tend to combine organizing, institutional advocacy, and other political activities in order to change society. Unlike campaigns, however, social movements can be dormant for some period, receding from public view while still keeping the infrastructure and historical memory that makes it possible to reemerge, organizing and mobilizing supporters in a new moment. Sometimes movements fade away entirely. They may shrink to a dedicated group of advocates who continue to educate and train core supporters. Their institutions and leaders may build coalitions and plan their next campaigns—until the next generation sees the injustice afresh and reinvents the movement for a new era.

Civil resistance campaigns tend to focus on confrontational and collective mobilization; social movements don't necessarily use civil resistance. Movements can involve a full range of nonconfrontational political activities, such as researching an issue and educating the public and political leaders about the problem, endorsing political candidates, writing and advocating for policy platforms, and arguing for their claims through the courts.

Like civil resistance campaigns, social movements are often carried out by a variety of organizations that are both complementary and competitive. More groups can mean more staffing, members, and reach, enabling the movement to accomplish more. But it can also mean tension among coalition partners as they debate the urgency and appropriateness of different goals and tactics. For example, the environmental movement has been made up of many organizations that emphasize a broad range of demands and tactics. From 350 to Greenpeace to the World Wildlife Fund to Extinction Rebellion to the Sunrise Movement, these groups endorse slightly different platforms and pursue their goals through different tactics—sometimes running their own campaigns individually and sometimes working collectively. For instance, Extinction Rebellion waged its First and Second Rebellions in spring and fall 2019, shutting down major thoroughfares in London and elsewhere with human blockades, encampments, street theater, and mass demonstrations. But it also participated in the Global Climate Strike on September 21, 2019—a campaign waged by a global coalition of environmental groups. The #FridaysforFuture walkouts and rallies, which began in August 2018 with Greta Thunberg's weekly protests outside the Swedish parliament in Stockholm, have similarly been integrated into a coalition that includes both long-standing climate organizations like Greenpeace as well as newer groups like the Sunrise Movement, working in a global campaign.

Many civil resistance campaigns emerge out of social movements, and many social movements have waged civil resistance campaigns. Although the terms are not strictly synonymous, the concepts are close enough that many people use the terms "campaign" and "movement" interchangeably.

What are the stages of a civil resistance campaign?

There is no standard formula. Some civil resistance campaigns are loosely organized and don't plan out next steps. One example might be the 2019 Hong Kong uprising, in which thousands of citizens poured into the streets to object when China appeared to be taking steps to erode the city's democratic rights and liberties, folding it into the autocratic state despite having promised it would not. Until the 2019–2020 COVID-19 pandemic, Hong Kong's leaderless movement simply kept filling the streets, apparently with few organized plans other than to stay there until the movement's demands were met.

Other movements, in contrast, have spent months or years planning strategy before mobilizing, first defining the campaign's goals, structure, leadership, and sequence of tactics. For instance, in 2000, when Serbia's youth movement Otpor wanted to remove the country's autocratic leader, Slobodan Milošević, from power, the group developed a specific plan to do so through free and fair elections. A small group of Otpor's leaders helped to bring together Serbia's opposition political parties into a coordinated effort to run a unity candidate against Milošević. They also helped to devise an election monitoring system, where their offices in Belgrade received independent reports of vote counts from districts all over Serbia. The movement trained thousands of youth activists, who were scattered around the country, about the theory of nonviolent resistance. Local youth then helped to mobilize their communities to vote, while also organizing small protests and street theater where they lived. Otpor also created a national communications network—through phone, email, posters, and newsletters—that broadcasted evidence of the electoral fraud. Otpor also mobilized hundreds of thousands of Serbs to descend on Belgrade at a critical point, flooding the parliamentary square with mass demonstrations. Milošević's security forces—seeing the massive opposition against him and sometimes recognizing their own acquaintances among the demonstrators—refused to comply with orders to violently disperse the crowds. Milošević fled.

The Serbian example shows the importance of strategic planning, preparation, and training prior to mobilization. Trainers associated with the King Center and other institutions associated with Dr. Martin Luther King Jr.'s teachings have adapted a six-step model from his writings. I quote this approach directly here:

1. *Information Gathering: To understand and articulate an issue, problem, or injustice facing a person, community, or institution you*

must do research. You must investigate and gather all vital information from all sides of the argument or issue so as to increase your understanding of the problem. You must become an expert on your opponent's position.

2. *Education: It is essential to inform others, including your opposition, about your issue. This minimizes misunderstandings and gains you support and sympathy.*

3. *Personal Commitment: Daily check and affirm your faith in the philosophy and methods of nonviolence. Eliminate hidden motives and prepare yourself to accept suffering, if necessary, in your work for justice.*

4. *Discussion/Negotiation: Using grace, humor, and intelligence, confront the other party with a list of injustices and a plan for addressing and resolving these injustices. Look for what is positive in every action and statement the opposition makes. Do not seek to humiliate the opponent but to call forth the good in the opponent.*

5. *Direct Action: These are actions taken when the opponent is unwilling to enter into, or remain in, discussion/negotiation. These actions impose a "creative tension" into the conflict, supplying moral pressure on your opponent to work with you in resolving the injustice.*

6. *Reconciliation: Nonviolence seeks friendship and understanding with the opponent. Nonviolence does not seek to defeat the opponent. Nonviolence is directed against evil systems, forces, oppressive policies, unjust acts, but not against persons. Through reasoned compromise, both sides resolve the injustice with a plan of action. Each act of reconciliation is one step closer to the "Beloved Community."*[44]

When is it legitimate to use civil resistance?

For centuries, philosophers have formally addressed this question in writing; those who've tackled it include Thomas Aquinas, Henry David Thoreau, Mahatma Gandhi, Jane Addams, and Barbara Deming. But their writings are just first forays into this difficult territory; all dissidents have had to grapple with this question for themselves. Some people think it is always legitimate for a person to engage in nonviolent resistance—so long as a person or group is genuinely committed to nonviolent action and accepts defeat along with victory.

Not everyone agrees. Civil resistance brings out masses of people to demand change in disruptive ways, disturbing a society's normal, everyday functions—school, work, travel—in the hopes of creating a better world. But mass disruption can have unintended consequences. Leaders can paint the movement as chaotic and crack down violently, suppressing dissent. Impatient movement factions can go rogue, becoming violent themselves. People can lose their jobs, homes, health, or lives.

What's more, some civil resistance campaigns may be using moral means to achieve immoral ends. What if a minority of the country launches a civil resistance campaign to overturn the outcome of a popular election, or to install a dictator or dictatorship? What if a group uses civil resistance to promote harmful policies that will restrict others' freedoms and human rights? All these outcomes have happened, and relatively recently. So what might be some criteria that help activists consider whether a civil resistance campaign is legitimate?

Scholar-activist Maciej Bartkowski in 2017 suggested ten criteria for a movement to consider, particularly when it is rising up against a democratically elected opponent.[45] Here these ten criteria are condensed and paraphrased into five:

1. **The resistance is unarmed and nonviolent.** Peaceful assembly is a widely recognized human right. Resistance may therefore be universally legitimate if it uses only nonviolent and peaceful means, and makes that commitment clear. When movement organizers haven't signaled that their campaign is peaceful or haven't committed to nonviolent discipline, opponents and allies alike often question the movement's legitimacy.

2. **The movement is collective, inclusive, and diverse.** A movement should be broad-based and inclusive, representing many different segments of society. If a movement does not draw in the support of several important segments of the population, or if it deliberately excludes or discriminates against certain

groups, observers may doubt its legitimacy. Like governments, movements are on much safer ground when they build broad-based coalitions that reveal widespread agreement about the movement's underlying claims.

3. **Civil resistance is the last resort.** Bartkowski suggests that before a movement plans to step outside normal, institutional channels to answer its complaints and claims, people must first exhaust normal, legal means for doing so. There is no need to break down the door if it is already open. As we discussed earlier, civil resistance can bring unintended consequences, from more intense repression to civil war. Those involved should carefully evaluate whether such a campaign's potential benefits genuinely outweigh the risks at a particular time and place.

4. **Turning to civil resistance is the exception, not the rule.** In addition to using civil resistance as a last resort, would-be dissidents should also pick their battles. People should not use civil resistance every time they lose politically. If overused, civil resistance becomes disruption for its own sake—tearing down normal life without justification. If civil resistance is never used, however, the powers that be may well take advantage of an overly compliant population. Civil resistance is needed when a situation is so grave that only drastic action can remedy it.

5. **The cause is just.** Generally speaking, I take this to mean that a movement is seeking to emancipate its members and others from cruelty, repression, and restriction, rather than seeking to elevate their own group above others or to impose discrimination and antidemocratic restrictions on outsiders. A movement aiming at exterminating another group, kicking them out of their homes, or discriminating against them is clearly unjust, even if its methods are nonviolent. Of course, this can be murky and controversial; some movements believe their cause is just, while others view it as fundamentally interfering with their own rights. For instance, many within the pro-life movement see their cause as saving unborn children from being murdered; others who mobilize for women's reproductive

rights believe that the pro-life movement is trying to control women's bodies and choices.

Like the just war doctrine, which lays out moral justifications for the use of armed violence, these five criteria could be subject to rationalization and abuse. But precisely because civil resisters claim that their methods and demands are just, peaceful, and widely shared, movements can succeed only if they can continually build and demonstrate their legitimacy.

Can nonviolent resistance be immoral?

In general, it's hard to convincingly argue that the *means* of nonviolent resistance could be immoral, even if they're highly disruptive. But because civil resistance is a method, not an ideology, people could use—and have used—this method to pursue immoral ends.

For instance, in Thailand in 2014, a group of pro-monarchy activists fomented a popular uprising, which ultimately deposed a democratically elected leader and demanded that a military-backed monarchy be restored.

In 2002, a popular uprising in Venezuela against the Hugo Chávez regime led to a popular coup. The coup was short-lived and was quickly overturned by pro-Chávez forces, which regained power; some people believe this incident was an unjust use of civil resistance. In 2013, the Tamarod ("Rebel") campaign mobilized millions of secular and nationalist Egyptians in 2013 to oust democratically elected Mohammed Morsi from power, bringing back a repressive military dictatorship under Morsi's minister of defense, Abdel Fattah al-Sisi. And in 2019, a popular uprising forced out Bolivian president Evo Morales, Latin America's first Indigenous president, who had unconstitutionally run for a fourth term; many argue that military leaders used the widespread popular protests as a pretext for a coup that installed right-wing civilian leaders to roll back Morales's leftist agenda and exclude Indigenous leadership from government positions.

In Europe and the United States, anti-immigrant groups organize mass protests and demonstrations, often relying on racist arguments and ideas, to demand that migrants be kept out of the country. And in the United States, pro-life groups have used various civil resistance tactics, such as harassing doctors and clinics that performed abortions, forming human blockades to prevent people from entering family planning clinics while shouting at patients entering them, and holding regular protests at clinics and on college campuses, and local and national rallies to promote abortion restrictions. If you believe women should have rights to reproductive healthcare that include terminating a pregnancy, you'd view such nonviolent resistance acts as ultimately immoral—even if you might support the tactics if applied toward a goal you share.

Gandhi and his associates were concerned about the immoral use of civil resistance too. Satyagraha—which Gandhi developed as a two-pronged technique that would lead to self-sufficiency as well as noncooperation with colonial laws—was a powerful method and way of life, which anyone could adopt and wield. In February 1919, the British colonial government in India passed the Rowlatt Act, which allowed Indians to be tried without jury and suspects to be detained without trial. Gandhi had visited towns and cities across the country, preparing people to mobilize resistance against the "obnoxious" Rowlatt Act through a nationwide "hartal"—a total shutdown that included worker strikes, voluntary school closings, and citizens' disappearance from public life. Gandhi saw that the laws affected all Indians so viscerally that the outpouring of anger could be channeled into a nonviolent mass uprising.

Preparing for the uprising, Gandhi wrote to renowned Indian poet and nationalist Rabindranath Tagore and asked for his support of the action. In response, Tagore wrote a word of caution:

> *Passive resistance is a force which is not necessarily moral in itself; it can be used against truth as well as for it. The danger inherent in all force grows stronger when it is likely to gain success, for then it becomes temptation. . . . Such a fight is for heroes and not for men led by impulses of the moment.*[46]

Tagore's warning was prescient. The hartal began across the country on April 6, 1919, and was widely heralded as a success, especially because Hindus and Muslims united to observe it—an important step in resisting the British Raj's divide-and-rule strategy. On April 8, the government arrested Gandhi. As news of his arrest spread, protests erupted around the country. In the city of Ahmedabad in Gujarat, protesters attacked Europeans, looted their homes, and torched a number of official buildings. The government declared martial law and dispatched troops to put down the riots. The troops killed dozens and injured over one hundred more. Gandhi canceled the satyagraha and launched a fast to atone for these incidents—as he put it, to "offer satyagraha against ourselves for the violence that has occurred."[47] He concluded that organizing a large-scale uprising had been premature, and the Indian independence movement needed to wait until nonviolence spread more broadly and was internalized as a way of life.

Moreover, civil resistance campaigns are increasingly met with counterprotests. A 2019 study by Nils Weidmann and Espen Rød suggests that in autocracies, one pro-government protest takes place for every seven antigovernment protests.[48] These numbers are remarkably consistent with trends in protest and counterprotest in the United States since Trump's inauguration; from 2017 to 2019, about 85% of protests were against Trump and about 15% (or one in seven) protests were held in support of him or his policies.

Counterprotesting can sometimes be an intentional strategy used by authoritarians to drum up and demonstrate public support for the status quo. Or it can simply be that protests and counterprotests often occur in tandem. Like civil resistance campaigns, counterprotests can win when they put up the numbers of participants necessary to divide their opponents and leverage existing power structures in their favor; they lose when they cannot. If progressive people want to avoid such outcomes, they need to out-organize and out-mobilize these more reactionary or regressive movements.

Is it fair to expect oppressed people to fight back against oppression using only civil resistance?

No. In the newspaper *Harijan*, Gandhi wrote, "Though violence is not lawful, when it is offered in self-defence or for the defence of the defenceless, it is an act of bravery far better than cowardly submission. . . . Every man must judge this for himself. No other person can or has the right."[49] It certainly cannot be fair to demand that people fighting oppression do so using methods prescribed by others, even if other observers believe that their methods will be counterproductive.

As the Black feminist activist Wilmette Brown wrote,

As long as Black people are denied self-determination, reliable allies, and the resources to liberate ourselves, we are forced to resort to our power to destroy—as the only power we have, and as the only way to get more power. In that context our violence is always in self-defence, and white people who have more power than we do, counselling us against violence, place themselves in the indefensible position of presuming to choose our weapons for us.[50]

Yet questions of justice and political effectiveness are often in tension. Most scholars of civil resistance stay agnostic on this question by leaving aside moral questions altogether and focusing on strategy, not morality. Others say that they do not judge what methods anyone facing oppression should use to fight it. But those are scholars and others on the sidelines. Within movements, activists can differ profoundly on whether civil resistance is effective and appropriate, and over who has the authority to dictate the methods used. These heated debates often fracture and confound movements, limiting what kinds of activities coalitions can agree upon.

For instance, scholar-activist Chris Rossdale studied the UK antimilitarism movement from World War I onward. He found that strict pacifists wouldn't partner with those who refused to rule out acts of violent self-defense; the pacifists argued that such tactics were both immoral and counterproductive.[51] On their side, those keeping such options open were not necessarily endorsing unlimited or uncontrolled violence—but they argued that pacifists and outsiders had no right to dictate what actions others could take in facing down much greater violence by their opponents, especially when those opponents' power and authority was in fact based on their monopoly on violence. Debates like these often create fault lines that can make it difficult for coalitions to work together and wage an ongoing struggle. The fault line is not about whether antimilitaristic direct action ought to be nonviolent; most agree that it should be, whenever possible. Rather, the division is over who has the right to dictate what another person decides to do when confronting a much more powerful and potentially lawless opponent. This set of arguments and concerns echoes the stance of civil rights icon Ella Baker, who said in the 1960s, "People under the heel had to be the ones to decide what action they were going to take to get (out) from under their oppression."[52]

Those who observe movements should practice humility and suspend judgment about whether movements' methods are justified—particularly when the observers are not subject to the types of oppression that movement is fighting. As the pacifist pan-African activist Bill Sutherland often said, "Our job is not to tell people how to free themselves. Our job is to get our government's boots off their necks."[53]

The most important thing for observers to do is to learn how to reliably show solidarity, share resources, and create opportunities whereby people can liberate themselves. Instead of asking why people seeking justice are resorting to violence and asking whether it is wise, people can ask themselves what nonviolent methods *they* can employ themselves to support people seeking justice in the face of oppression.

2

HOW CIVIL RESISTANCE WORKS

What can they do
to you? Whatever they want.
They can set you up, they can
bust you, they can break
your fingers, they can
burn your brain with electricity,
blur you with drugs till you
can't walk, can't remember, they can
take your child, wall up
your lover. They can do anything
you can't stop them
from doing. How can you stop
them? Alone, you can fight,
you can refuse, you can
take what revenge you can
but they roll over you.
Two people can keep each other
sane, can give support, conviction,
love, massage, hope, sex.
Three people are a delegation,
a committee, a wedge. With four
you can play bridge and start
an organization. With six
you can rent a whole house,
eat pie for dinner with no
seconds, and hold a fund raising party.
A dozen make a demonstration.
A hundred fill a hall.
A thousand have solidarity and your own newsletter;
ten thousand, power and your own paper;

a hundred thousand, your own media;
ten million, your own country.
It goes on one at a time,
it starts when you care
to act, it starts when you do
it again and they said no,
it starts when you say We
and know who you mean, and each
day you mean one more.

—Marge Piercy, "The Low Road"[1]

Over the past century, nonviolent revolutions have succeeded more often than violent revolutions. In fact, in just the past ten years alone, we've seen spectacular people power victories in places as diverse as Sudan, Lebanon, Armenia, Bulgaria, Tunisia, and Thailand. But nonviolent resistance does not always succeed. In the past decade autocratic regimes in Bahrain, Turkey, Iran, Venezuela, and Russia crushed or outmaneuvered mass movements that were trying to challenge them.[2] Why?

This chapter shows why mass participation, defections, tactical innovation, and resilience against repression have helped people to overcome long odds and succeed using civil resistance. In doing so, I take on some of the most common questions about how nonviolent movements succeed, and whether there are situations in which nonviolent resistance is impossible. I also try to debunk some common myths.[3] Those include the idea that civil resistance works by morally converting the opponent; that civil resistance only works in democracies, against weak or ambivalent opponents, or to reform rather than overthrow the government; that violent resistance is more effective than civil resistance; that using a single method of civil resistance—like protest—is enough to create change; and that social media and digital technology always work to the advantage of nonviolent dissidents.

What makes civil resistance campaigns effective?

A common misconception is that nonviolent resistance is only possible in a few situations: when an opponent is too weak or incompetent to prevent or defeat the movement, when the campaign is making fairly straightforward demands for reform, or when a free and open political system makes it easy for people to gather together and organize for change.

But this intuition is wrong. Civil resistance campaigns have worked against weak and strong opponents. They have won reformist and radical demands. And they have done so in incredibly tough political environments where open displays of dissent were nearly impossible.[4]

In fact, the effectiveness of a nonviolent revolution depends much more on its political power than on its moral righteousness. When we look back at the record of such movements, four key factors emerge as critical in explaining their success or failure. Let's look at these in turn.

Mass participation, drawing from all walks of life

The single most important influence on a civil resistance campaign's success is the scale and range of popular participation. The larger and more diverse the campaign's base of participants, the more likely it is to succeed.[5] Mass participation seriously disrupts the status quo; makes continued repression impossible to sustain; prompts defections from its opponent's institutions and supporters, including, often, the security forces;[6] and constrains the power holder's options. Ignoring a large-scale campaign becomes politically impossible. But even the most brutal opponent finds it difficult to indefinitely crack down on large numbers of peaceful people working together to refuse to cooperate with the regime and to disrupt everyday life—particularly when the campaign varies its methods and approaches.[7]

Let's look at how large-scale participation impacted the Sudanese Revolution of 2018–2019, during which a mass movement skillfully and creatively confronted the brutal dictatorship of President Omar al-Bashir, who had been in power for thirty years. Al-Bashir's government had committed genocide in Darfur in the early 2000s and had violently suppressed previous nonviolent uprisings in Sudan in 2011 and 2013. In December 2018, al-Bashir's security forces killed dozens of protesters who had organized spontaneously against the tripling of the price of bread. In response to the violence, protests spread throughout the country, calling for al-Bashir to step down. Students, workers, tea sellers, taxi drivers, civil servants, doctors, lawyers, and other professionals banded together through a coalition that included the powerful Sudanese Professionals Association (SPA). The SPA began to plan for a long-term struggle, training people in the theory and practice of nonviolent resistance and setting forth a strategy for keeping the pressure on al-Bashir through mass demonstrations paired with work stoppages and strikes.

By April, reports emerged that some police and security forces had defected to the side of the protesters, refusing to carry out orders to shoot and kill activists organizing in their towns and villages. By then, hundreds of thousands of people were active in the movement, which included people from all walks of life within Sudan. Al-Bashir's attempts to claim that the movement was organized by Darfuris—a marginalized group—was met with the slogan "We are all Darfuris!"— a powerful rebuke of al-Bashir's attempts to destroy the unity of the movement and scapegoat an already marginalized population.

In the midst of widening participation throughout Khartoum and other Sudanese cities, on April 11, 2019, some Sudanese military officers removed al-Bashir in a coup and established a transitional military council (TMC). But hundreds of thousands of Sudanese people stayed in the streets, calling for the coup leaders to hand over power to civilians and begin a democratic transition. By June, the TMC had grown desperate to suppress the protests. Security forces attacked a sit-in outside the regime's military headquarters in Khartoum, killing, raping, and mutilating hundreds of people in what is now known as the Khartoum Massacre. But instead of falling into disarray, the SPA warned dissidents of an ongoing campaign of intimidation and violence by the TMC, and called for Sudanese people to shift their methods from street protests to a three-day general strike in which people stayed home from their shops, schools, workplaces, factories, and government offices. The strike took place from June 9 to June 11 and quickly demonstrated the power of the movement to wield people power in a disciplined and disruptive manner. But the strike also cleared the streets, keeping people relatively safer from state violence, while also keeping the pressure on the TMC to accommodate the SPA's demands of more civilian oversight and participation in the transition process. By June 12, the TMC had capitulated. Talks resumed with the SPA, perpetrators of the Khartoum Massacre were arrested and tried, and a new constitution was agreed upon in the following months. Although the path ahead is bumpy, the country is on its way to an unexpected democratic transition as I write. This case shows how massive popular participation translates into genuine people power.

Shifting the loyalties of the regime's supporters

Civil resistance works by fomenting enough power from below that grassroots civil society can essentially disrupt or co-opt those responsible for implementing and enforcing the power holder's plans and policies. That leads us to the second key factor: a movement's ability to shift the loyalties of people within the adversary's pillars of support.

Achieving that requires campaigns with many different communities supporting it: women, youth, students, elderly, professionals, taxi drivers, merchants and small-business owners, religious figures, civil servants, and more. The broader the array of supporters, the more likely the movement is to represent the full range of society with diverse spheres of influence—which means more ways to reach people situated within the opponent's pillars of support.

It's important not to underestimate how social power can dramatically affect the status quo. Even people who feel they have no ability to influence the political system have social power. Everyone has at least some relationships through which they can challenge or reinforce others' behavior. And social approval and disapproval are powerful influences on human behavior. A desire to maintain approval or easy relationships with family members, friends, peers, and neighbors can convince even those within a regime that they cannot keep supporting the system. People at every level influence the social milieu and attitudes of some key part of the regime, whether that's foot soldiers on the front lines, generals plotting strategy, civil servants like diplomats, or people working on the electric grid.

This is true even when people do not have other legal options for political participation, like voting. In an earlier era, abolitionist Angelina Grimke made this point in her 1836 pamphlet *Appeal to Christian Women of the South*, before white women in the US had the right to vote:

> But perhaps you will be ready to query, why appeal to women on this subject? We do not make the laws which perpetuate slavery. No

legislative power is vested in us; we can do nothing to overthrow the system, even if we wished to do so. To this I reply, I know you do not make the laws, but I also know that you are the wives and mothers, the sisters and daughters of those who do; *and if you really suppose you can do nothing to overthrow slavery, you are greatly mistaken.* (emphasis in original)

In the nineteenth century, Grimke was acknowledging that even though white women in the southern United States could not vote, serve on juries, or hold political office, they still held the power to subvert or challenge some of the everyday injustices and indignities faced by enslaved people, and could also challenge the morality of slavery when speaking to their husbands, relatives, friends, and children. With their pressure, Grimke believed that over time, white men who made laws in the South would begin to make some concessions, if only to ameliorate their marital distress. (Of course, southern white women did not take up Grimke's call, and there was no sustained, widespread civil resistance against slavery among white southerners—women or men—before the Civil War.)

When movements do manage to pull key regime figures and loyalists to their side, they are more likely to succeed than movements that do not. And shifting these loyalties does not require melting opponents' hearts or appealing to their morals. Often it means hurting the wallets of key economic or business elites, threatening the business or professional interests of important military or security officials, or simply sidelining powerful opponents within the regime as reform-minded elites begin to sense a shift in the political winds and collectively cast aside perceived holdovers.

Of course, each campaign has its own peculiarities. For instance, in highly racist or ethnically divided societies, it can be impossible to persuade security forces—who typically represent a privileged ethnic or racial group—to defect.[8] Many regimes seek to insulate themselves from the risk that police, military, and others will defect by hiring foreigners or mercenaries to supply security; for instance, Bahrain imported Pakistani and Saudi police to put down a 2011 mass movement against the monarchy there. Or regimes exploit existing racial or ethnic divisions within the society, as when South Africa's apartheid-era regime employed disproportionately white South Africans for the security forces. But the loyalty of other key groups, such as economic and business elites, can often weaken if people power imposes enough costs on them. For instance, in apartheid-era South Africa, white business owners ultimately began to support ending apartheid—and pressured the South African government to negotiate with the African National Congress (ANC)—after Black townships boycotted their goods, international corporations divested from the South African economy, and international organizations imposed sanctions on the apartheid government. This pressure from below forced the regime to comply with the opposition's demands.

Using a wide variety of tactics, not just demonstrations

Movements that shift among various tactics are more likely to succeed than movements that rely too much on a single method, like protests or demonstrations. Nonviolent campaigns that draw on their vast human capital to create new and unexpected tactics are better at maintaining momentum than movements that become predictable and tactically stagnant. When movements are especially large, they can afford to retreat from the streets so long as they impose other kinds of pressure.

Let's look at another historical example to see how this works. In 1940 the Nazis invaded Norway and installed a puppet government, run by Vidkun Quisling. In February 1942, Quisling's government attempted to change the curriculum in Norwegian schools to reflect Nazi ideology and propaganda, and ordered Norwegian schoolteachers to join a Nazi teacher association.[9] Up to ten thousand—over 83%—of Norway's teachers refused, went on strike, or continued teaching underground. With schools closed, tens of thousands of children also stayed home. That led a critical pillar—parents of school-age children—to align with the teachers' movement, with hundreds of thousands of parents writing letters demanding an immediate reversal of Quisling's policy in order to return the country to a status quo. In response, Quisling's gestapo rounded up one thousand teachers, jailed them, and publicized news of their inhumane treatment to try to frighten teachers to comply with his orders, but the teachers did not capitulate. Instead, community members raised funds to support families of striking and incarcerated teachers in an act of solidarity. Next, in April 1942, he sent nearly five hundred teachers to a concentration camp in northern Norway, near the Arctic. He was dismayed to learn that Norwegian farmers gathered along the train tracks to sing and hand out food to the prisoners as they rode north on the train. Still, the teachers did not capitulate. By November 1942, Quisling reached the conclusion that he could escalate his brutality, but reasoned that he could not do so and maintain legitimacy among the Norwegian population upon whose acquiescence he depended to stay in power. He abandoned his attempts to Nazify the Norwegian curriculum, as well as other attempts to consolidate Norwegian public and cultural institutions with Nazi control.

This case—and many others—show how a strike, combined with collective support from a broad base of a population, can be truly threatening to a regime's grip on power. It also shows how movements can prepare for such large-scale noncooperation by creating strike funds, stockpiling of food and water, and practicing other kinds of community self-reliance—all of which can make this approach durable. Such techniques are most effective when large numbers of people participate.

Discipline and resilience in the face of repression

Fourth, movements tend to succeed when they develop staying power, which means cultivating resilience, maintaining discipline, and sustaining mass involvement even as the government cracks down on them violently. What's most important is remaining organized, no matter what the regime throws at them—neither fighting back with their own counterviolence or reacting or retreating in disarray. The movements that manage to achieve this usually have clear organizational structures; succession plans in place in case a leader is imprisoned, killed, or otherwise sidelined; and contingency plans for how to respond when repression escalates.[10] It also involves keeping a broad range of people, in mass numbers, involved even while coming under fire, because cracking down on a highly diverse movement is more likely to backfire against the opponent. It is much tougher (though not impossible) for regimes to get away with targeting civilians who are considered mainstream or even close to the regime's social circles than it is to target smaller-scale crowds who are not perceived as representative of the society as a whole.[11] After all, police and military forces are rarely comfortable being asked to use violence against people who may include their children, cousins, accountants, priests, or imams. Because of this potential for backfire—as well as the skillful maneuvering of nonviolent campaigns between methods of concentration and methods of dispersion—nonviolent campaigns can be far more successful than violent campaigns, even when the regime is actively attacking and killing the nonviolent participants. In fact, from 1900 to 2019, maximalist nonviolent campaigns that were facing violent repression succeeded 45% of the time, while violent ones only succeeded 22% of the time.

Each of these four factors—large-scale participation, loyalty shifts, tactical innovation, and resilience in the face of repression—is more easily managed when a movement is well organized and prepared for a long struggle. Don't be fooled by how seemingly quickly many regimes collapse when they face a mass nonviolent uprising. Organized, disciplined campaigns often follow months or years of planning and organizing that precede the mass mobilization. For instance, Serbian activists associated with the Otpor movement—which helped bring down Slobodan Milošević in 2000—often say that 95% of their effort went into planning, training, preparation, and follow-up like distributing photos and videos from an action, writing op-eds to interpret the action, engaging in recruitment efforts, and the like.[12] Only 5% of their effort went into the actions themselves. Similarly, student activists involved in sit-ins to desegregate public accommodations in Nashville, Tennessee, during the US civil rights movement often met every morning before classes began to plan, prepare, and strategize.[13]

What those stories show is that successful nonviolent campaigns are rarely spontaneous. They require time, effort, and planning. In fact, on average, successful mass nonviolent mobilizations last for sixteen months—not including phases in which movements were planning, training, and strategizing before they first launched into mass action. But do keep in mind that this is significantly shorter than the average successful violent campaign, which lasts over five years.

To make civil resistance work, campaigns must be large, they must be innovative and sustained, and they must signal to the regime's communities of support that the political winds have shifted irrevocably—and that switching sides is in their own long-term interests. Size, unity, creative tactical innovation, and leverage through defections are what make nonviolent resistance campaigns successful.

How do nonviolent civil resistance campaigns attract large followings?

So how *does* such a movement attract masses of people from every walk of life? That involves what sociologist Douglas McAdam calls "cognitive liberation"[14]—a process in which a large number of people collectively decide that a grave injustice has taken place, that they must take action to change the situation, that they have to get involved with the collective cause to create the change they want to see, and that they cannot go back to the time when they were unaware of the injustice or were willing to tolerate it rather than risk taking action. Yes, that's a big leap. But McAdam argues that movements are more likely to set off cognitive liberation when they frame their claims in a way that resonates with people from every walk of life, when some political event both motivates and facilitates collective action, and when the movement is well organized enough to mobilize a sustained challenge.[15] I look more closely at each of these elements below.

How do successful civil resistance campaigns get going?

Civil resistance campaigns launch for myriad reasons. Injustices and insults to dignity accumulate over so much time and across so many people—and people start coming together to resist that mistreatment in so many ways—that precise beginnings are hard to pinpoint. The reasons for such mass mobilization thus resist generalization.

Of course, that hasn't stopped academics from trying. In a study published in 2017, Jay Ulfelder and I evaluated numerous leading sociological theories of protest and revolution. Some such theories emphasize collective grievances; others focus on how political opportunities open up during periods of regime weakness or transition; others look at more gradual processes of liberalization that suddenly snowball into a successful mass movement; still others look at whether mass movements had the right resources available—meaning communications, youth with free time, and existing organizational networks into whose membership and experience they could tap.[16] We wanted to know whether any of these could accurately explain or predict how civil resistance campaigns get going.

To our surprise, none of these standard theories accurately predicted where nonviolent uprisings occurred across countries, at least since 1955.[17] They're just too varied.

That said, a few key factors correlate with the beginning of civil resistance uprisings. First, having a large population makes it more likely that a campaign will break out in any given year. Simply because they're so big, large countries like China, India, the United States, and Russia are more likely to experience most kinds of political events. Another factor is having a "youth bulge," or people ages fifteen to twenty-four making up a disproportionate part of the population.[18] This is important, since youth activists—particularly students—tend to drive protest and resistance, in part because they have the time; they have more to gain with less to lose; and they are often concentrated in centralized places like schools.[19] If most people have telephone subscriptions, civil resistance campaigns are more likely to start. That's also true if much of the population lives in cities, concentrating large numbers of people near each another for easier discussion, coordination, and mobilization.[20] Having a large manufacturing sector may help with bargaining power, enabling large groups of people to withhold labor that's essential to the economy.[21] And existing social organizations—such as organized labor or professional associations, religious institutions, or schools and universities—can be especially important in channeling dissent into durable political power.[22]

All these factors open up the *opportunity* to mobilize large-scale resistance. But what *motivates* people to launch high-risk collective action, particularly when the opponent has all the guns and may be willing to using them? Let's look at both short-term triggers and longer-term motivations. Short-term triggers are unique to each movement; they're difficult to anticipate and not necessarily easy to recognize as they are happening. For instance, in December 2010, fruit vendor Mohammed Bouazizi set himself on fire in Sidi Bouzid, Tunisia, in furious despair that local police kept harassing him, demanding bribes, or confiscating his wares, while the governor refused to hear his complaint. Most people believe that his protest triggered the Dignity Revolution in Tunisia in December 2010, leading to the Arab Spring more generally. But many others had self-immolated in Tunisia out of political defiance and despair before that,[23] to no effect. Few know why it was Bouazizi's act of defiance and desperation that set off a revolution.

Similarly, in Sudan in December 2018, in the midst of an economic crisis, the government announced it would no longer subsidize food or fuel. Sudanese people took to the streets to protest—and stayed there until they brought down the regime of autocratic president Omar al-Bashir in April 2019. And a proposed tax on WhatsApp in cash-strapped Lebanon triggered its 2019 October Revolution, during which hundreds of thousands of Lebanese engaged in protests, demonstrations, and strikes, leading the prime minister to resign. Triggers are notoriously impossible to anticipate or to generalize.

Many people assume that economic frustration is the most common reason for mass uprisings. But Ulfelder and I found that economic hardship—as measured by poverty, inequality, inflation, or economic shocks like a sudden decline in economic output—didn't systematically predict the beginning of mass civil resistance campaigns, at least between 1955 and 2013. So what did? Political offenses, like authoritarianism, and visible human rights abuses, like torture, beatings, political imprisonment, or arbitrary killings committed by police or the government were the primary culprits.[24] In fact, we found that a decline in a country's human rights practices from one year to the next regularly led to determined civil resistance. Or to put it differently, as a country became more repressive, the country became more likely to experience a nonviolent uprising.

Why would an *increase* in repression prompt a nonviolent uprising? Wouldn't you think it would frighten citizens into staying quiet instead? Political scientist Wendy Pearlman interviewed activists involved in the Arab uprisings and found that very strong collective emotional states—like outrage combined with pride, joy, and hope—can push people to overcome fear and leap into resistance.[25] That collective anger can be a reaction to widely perceived injustices, such as an assassination or police killing of a respected individual or someone perceived as innocent. In the United States, in May 2020, mass protests erupted across the country in response to the police killing of George Floyd, an unarmed Black man, in

Minneapolis, Minnesota. Or that sense of collective outrage could be motivated by the passage of an unjust or unpopular law, like the Extradition Bill in Hong Kong, which allowed for political prisoners to be extradited to the Chinese mainland for trial and punishment and prompted widespread outrage that residents of the once-democratic territory could suddenly become subject to China's harsher justice system. And what about the hope? That can come from a sense that citizens working together can do something about the injustice.

Once people have the opportunity and motivation to mobilize, why do they choose nonviolent action rather than armed resistance?

One influence is a country's recent protest history. People who've recently been involved in or aware of protests and other nonviolent methods may simply be more familiar with those approaches, recognizing them as a language they share with others and using them to wage another nonviolent struggle.[26] In the United States, the democracy movement that emerged in advance of the 2020 elections was built from the massive coalition of groups that had mobilized for Black lives, immigrant rights, women's rights, gun control, environmental justice, economic justice, and voting rights in the years before. The coalition had organizational capacity to harmonize messaging, share resources, and mobilize and amplify rapid responses to voter harassment, vote tabulation interference, or subversion of the state-by-state certification of the results.

Familiarity with nonviolent action can cross borders: being geographically close to another country that has had a nonviolent uprising can prompt people to think that it might be the time for them to rise up as well.[27] That's why we often see people power movements occurring in regional waves, like the Eastern European color revolutions or the Arab Awakenings—what political scientist Mark Beissinger calls "modular revolutions."[28]

In sum, a few factors do seem to make civil resistance campaigns more likely. But it's also helpful to keep in mind which factors do *not* appear to prompt such campaigns.[29] These include a country's wealth or poverty; its level of education; recent armed conflict; ethnic or linguistic fragmentation; the type of autocracy (military, personalist, single-party, or monarchy); and economic growth or inflation. These factors might be part of the reason why a particular country's population revolts. But they don't seem to have any systematic relationship to whether a particular country will see a mass civil resistance uprising in any given year.[30]

In fact, even though the occurrence of mass movements has increased dramatically over time, popular uprisings are fairly uncommon in any given year. In the most active decade in recorded history—2010–2019—sixty-eight countries experienced at least one such nonviolent revolution. That's about a third of the countries in the world.

Is there a formula for effective civil resistance campaigns?

No universal formula is likely to exist. Every country, every citizenry, every outrage is unique. At the same time, we do find some striking patterns that seem consistent across successful campaigns.

First, there's a critical mass required to alter national governments.[31] No movements have failed after getting 10% of the nation's population to be actively involved in their peak event. Most succeed after mobilizing 3.5%. More on this later.

Second, movements seem to build pressure in ways that a metaphor from Newtonian physics can help explain. Some movements strategize how they can generate and maintain momentum over time by seizing on moments of political opportunity, building their base, sequencing their tactics, and blocking opposing coalitions. In a 2019 study in *Nature Human Behaviour*, political scientist Margherita Belgioioso and I found that a movement's momentum was remarkably good at predicting whether the government would fall on any given day.[32] In Newtonian physics, momentum equals mass times velocity. In movements, mass relates to size, or the number of people participating. Velocity relates to speed, or the speed with which resistance against the opponent is happening. We drew on data on protest events in Africa from 1990 to 2014 to create proxy indicators for mass and velocity. We looked at how many people were protesting on any given day in the country, using that as a measure of mass. Then we multiplied that value by the number of protest events in the prior week, using that as a measure of velocity. This simple metric—mass × velocity = momentum—can be a powerful tool for movements attempting to gauge progress.

Third, many people have identified key movement challenges that, if overcome, generally lead to success. I mentioned four of them above: diverse, large-scale participation; shifting the loyalty of groups or sectors formerly committed to the regime; tactical innovation; and staying power. Others have developed their own checklists. For instance, Peter Ackerman and Hardy Merriman published in 2014 a "Checklist for Ending Tyranny" that offers six items by which movements can evaluate their progress and power.[33] They include three capacities and three trends. For capacities, they suggest working to build (1) the ability to unify people, (2) operational planning, and (3) nonviolent discipline. For the trends, they suggest watching for (1) increasing civilian participation in civil resistance, (2) diminishing impact of repression and backfire, and (3) increasing defections from the movement's adversary.

Who participates in civil resistance campaigns?

All kinds of people, from all walks of life. In fact, the inclusive nature of civil resistance is a major reason nonviolent action is so successful. Nonviolent action is a method of fighting back against injustice that does not require intense physical training, long-term deployments away from home and family, or an unconditional willingness to use violence against opponents.

Therefore, nonviolent campaigns are more likely to bring in women, minorities, children, the elderly, people with disabilities, people with moral commitments to nonviolence, parents of young children, marginalized groups, and others who would not necessarily volunteer for armed struggle.[34] As a result, nonviolent movements tend to have more people involved than do armed struggles. From 1900 to 2019, the average nonviolent revolution brought in the active participation of 1.6% of the national population at its peak. That's four times larger than the average armed insurgency, which yielded only 0.4% active participation.

Nonviolent resistance even enjoys a participation advantage in countries where civil war is underway. At the height of Ukraine's civil war in 2015, for instance, researchers Maciej Bartkowski and Alina Polyakova conducted a survey among Ukrainians living in the war-torn east about how they would respond to a Russian invasion of Ukraine. Respondents were asked whether they would participate in specific tactics such as strikes and work stoppages, noncooperation, protest, attempts to persuade or insult occupying forces, symbolic displays of national unity, and other methods. Over 70% reported that they'd be willing to get involved in at least one of these actions. But only 35% of Ukrainians said they would be willing to participate in armed action, even to defend their own towns.[35]

How are women involved in civil resistance?

Women are regularly at the forefront of civil resistance movements.[36] Examples include nuns positioning their bodies between security forces and activists in the pro-democracy movements in the Philippines and Burma, queer Black women organizing the Black Lives Matter movement in the United States, tea sellers holding a sit-in outside Sudan's military headquarters, grandmothers resisting dictatorship on behalf of their grandchildren in Algeria, poets and playwrights chronicling the January 25 Revolution in Egypt, and young women at the forefront of the global climate movement today.

What's more, having women involved in civil resistance campaigns is vital to their success. Since World War II, very few civil resistance movements that excluded women at the front lines succeeded.[37]

For one thing, movements that exclude women cut themselves off from at least half the population. That hurts the crucial variable—mass participation—that makes or breaks the campaign's political power.

Second, having women involved gives a movement more social networks to use to persuade those supporting the opponent to defect.[38] Because of traditional gender roles, women often have information about where and how to buy or boycott certain products or producers, what supplies various communities will need to sustain a long-term strike, and whether their military husbands or sons will report for duty on any given day of the week. What's more, as Angelina Grimke recognized, they also have social power and influence that can dramatically increase the political leverage of a movement.

Third, with women involved, movements have vastly more opportunities for tactical innovation. Women in Chile are credited with inventing the *cacerolazo*, or pots-and-pans protest, first used in 1971 to protest food shortages under Salvador Allende's government. The method, which also called a "noise barrage" in the Philippines or "casserole" in some English-speaking countries, involves people staying inside their homes (and therefore usually out of harm's way) and banging on empty pots and pans at a coordinated time of day. In a city, this makes it possible for thousands to be involved, generates deafening noise, delivers a powerful impression of unanimous disgust or even rage, and starkly symbolizes a universal, apolitical grievance: hunger. It may not be surprising that women would invent such a protest tactic; often, in traditional societies women are the ones who spend hours in the kitchen or who feel especially comfortable protesting from inside their own homes. The innovation illustrates how women expand a movement's tactical possibilities—both because more people means more imaginations involved, and because, as in this example, women's specific social positions give them unique opportunities for meaningful and creative action.

What's more, having women involved—whether alongside or independent from men—helps to convey the universal and apolitical nature of the grievances that the movement represents. For instance, in Argentina's capital city, Buenos Aires, the Mothers of the Disappeared—also known as the Mothers of the Plaza de Mayo— conveyed such universal claims when they organized protests against the right-wing military junta that, backed by the United States, disappeared thousands of people suspected of opposing the regime during what became called the Dirty War, from 1976 to 1983. This group of mothers began to meet each Thursday in the large Plaza de Mayo in Buenos Aires, demanding to know where their children were. Despite the risk of being disappeared themselves, they protested for decades, eventually wearing white scarves to symbolize peace—and deploying powerful moral claims as mothers to demand accountability and justice for their loved ones. Their efforts helped to inspire courage among those participating in a broader movement against the dictatorship, ultimately resulting in a transition to democracy in 1983. Mothers, wives, and sisters have sought justice for the killings of their loved ones during many war-time contexts, from Bosnia to Sri Lanka to Liberia.

Emulating the Mothers of the Plaza de Mayo, women living in Chile under the right-wing dictator General Augusto Pinochet used a similar technique to protest the regime's kidnapping, torture, and killing of thousands of people who opposed it. The women would arrive in the main parliamentary square and silently dance *la cueca*, Chile's national dance, holding photographs of their missing loved ones. This powerful method symbolized the injustice of the regime's violence, which killed people with impunity, and highlighted the women's moral claims to justice. Women's collectives that formed during this time created a powerful backbone for the pro-democracy movement that emerged in the mid-1980s. Ultimately, they helped to organize "No" votes in a referendum during which General Pinochet sought to renew his grip on power by asking the public to extend his term in office. The "No" votes won decisively, with nearly 56% of the vote. Pinochet's military officers backed the result, and elections were held in 1989, removing him and the dictatorship from power. These powerful symbolic performances of *la cueca* caught the attention of the international community, inspiring Sting's 1987 protest song "They Dance Alone." Along with other artists and the Mothers of the Plaza de Mayo, Sting performed the song at an Amnesty International solidarity concert in neighboring Argentina in 1988.

Women have always developed new and creative tactical innovations that have added important methods to the tactical toolkit that we take for granted today. In the nineteenth century, the Ladies Land League in Ireland created new noncooperation tactics in hopes of securing Irish independence from British rule. Operating under an inherited feudal situation, Irish women were often responsible for cultivating crops and paying rent to landowners, many of whom were nonresident Englishmen. But their efforts did not guarantee land rights, such as protection against arbitrary eviction, or provide opportunities for social or economic mobility. To reduce British economic power over Ireland, they launched a campaign in which they refused to pay rent and refused to help bring in the harvest. In 1880, one of these campaigns targeted Captain Charles Boycott, a land agent in County Mayo, with ostracism. Members of the Ladies Land League along with local shopkeepers, blacksmiths, bakers, cooks, laundresses, maids, postmen, and others refused to serve him, forcing him to leave for England—and coining the term "boycott." That technique spread throughout Ireland. A year later, a comprehensive land reform bill in the British Parliament conceded to the boycotters' demands and established joint ownership between landlords and tenants, a fair rent commission, and guarantees against eviction.

Sometimes, women have used conservative gendered expectations of how women and men are supposed to behave and turned them inside out to create power. For instance, inspired by the 2010 Dignity Revolution in Tunisia, thousands of Egyptians began to protest the dictatorship of President Hosni Mubarak in early 2011, ultimately culminating in a mass uprising in which millions of Egyptians took part. In mid-January 2011, twenty-five-year-old Asmaa Mahfouz posted a YouTube video in which she called on the men of Egypt to rise up against Mubarak—and to demonstrate their courage by joining the women who were already protesting in Tahrir Square, where thousands of Egyptians were assembling in anticipation of large-scale mobilization on January 25. By doing so, she tried to redirect Egyptian masculinity against the regime.

Similarly, women have used gender roles to shame police and security forces about how they're treating protesters, pushing them to be more restrained. For instance, the environmentalist and feminist Green Belt Movement in Kenya has creatively used gender-based social taboos to confront security forces. At one 1992 sit-in protesting deforestation and environmental degradation, police began to beat protesters. Women on the front lines of the demonstration undressed, bore their breasts to publicly shame and repel the police, and de-escalated the situation. That's especially powerful in Kenya, explained Wangari Maathai, leader of the Green Belt Movement and 2004 Nobel Peace Prize Laureate, when she said that the women "resorted to something they knew traditionally would act on the men. . . . They stripped to show their nakedness to their sons. It is a curse to see your mother naked."[39] In Uganda, women opposing authoritarianism have used similar tactics.[40] In Israel, women have stripped to disperse ultrareligious men. And originating in Ukraine, the antiauthoritarian feminist collective FEMEN has routinely used public nudity as an important form of performative street protest against patriarchy.

How can civil resistance movements prompt a regime's supporters to defect?

When a regime's key loyalists stop supporting the power structure, scholars call that "defection."[41] No power structure can function without daily efforts and passive support from a wide variety of groups, from society's bottom to the top: police and soldiers, business owners and bankers, teachers and lawyers, truck drivers, garbage workers, diplomats, and more. And all these groups can be persuaded to think that it's no longer in their interest to keep working—directly or indirectly—for the regime.

Prompting defections is important, because defections are key to change. In reviewing the historical record of more than one hundred civil resistance campaigns between 1900 and 2006, Maria Stephan and I found that security-force defections dramatically increase the chances for nonviolent resistance to succeed.[42] Among these cases, the nature of security force defection varied widely—from generals openly refusing to carry out orders, to officers pretending they did not receive orders, to soldiers shirking their duties or putting down their weapons.

More recently, scholarship has found that organized labor—particularly in manufacturing—can shift the balance of power from below.[43] When factory workers walk out of their workplaces—or lock themselves into their workplaces but refuse to do any work—business owners may pressure the regime to accommodate the movement. Union leaders who back a mass movement can bring along a wide range of abilities, like negotiation, as well as a large number of workers who can quickly coordinate collective actions like strikes or stay-at-homes, adding to the economic pressure against a regime.

To prompt such defections, movements need to get people who have gone along with the status quo to wonder whether doing so is actually good for them individually or collectively. They might do this for a variety of reasons, which vary with each group.[44]

Security forces—police, militias, militaries—tend to defect if they share ethnic or social ties with protesters or their social networks; if they think that the government or senior officers have treated them unfairly; or if they feel that competing security forces—like rival branches of the military or elite police units—are treated better than their own units.[45] For instance, in the summer of 2011, a group of Sunni conscripts in the Syrian Army refused orders to shoot live ammunition at unarmed protesters who included people from the country's Sunni majority. If security forces have family members or other loved ones or family members opposed to the regime, they're susceptible to pressure at home as well. One Serbian policeman told journalists that he didn't follow orders to fire into a crowd protesting Milošević in 2000 because he thought he saw his child among the protesters.[46]

Similarly, strikes, boycotts, and other consumer or labor actions can influence the wallets of business owners, bankers, and other economic elites, who abandon loyalty to the status quo system if it's becoming too expensive. Examples include transportation workers during the California Farm Workers' Movement, who in the 1960s refused to transport grapes from farms to distribution centers in solidarity with farmworkers who were striking for higher wages and fairer working conditions. In the 1980s and 1990s, an international campaign of sanctions and divestments combined with domestic consumer boycotts pushed many South African business owners to change sides and oppose apartheid. That's why some Palestinian self-determination activists have been working on a campaign of consumer boycotts, international sanctions, and corporate divestments against Israeli companies that profit from Israel's occupation of the West Bank—a campaign that's potentially so powerful that the US Congress has considered legislation to quash it on college campuses. Within the United States more recently, gun control activists have been pressuring retail outlets to stop selling military-grade firearms—leading the megastore Walmart to stop selling AR-15 semiautomatic rifles, for instance.

Civil servants are another group without whose support no regime can function. They may refuse to continue working for a variety of reasons: if, like security forces, they have friends and family in the movement, or feel aggrieved for the reasons the movement is championing; when they've been underpaid or mistreated; or when they considered themselves honor-bound to uphold the rule of law or professional norms during a crisis. For instance, during the Nazi occupation of Norway, teachers refused to teach Nazi-approved textbooks and went on a multiyear strike, during which they taught in underground schools in homes and other private spaces. During the Central African Republic's democracy movement from 1990 to 1993, health workers, unemployed civil servants, and the federation of trade unions went on strike—creating a level of mass noncooperation that ultimately forced President Kolingba to resign and paved the way for the country's first free and fair elections in 1993. Upon his inauguration, the new president Ange-Félix Patassé paid twelve months of back pay to public sector workers.[47] And during Tunisia's Dignity Revolution in 2010–2011, thousands of lawyers and teachers went on strike in the uprising's final days—bringing much of the public sector's work to a halt and further isolating the regime.

I don't want to give the wrong impression: movements do not necessarily have to actively persuade or convert people in all of these groups to create this effect. However, because each context is so unique, many activists and organizers have found it useful to conduct a "pillar analysis" (since the term "pillars of support" is fairly standard usage) as they develop a campaign strategy. In a pillar analysis, illustrated in Figure 2-1, movements map out which groups or sectors prop up the status quo and are therefore blocking the movement's progress.

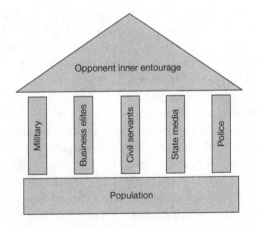

Figure 2-1 Sample Pillar Analysis for a Government

A wide variety of people from the broader population are involved in each of these groups or institutions. All of these people have their own personal interests, which may or may not align with their superiors'. Many movements try to examine different influential subgroups within each "pillar." The analysis involves assessing the movement's potential for affecting or disrupting people in each of these smaller groups, as depicted in Figure 2-2. Each concentric circle or half-circle depicts, roughly, the groups' proximity to power. Groups that are within the pillar but less proximate to power may have less robust loyalty to the center.

Here, we can see that even if the subgroup or groups central to the pillar remain loyal to the regime, that core still relies on various other people to maintain its hold on power. A general may remain loyal to the regime, for instance, but if his officer corps or enlisted troops refuse to cooperate, he would be facing a difficult referendum on his own authority. A foreign ally deciding to withhold support

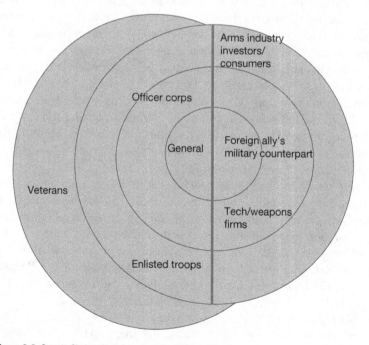

Figure 2-2 Sample Circles of Influence Exercise: Military Pillar

because of public pressure at home might significantly weaken a military's strength and resolve as well.

Enough defections within critical pillars of support can make it very difficult for a regime to maintain a grip on power.

What's the difference between defections and coups?

In a coup, the military ousts the current leader and seizes power for itself.[48] In other words, the security forces defect—but take power rather than placing themselves under civilian rule.

For instance, in Egypt in 2013, after several days of demonstrations and protests by the well-organized, millions-strong Tamarod campaign against Mohammed Morsi's regime, the Egyptian military declared that it had no choice but to remove him and install strongman Abdel Fattah al-Sisi in power. Tamarod organizers and military elites may have coordinated on the plan for months. As early as February 2013, some senior Egyptian army officers were in private talks with liberal opposition groups, asking them whether they would approve of the military ousting Morsi. You could argue that there was too much collusion between nonviolent people power and security forces—or at least that the former trusted the latter too much. This suggests that rather than being a protest-induced defection, it was a popularly backed coup. Al-Sisi moved quickly to crush remaining pro-Morsi oppositionists, massacring hundreds of Muslim Brotherhood activists who were protesting the coup in August 2013 and jailing up to sixty thousand human rights and pro-democracy activists in a wave of mass arrests. Human rights groups have expressed grave concern for the welfare of political prisoners, citing summary executions, torture, and disappearances as relatively common in al-Sisi's Egypt. And al-Sisi has accumulated extensive powers by passing self-serving laws through his rubber-stamp parliament, allowing him to remain president until at least 2030, allowing the military to intervene in domestic politics, and allowing his government greater powers over judicial appointments. Backed by the US Trump administration, al-Sisi's government has quickly silenced any visible opposition to these efforts.

Such a cautionary tale suggests that defections can come in various flavors. Let's call them "full defection," "partial defection," "shirking," and "outright disobedience."

In "full defection," an entire institution—the army in Egypt, for example—openly withdraws its cooperation and seeks to replace the ruler with its own leadership. This amounts to a coup.

As the term "partial defection" suggests, in this variant only part of the institution withdraws its support. Maybe some dissatisfied group within the armed forces realizes it couldn't successfully stage a coup—but calculates that they have enough strength to seriously challenge the regime. This might mean civil war, as happened in Libya and Syria in 2011, where factions within the military rebelled but a sizable number of troops remained loyal to, respectively, the Muammar Qaddafi regime in Libya and the Bashar al-Assad regime in Syria. In these cases, the defectors joined the civilian opposition movements—but took their guns with them.

"Shirking" is a form of defection in which regime functionaries disobey discreetly and with plausible deniability. In general, this form of defection looks like foot-dragging, calling in sick, or intentionally doing a bad job. It is easy for such defectors to deny that their shirking is intentional or political; as a result, such activities aren't as risky as full or partial defection or outright disobedience. As Serbian organizer and trainer Ivan Marović is fond of saying, "People get in trouble for insubordination, but not so much for incompetence. Commanders tolerate incompetent fools and punish smart dissenters."[49] When there is evidence of shirking, the security forces' loyalties may be vulnerable to costlier forms of defection, too.

In "outright disobedience," former loyalists refuse to carry out orders—but without fully aligning with the movement. A dictator might order the police or military to shoot down unarmed demonstrators, only to have security forces refuse. This allegedly happened in Tunisia in early 2011, when senior military commanders refused to obey Ben Ali's orders to attack unarmed protesters. The military did not then join the demonstrators in the streets, or put a gun to Ben Ali's head, carrying out a coup. They simply said "No" and allowed the political consequences to unfold. Ben Ali quickly resigned, initiating Tunisia's revolutionary transition to democracy.

Something similar happened during the 1986 People Power Revolution in the Philippines. After several senior military commanders defected, President Ferdinand Marcos sent tanks and armored personnel carriers to confront them. As loyalist troops approached the camp, civilians formed human barricades in front of the tanks. Demonstrators offered candy, food, cigarettes, and flowers to the troops, asking them not to proceed. Eventually, the tanks began to advance. Loyalist commanders ordered troops to clear the crowd with live fire and to attack the camp with mortar and cannon rounds, whether civilians remained in the way or not.

But Catholic nuns knelt in front of the tanks and began to pray, stopping them in their tracks. The officer in charge stalled by claiming to his superiors that his troops were trying to get into position. With nearby marines taking aim at unarmed protesters, breaking into tears, and retreating, the tanks ultimately withdrew without firing a shot. Fighter jets deployed to attack the area refused to fire, with one pilot citing the inevitability of widespread civilian casualties and another noting, discouraged, that the crowds below had organized in the shape of a cross. Within days the Marcos regime was finished, and a new civilian government led by Corazon Aquino was elected to power.[50]

Regardless of whether outright disobedience occurs at the higher or lower levels of command, however, the political consequences can be identical: the person in power often departs from office upon realizing that the security forces' cooperation and acquiescence have been lost. For civil resistance movements seeking greater civilian control over the outcome, outright disobedience is almost always the most promising form of defection, since it means that security forces are prepared to submit to popular will.

Whatever form a defection takes, however, the greatest challenge is to ensure that the movement is driving the defections. The movement should be compelling those in power to do something they might not have wanted to do otherwise, rather than just allowing them to do what they meant to do all along. The Egyptian army apparently wanted to get rid of Morsi, and it seems to have used the movement to do it. But defections can carry risks for nonviolent campaigns, as we can see in Libya and Syria as well as Egypt.

In Libya and Syria, nonviolent action led to early defections among the armed forces. But the defectors regrouped as armed challengers, and undermined and replaced nonviolent campaigns with armed struggle.

On the other hand, the Serbian policeman mentioned earlier had no intention of disobeying orders, but the movement forced him to do so, just as overwhelming civilian pressure made Filipino troops reevaluate their position. Establishing and maintaining movement control over defectors greatly reduces the chances that they will turn around and launch a civil war or consolidate power into a military junta.

Of course, civil resistance campaigns cannot always control the form that defections will take. Those belonging to certain pillars of power may never be willing to defect in any overt form. Consider the anti-apartheid movement in South Africa: security forces continued attacking Black people in the townships up until the end, even as boycotts of white business, international sanctions, and divestment campaigns forced the South African government to the negotiating table with the ANC.

Such cases suggest that civil resistance campaigns should often focus on bringing about shifts within several different pillars of support, not just one—say, among economic and business elites, state media, state education systems, religious authorities, and civilian bureaucrats. Compared with security forces, these groupings' loyalty shifts are easier to manage and less risky to society in the long run.

In the meantime, the historical record shows that the people and the military are rarely "one hand," as protesters chanted in 2011 (and against in 2013) in Egypt. Instead, security forces have their own interests and can easily manipulate a campaign to suit their own purposes and undermine the movement's agenda.[51]

Historically, movements with massive and diverse participation, nonviolent discipline, and the ability to withstand repression have been able to force those in power to change. But only when a campaign pressures elites to suspend or reevaluate their own interests do they tend to step out of the way of genuine transformation.

How do campaigns attract more supporters, even while being attacked by the regime?

Having a just cause isn't enough to bring in a movement's supporters and prompt those involved in the regime to defect. Historically, organizers and activists have taken vigorous steps to encourage both. Some find it useful to visualize where they might find the full range of supporters and opponents. For instance, the organization 350, a climate justice group, has used an exercise called "The Spectrum of Allies," as shown in Figure 2-3. Groups draw five wedges in a half-circle, from left to right, one each for active supporters, passive supporters, those who are neutral or uninvolved, passive opponents, and active opponents—and fill out worksheets underneath with the groups or sectors that belong to each wedge. The activists then consider what arguments or actions might move each group. Instead of attempting to mobilize neutral parties or passive or active opponents at the outset, many movements start by trying to pull passive supporters into the active camp through consciousness raising, small-scale actions such as teach-ins or low-risk protests, legal and institutional advocacy (where possible) like letter-writing drives to public officials, filling out petitions, filing lawsuits, and other organizing efforts. Once they've expanded the numbers of people who are actively working with them, they begin to appeal to people who have been neutral to try to make them into movement supporters, whether passive or active. For example, movements may call on churches—often considered apolitical—to

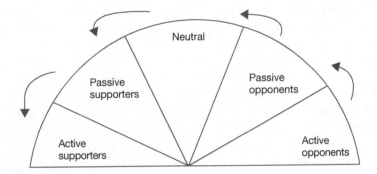

Figure 2-3 The Spectrum of Allies

provide space for organizing meetings and planning sessions, or even to house politically persecuted individuals seeking protection from state violence. At the same time, organizers try to encourage passive and active opponents to defect.

Here's what's key: organizers are not necessarily starting out by trying to persuade active opponents to support the movement. Instead, they want to get passive opponents—for instance, business owners or certain groups of police—to stay neutral in a conflict, or at least to stop supporting the active opponent, in the ways discussed earlier: withholding political support or refusing to follow orders.

We can see how this worked, in Serbia on October 7, 2000, when police refused an order to fire on demonstrators who were calling for the resignation of dictator Slobodan Milošević. Most of the police did not join the protesters. Many may not have even supported the movement's aim of reforming the country away from Milošević's socialist and ultranationalistic legacy. But in a critical moment in the campaign's momentum, the police shifted from being active to passive opponents, meaning that Milošević could not rely on this necessary pillar of support in a crisis. He stepped down that day.

Very occasionally, movements have actually encouraged some active opponents to switch sides and join the movement altogether, but such instances are rare, and they do not appear to be necessary for movements to succeed.[52] In other words, successful movements do not necessarily need to turn mortal enemies into active supporters. Civil resistance is not about converting the opponent or melting the hearts of brutal dictators. It is about pulling their supports away in key moments—and taking away their options.

Which civil resistance tactics are most—and least—effective?

There is no general rule here. Research tells us little, because we don't have the data sources that would give us this kind of detail. However, there's a growing consensus about a few approaches.

First, economic noncooperation seems to work very effectively to make opponents suffer immediate and direct costs. Strikes are fairly reliable ways to win short-term concessions on labor rights, wage disputes, and workplace practices.[53] And strikes work for more than winning labor disputes; they can be powerful tools in struggles for rights and justice as well when they're combined with broader civil resistance campaigns. General strikes are particularly powerful. Boycotts are also effective methods of noncooperation when entire communities abide by them. As I referenced earlier, during the South African anti-apartheid movement, Black-led boycotts of white-owned businesses proved to be an incredibly important tactic of economic noncooperation. While they continued to work and collect paychecks, they simply refused to spend their money at white-owned shops and businesses. After several months, this forced white businesses to approach key political elites to demand reforms.

Second, it's essential to build momentum through a sequence of tactics that increasingly build pressure on people who are upholding the status quo while protecting participants as much as possible. This often means starting from safer actions that bring in more and more supporters and building to riskier actions once large and diverse constituencies have become involved. That approach makes movements more resilient in the face of government repression while consistently disrupting the opponent's rule.[54]

The opposite approach—starting big and then reducing the size and diversity of those involved—seldom leads to long-term victory. Tactics that alienate the population at large are the least effective; movements generally discover what's unpopular as they proceed, and learn what to avoid.

Overreliance on any one tool makes a nonviolent uprising predictable. And predictability means vulnerability, whether on the battlefield or on the streets.

How do social media and digital technology affect nonviolent campaigns?

Social media have given movements amazing tools for rapid communication and coordination and made it easier for movements to spotlight injustices, broadcast their claims, and make their messages go viral. During the coronavirus pandemic of 2020, digital organizing became a particularly important method for movements to stay connected and build capacity amid physical shutdowns and multiple overlapping crises.[55] Social media platforms like Facebook, YouTube, and Twitter; anonymous browsers like Tor; webcasting services like Zoom; and apps like WhatsApp, TikTok, and Telegram have been important in supporting mass mobilization in cases as diverse as Lebanon, the United States, and Belarus. But these same tools, if captured by the other side, can be turned against the opposition—like any other weapon. As in battle, opposition strategists must always have backup plans for how to communicate and coordinate with other activists if any communication method is dismantled or intercepted.

Overall, have social media been good or bad for activism? Views are divided. Optimists suggest that new media give activists the edge over their opponents—making it easier to communicate with other people directly, quickly, and effectively, and eliminating the filter of journalists' interpretations, editorial boards, or censors.[56]

Social media also create a new public sphere, which is especially useful when none other exists, advancing dialogue among new groups of people.[57] Through such dialogue, activists and dissidents can hammer out new policy alternatives or institutional designs. For instance, in the aftermath of the successful 2009 Cutlery Revolution, which overthrew a corrupt government in Iceland, the population developed plans to create the world's first "Wikipedia Constitution"—a crowdsourced document created collectively on the internet.

Perhaps most important for civil resistance purposes, social media allow extremely rapid mobilization. Facebook event pages and the amplifying effects of Facebook, Twitter, WhatsApp, and Instagram allow people to communicate with masses of others in seconds. These platforms let people share important news and updates just as swiftly. If a situation becomes too dangerous or a group needs medical or legal assistance, social media can bring a near-immediate response. We've seen the results around the world, particularly in the successful revolutions in Tunisia in 2010–2011 and Sudan in 2019.[58]

But while some believe social media created these revolutions, Facebook, Twitter, YouTube, and so on may be better described as *characteristics* of the recent uprisings, not necessarily *causes*. As political scientist and nonviolent resistance practitioner Mary Elizabeth King has noted, movements always grab the newest available technology of their era.[59] But so do their opponents. As a result, movements that rely solely on digital media to coordinate a revolution are quite vulnerable.

That leads us to the pessimists' views on digital technology, which include a number of concerns. First, social media have given some people the feeling that simply by retweeting, liking, or clicking on a link they're involved in a movement. Skeptics argue that this "clicktivism" gives people a false sense of direct participation that may actually reduce their involvement in more disruptive and effective kinds of direct action.

Second, the ability to coordinate large-scale mass protests on short notice has an important downside. As Zeynep Tufekci has argued, movements that want to make change first have to build the staying power and organizational structures that enable longer-term struggle.[60] Digital technology makes it easy to skip the critical steps of building relationships, developing ongoing coalitions, planning strategies, building alternative institutions, and preparing a population for a long struggle. With the convenience of social media, many movements may fall into the trap of organizing only in the short term, moving from one event to another, while failing to absorb their base of supporters into long-term movement adherents. Every movement faces the temptation to put tactics before strategy. Social media dramatically increase that temptation.

Third, the failure to build a sustainable organization also means that movements that organize on social media are failing to expand their constituencies to bring in others from different social networks. Perhaps even more than in the physical world, people select their own online social networks, news sources, and information feeds that deliver the social contact and intellectual perspectives they find comforting. Many studies find that social media tend to exacerbate the human tendency to atomize into small, cohesive groups rather than enduring the friction of collaborating with people who have different views or experiences. That makes it harder for online movements to reach and influence regime supporters, disrupt the regime's complacency, or bring in broader coalitions of supporters.[61]

Still more important, oppressive regimes can (and do) use social media too. Authoritarian regimes have lots of resources, and they think strategically about the best way to use those resources to restore calm and maintain power. At first, regimes reacted to activist digital media directly, by shutting down the country's internet, as Hosni Mubarak did in Egypt in 2011, as the Iranian regime did in 2019 when Iranians began to protest en masse against the government, and as the Indian government did in Kashmir in 2019 when Muslim Kashmiris began to protest human rights abuses by Indian occupation forces. But most governments have caught on pretty quickly that there was a smarter response. As political scientist Anita Gohdes has found, activists' increasing reliance on the internet has made it easier for governments to track political dissent, identify key participants and organizers, disrupt those networks, and prevent them from being able to successfully organize.[62]

Further, regimes use these tools to organize their own supporters and spread false news or compromising information meant to damage people associated with the movement. Political scientist Seva Gunitsky argues that many authoritarian regimes now create their own digital messages and messengers, circulating propaganda and counter-analysis that defeats movements' claims to legitimacy. "Deep fakes"—video-recorded "evidence" that has been altered digitally—can make it especially difficult for movements to counteract propaganda.[63]

What's more, just as the internet can help activists organize, it can help government loyalists and counterprotesters to coordinate responses as well. During Bahrain's failed uprising in 2011, that's how the regime used Facebook: to organize counterprotests and deploy loyalists to intimidate protesters with threatening messages and harassment. Patrick Meier reports that during a failed uprising against Omar al-Bashir in Sudan in 2011, the government used Facebook to create loyalist squads in remote areas to "defend" the regime—and even set up mock protest pages to trap the opposition. In one case,

> Thousands of activists promptly subscribed to this group. The government then deliberately changed the time of the protests on the day of to create confusion and stationed police at the rendezvous point where they promptly arrested several dozen protesters in one swoop. There are also credible reports that many of those arrested were then tortured to reveal their Facebook (and email) password.[64]

What are activists to do? In some cases, they have tried to think like the opponent, anticipate problems, plan responses, and switch up encrypted platforms and sources of communication. This may

even involve printing paper pamphlets and other materials to distribute in person, as Egyptian activists did in 2011, to avoid detection online.[65] And many activists develop a Plan C as well—a
covert way to continue communicating and coordinating if they
can no longer distribute literature.

What is the 3.5% rule?[66]

The "3.5% rule" is the idea that no revolutions have failed once 3.5%
of the population has actively participated in an observable peak
event like a battle, a mass demonstration, or some other form of mass
noncooperation. I coined the term during a 2013 TEDx talk. Various
movements around the world—from Extinction Rebellion in 2018–
2019 to the 2016–2017 Candlelight Movement in South Korea—have
since used the 3.5% figure to inspire participation and to gauge their
capacity for creating change.

Other scholars interested in revolutions and mass protest also
have some hunches about this. Mark Lichbach, for example,
mentions a "5% rule" in his 1994 book *The Rebel's Dilemma*.[67] His rule
referred to the idea that (a) no governments could withstand a challenge from 5% of the population, and (b) no rebellions could hope
to mobilize more than 5% of the population anyway, because many
people would rather "free-ride"—benefit from others' risks without
taking any themselves.

Does this mean that if a movement just gets 3.5% of the population into the streets, it will always win?

Not necessarily. First, the data behind this figure describe what's
happened in the past, not what *must* always happen in the future.
This historical tendency existed before anyone was conscious of it.
No one knows whether the rule will hold once people consciously
attempt to reach the threshold—especially if they do so without all
the strategizing, community organizing, and training and preparation that these earlier movements had to undertake to mobilize such
huge numbers.

Second, it's hard to imagine that before digital media, a movement that mobilized 3.5% of the population could have done

so without widespread public sympathy. Although there is no way to reliably measure public opinion of the governments or the maximalist movements challenging them, it is highly likely that successful revolutionary movements enjoyed overwhelming public sympathy and support, even if only a relatively small number actively participated. It may be, for instance, that 80% of the population wanted Hosni Mubarak to leave office in 2011, even though only about 1% of the population filled the streets to depose him.

Third, the way that I calculated the 3.5% rule relies on a snap-shot in time. It estimates participation at a peak event (usually either mass demonstrations in the case of nonviolent campaigns, or the maximum total fighters in armed campaigns). It does not account for the way that participation might build over time. It may be that what matters are the cumulative effects of mass participation and disruption. Momentum—which, as you recall, accounts for both mass *and* velocity—might be a better predictor of success than raw numbers themselves.[68]

Finally, the finding is based on very rare events. From 1945 to 2014, only 18 of 389 resistance campaigns surpassed the 3.5% threshold. That's less than 5% of all of the revolutions that took place during that period.

Are there any exceptions to the 3.5% rule?

Data published in 2019 suggest that the 3.5% rule still holds except for two cases.[69] The first was a 1962 revolt in Brunei, during which a reported four thousand people—4% of Brunei's total population of ninety thousand—launched an armed uprising that failed.

But Brunei is a small monarchy that presents a quite unusual case. There, the North Kalimantan Liberation Army was attempting to overthrow a sultan backed by the United Kingdom; the insurgents' goal was to prevent the sultan from joining Brunei with Malaysia. After only ten days, the sultan swiftly put down the revolt. Brunei's military stayed loyal to the regime. The unusual factor is that the British government diverted regional patrols to help shore up Brunei's stability. A year later, the sultan decided that Brunei would not join Malaysia, but kept his hold on power. By our strict criteria, this case would be considered a failure—despite the fact that the campaign's preferred outcome was achieved over a year later.

The second exception was a failed Bahrain uprising against King Hamad in 2011–2014. On February 22, 2011, one hundred thousand people reportedly participated in a major demonstration, constituting over 6% of the population. Over the next few weeks and months, Bahrain cracked down violently, dispersing demonstrators with live fire, rounding up oppositionists and throwing them in jail, and torturing political prisoners. After a few weeks, most of the demonstrators went home, and dissent largely faded away.

A couple of things may be going on with Bahrain. First, the opposition was up against an especially formidable foe. Bahrain is a monarchy in which a minority sect stays in power with the backing of Saudi Arabia, a powerful regional force, and of the United States. As with Brunei's regime in the 1960s, Bahrain's leaders could rely on outside forces, including Saudi troops and private security forces. That reduced the chances for security force defections. Because there was little sustained organizing or leadership within the movement, protesters were not able to shift to strikes and other forms of noncooperation. People drifted away from protests and marches after the government killed nearly one hundred people and arrested key protesters.

In these two cases, mass participation was quite short-lived. Perhaps the 3.5% threshold works only if large-scale participation can be sustained over a longer term. Or perhaps the 3.5% rule doesn't apply to small monarchies backed by overwhelming foreign military reinforcement. Leaving aside such rare circumstances, the rule appears to persist. But it is more of a rule of thumb than an iron law.[70]

Which campaigns have featured the largest percentages of popular participation?

Figure 2-4 shows all of the revolutions that mobilized at least 2% of the population between 1945 and 2014.[71]

As this figure shows, twenty-four of the largest thirty-two revolutions achieved outright success (75%), while twenty-seven out of thirty-two (84%) achieved either major concessions or full success.

Of course, many other mass mobilizations have brought out millions of people but didn't necessarily transform into

Figure 2-4 Revolutions with at least 2% Popular Participation during Peak Mobilization, 1945–2014 (n = 32)

revolutionary movements that brought lasting change. Some of the largest include:

- United States, 1969. Millions of people walked out of classes and college campuses and staged mass demonstrations to protest the draft and the Vietnam War in the so-called Moratorium to End the War in Vietnam.
- United States, 1970. Millions of people organized teach-ins, community projects, consciousness-raising actions, and protests for environmental justice, culminating in the first official Earth Day.
- Worldwide demonstrations, 2003. Around the world, a reported 10 million people took to the streets to protest the George W. Bush administration's preparations for war against Iraq.
- United States, 2017. Four million people turned out for the Women's March, a protest against the presidential inauguration of Donald Trump, filling streets in Washington, DC, and in cities and towns around the country, making it the largest single-day demonstration in US history.[72] The 2017 Women's March probably included around 1.8% of the US population. That's an impressive number for sure, but just above the average size for a civil resistance campaign—and just over halfway to the critical threshold observed for revolutionary change.
- India, 2020. Millions turned out for a general strike after Prime Minister Narendra Modi's legislature passed a Citizenship Amendment Bill that grants citizenship to immigrants from Pakistan, Afghanistan, and Bangladesh—but only if they are not Muslim. The bill was widely perceived to be an attack on India's 195 million Muslims, a minority group in an increasingly right-wing Hindu nationalist state.

Does the 3.5% rule apply to campaigns that aren't aimed at major results like removing a national leader or achieving independence—say, campaigns for climate action or against local governments, corporations, or schools?

No one knows. The 3.5% rule was derived from a very specific category of revolutions that had a specific, clear, major goal—albeit one very difficult to achieve. Other types of campaigns may be able to succeed with a similar level of popular participation, but we don't have reliable worldwide data about participation in other kinds of movements yet.

What does it mean for democracy that a minority of only 3.5% can oust any government?

Keep in mind that most movements that can bring 3.5% of the population out into the streets actually have a much broader base of support. Although there is no way to reliably measure public opinion across all national crises, in most cases in which that large a proportion of the population was willing to turn out publicly, the movement had overwhelming public support. Consider the US civil rights movement's successful actions in 1964 and 1965. While only a few hundred thousand people were actively involved in marches, sit-ins, boycotts, and other actions, the majority of Americans favored some sort of comprehensive civil rights legislation.[73] Being able to get 3.5% of a population to take action in a cause almost surely tells you that the majority of people support that cause. Getting such a sizable minority into the streets is probably the result, not the cause, of the movement's popular support.[74]

And keep in mind as well that although the 3.5% rule refers to a single peak event, civil resistance as a technique seldom involves one event that brings large numbers of people into the streets. We're talking here about an ongoing, well-organized campaign with a clear goal that shifts among various tactics as needed.

Does a civil resistance movement need a clear, single cause to succeed?

Most movements aren't aimed at a single goal; they have comprehensive platforms and demands. Usually, those claims and demands are argued over fiercely within the movement, especially as the movement brings in a more diverse array of supporters from across the social spectrum.

Many activists believe that what's more important than having a single goal is having a goal that's clear and specific. For instance, "Mubarak must go" is a much clearer and more concrete slogan than "We are the 99%." Progressive elements of the Egyptian January 25 Revolution and of Occupy Wall Street actually shared similar platforms about economic justice, government accountability, and the deeply unequal aftermath of the global financial crisis of 2008— but ousting a dictator is a concrete goal, while general objections to economic inequality are not.

A number of civil resistance campaigns underway in 2019 had clear goals. The 2019 Hong Kong democracy movement, which spent six months in the streets objecting to mainland China's efforts to override its civil rights and liberties, also has clear demands, which it articulates collectively: the chief executive's resignation, investigations of police brutality, the release of protesters from prison, retraction of the term "riots" to describe the uprising, and expansion of voting rights in Hong Kong. The climate change movement Extinction Rebellion has three clear and concrete demands of the UK government (and governments around the world more broadly): for those in power to tell the truth about climate change, for a global citizen's assembly to address the climate crisis, and for all governments to achieve net zero greenhouse gas emissions by 2025.

Often, it's easier to demand the end of something bad than to articulate a clear demand for something good. This is why, ironically, it's often easier for people power movements to remove a brutal dictator from power ("The people want the fall of the regime") than to agree on who should govern or to articulate how governments should be chosen. Bringing down a dictator requires firmness; creating a government requires time, negotiation, and compromise.[75]

Aiming for a clear and concrete goal can mean that movements have to temporarily let go of other claims, or at least aim at a sequence of goals so that each win leads the movement toward more abstract ultimate goals. For instance, the civil rights movement had clear and concrete goals—to desegregate the country—among broader, longer-term goals such as ending racist practices and policies, fixing the roots of poverty, and ending US militarism. But how to address these demands, and in what order, was extremely controversial between the movement's moderates and radicals.

And that's one of the most difficult parts of building and sustaining a coalition at this scale and scope: negotiating and prioritizing different demands from different points of view. Civil rights organizer Bernice Johnson Reagon once said that if you're comfortable with everyone in your coalition, you're not in a coalition. Maintaining a winning coalition is much more difficult than selecting a clear and concrete objective; it often requires skilled mediators and a movement-wide willingness to resolve conflict through some accepted process.

Which types of organizational structures are most effective?

There is no general consensus yet. Some successful civil resistance movements have had an accepted leadership that helped the movement navigate through essential challenges. Those leaders define the collective vision, communicate expectations and enforce movement norms, coordinate public relations, make strategic decisions, and negotiate and bargain on the movement's behalf. For instance, during 1987 to 1990 the First Palestinian Intifada—an uprising against Israel's occupation of the West Bank and Gaza Strip and growing inequalities between Israelis and Palestinians—featured a coalition-based leadership council.[76] Several hundred civic groups joined together and agreed to a senior leadership that developed and implemented plans, created a list of movement demands, and negotiated with the Israeli government, mediated by the United States. However, eventually those talks were undercut by secret negotiations in Oslo held between the Israeli government and the Palestine Liberation Organization (PLO), an exiled militant organization led by Yasir Arafat, which did not have as firm a foundation in the Palestinian grassroots at the time.

Similarly, in 1980, the Solidarity movement in Poland—a labor group that protested against and eventually unseated the Soviet-imposed Communist government—had a shared leadership structure drawn from various trade unions. These agreed-upon leaders undertook various critical tasks. After biding their time organizing trade associations, underground universities, community relief funds to support jailed dissidents' families, and illegal press for nine years, the leaders negotiated various concessions from the Polish communist party. Having secured the chance to compete in national elections from the communist regime, Solidarity ran candidates; campaigned on a pro-democracy, anticorruption platform; and won national elections in July 1989.

Other civil resistance movements have adopted a leaderless resistance approach, for both tactical and ideological reasons. Tactically, governments have a harder time decapitating a movement through arrests or subverting it through infiltration if a movement does not have clear leadership. Ideologically, leaderless movements can genuinely appeal to people who are fighting against oppressive structures, hierarchy, and corruption.

But a leaderless resistance approach brings some major strategic liabilities over the longer term, particularly if movements do not find a way to build and sustain some organizational form that can coordinate many groups and demands into effective action.[77] First, if those in the movement do not assign certain tasks—like negotiation, public communications, coalition-building, or strategy—to a cohort of trusted leaders, movements cannot necessarily negotiate with opponents who might be willing to make concessions. In other words, they have trouble accepting yes for an answer.

Second, leaderless movements have a harder time managing public relations crises, as when some in the movement alienate the public at large through violence or militancy. A movement without a spokesperson cannot credibly denounce or contextualize street fighting or provocateurs, thereby making it easier for those outliers to weaken or undermine a movement's public image and legitimacy.

Third, leaderless movements have a hard time building working relationships with other organizations, which they need if they want to have leverage over their opponents. Building coalitions is essential if the movement wants to expand its supporters and erode the opponent's. Without movement figures assigned the job of pursuing coalition partners and making credible commitments to reciprocate, movements have a tough time expanding enough to achieve their goals.

Fourth, movements typically need ways to evaluate strategic decisions, to change course, and to move in new directions. Leaderless movements may improvise in the short term, but without some agreed-upon central authority that has the power to change tactics and communicate new plans, movements will have a hard time sustaining the disciplined self-reflection, adaptability, and coordination needed to succeed. For instance, the Polish Solidarity movement mentioned earlier achieved its victory just weeks after the Chinese government massacred a different pro-democracy student movement at Tiananmen Square in Beijing. One of the key differences between the Polish movement and the Chinese movement was the former's ability to make crucial strategic decisions at key points in the conflict.

Let's look at how leaderless resistance played out in the Chinese case. Prior to the massacre at Tiananmen Square, Chinese student representatives had snubbed offers by the Chinese Communist Party leadership to engage in dialogue in May 1989, in large part because of internal disputes about whether the selected student representatives had the right to negotiate on behalf of the broader movement. Instead, charismatic individuals within the student movement began to argue for more confrontational tactics, such as a hunger strike and nonviolent occupation of Tiananmen Square to coincide with Soviet premier Mikhail Gorbachev's scheduled visit in mid-May. On May 20, the Chinese Communist Party declared martial law and announced its intent to clear the square, issuing a grim warning to the protesters to leave or face overwhelming firepower. Although massive protests in Beijing prevented the Chinese People's Liberation Army (PLA) from approaching the square on its first attempt, the sit-in in Tiananmen Square descended into crisis with internal squabbles, disputes over next moves for the opposition, and disagreements about whether to violently attack the military or maintain nonviolent resistance. Those individuals who tried to assert leadership in the midst of the crisis were accused of betraying the movement's democratic values, or of colluding with the state. In the days before the massacre, as army units approached the square, university professors and intellectuals negotiated with the PLA leadership, securing a promise that students would be unharmed if they voluntarily vacated the square. But few students left, insisting that their professors had no right to negotiate on their behalf. On June 4, 1989, the PLA attacked the movement with overwhelming force, killing hundreds to thousands, and wounding thousands of others. The massacre effectively demobilized the Chinese pro-democracy movement.

Of course, the need to develop and recognize leadership is often in tension with the need to avoid re-creating or reinforcing oppressive structures. Many progressive movements chafe at centralized organization, particularly if it puts privileged individuals within the movement into key decision-making roles, while excluding others.

This tension is an old one. In 1970, the feminist activist and scholar Jo Freeman delivered a talk, later adapted into an essay, titled "The Tyranny of Structurelessness."[78] In it, she critiqued precisely this aspect of the second-wave women's liberation movement, arguing that:

> A great emphasis has been placed on what are called leaderless, structureless groups as the main—if not sole—organizational form of the movement. The source of this idea was a natural reaction against the over-structured society in which most of us found ourselves, and the inevitable control this gave others over our lives, and the continual elitism of the Left and similar groups among those who were supposedly fighting this overstructuredness. . . . The idea of "structurelessness," however, has moved from a healthy counter to those tendencies to becoming a goddess in its own right. The idea is as little examined as the term is much used, but it has become an intrinsic and unquestioned part of women's liberation ideology. . . . [M]ost groups were unwilling to change their structure when they changed their tasks. Women had thoroughly accepted the idea of "structurelessness" without realizing the limitations of its uses. People would try to use the "structureless" group and the informal conference for purposes for which they were unsuitable out of a blind belief that no other means could possibly be anything but oppressive. If the movement is to grow beyond these elementary stages of development, it will have to disabuse itself of some of its prejudices about organization and structure. There is nothing inherently bad about either of these. They can be and often are misused, but to reject them out of hand because they are misused is to deny ourselves the necessary tools to further development.[79]

Movements may overestimate the value of leaderless resistance, which can doom a movement's ability to move from consciousness-raising to tasks that require long-term coordination and resources. Although leaderless resistance may appeal ideologically to people who distrust authority, it brings serious strategic disadvantages to any civil resistance effort. This doesn't mean that all campaigns need strict hierarchies or single leaders at the helm. But they do require some sort of leadership, coordination, and organization to be effective.

Freeman also makes the point that even when movements appear to lack a formal structure, every human group has an informal structure or hierarchy, with some individuals rising into positions of authority—even when such authority is not formally acknowledged. As such, all movements have formal or informal leadership, with varying levels of accountability. The key challenge for movements, then, is to develop organizational structures that reinforce democratic procedures, assign tasks, and hold those entrusted with those tasks accountable for their actions.[80]

Is a charismatic leader necessary?

Definitely not. As political scientists Maria Stephan and Adam Gallagher point out, it would be hard to identify a single charismatic leader in the 2019 revolutions in Sudan, Algeria, or Lebanon.[81] This is true for most mass uprisings over the past century, many of which have succeeded without a Gandhi, King, Aquino, or Mandela as a figurehead. Indeed, the ongoing Movement for Black Lives in the United States has moved away from individualistic leadership models, instead adopting a federated, coalitional structure that prioritizes active coordination with and accountability to frontline organizers and activists.[82]

In fact, movements that overemphasize particular personalities without developing skilled leadership throughout the organization, from street groups to governments-in-waiting, are much more vulnerable to being decapitated, co-opted, or simply making fatal mistakes than well-organized movements with strong leaders throughout, organizing at local levels and developing those who will lead a longer-term transformation.

There are also strong political reasons for avoiding entrusting a single figurehead with the movement's image. Many movements are actively resisting rigid hierarchy and authoritarian leadership. Movements that are too closely associated with a single individual or personality may make people uneasy if they're looking for a more democratic, accountable system. The consensus seems to be that if a movement wants to appeal to a broad range of people, it's best not to rely too much on a single personality.

Does nonviolent resistance only work in democracies, in developed countries, or in more liberal cultures?

No. Although they have not always referred to their efforts as such, subjugated peoples have been practicing civil resistance against imperial, colonial, totalitarian, autocratic, and other oppressive regimes for millennia. Civil resistance as an approach was forged in decidedly undemocratic contexts: among peasants in tsarist Russia, among enslaved people and laborers in British colonies throughout the Americas, among Hindus and Muslims in imperial India, and among descendants of enslaved Africans in the Jim Crow South. Early thought-leaders and practitioners were almost always people who were marginalized, mistreated, or oppressed in their home countries. Individual protests may be more common in democracies that protect the right to peaceful assembly. But protests aren't the same as mass movements—and mass movements are no more likely to work in democracies than in autocracies. In fact, among the one hundred biggest nonviolent campaigns since World War II, only 25% of them were in democracies. Why?

First, in democracies, people already have a political pressure valve: elections give them a chance to weigh in on the government and its policies. In the run-up to elections, political oppositionists often shift from movement-building to electioneering. The fact that voting is the primary method through which people participate in democratic politics also tends to remove the sense of urgency and necessity to engage in extra-institutional forms of nonviolent resistance. In contrast, in autocracies, where elections are either rigged or nonexistent, mass mobilization is often the only method through which people can express dissent.

Second, movements often grow under autocratic systems when those systems have lost their legitimacy slowly and over time.[83] The longer a single dictator endures, the easier it can be for citizens to identify that dictator (or dictatorial system) as the source of their woes, and to agree en masse that he must go—even if they have a broad range of ideas about what should replace him. In democracies, however, movements tend to focus less on individual opponents and more on policies and systems that they want to change. Those movements, however, have a harder time agreeing on which reforms are most urgent among the economic, social, and political policies under discussion. As a result, democracies often have a variety of interest groups that do not always coordinate either their actions or their demands. In fact, they often compete with one another.[84]

Nor does there appear to be any specific culture in which civil resistance is more likely. Civil resistance takes place worldwide, with campaigns just as likely to begin in Southeast Asia and the Middle East as in Europe and Latin America.[85] In fact, Africa may be the region in which civil resistance has been particularly effective, perhaps because most African countries have a comparatively high proportion of young people.[86]

Neither does civil resistance grow exclusively from Western liberal values or "Judeo-Christian" beliefs. Gandhi drew his inspiration from his Hindu faith. The Dalai Lama invokes Buddhist teachings in his expressions of support for nonviolent resistance. Islamic teachings on peace and justice have animated many nonviolent movements in the Muslim world.[87] All of the world's major religions include texts and practices that provide ample justification for civil resistance, as well as examples of religious followers who have used it. Indeed, every major world religion has the seeds of civil resistance (or nonviolence more generally) within its scriptures.[88]

Why do nonviolent campaigns sometimes fail?

Recall the four features of a successful movement discussed earlier: large-scale participation, loyalty shifts, tactical innovation, and resilience in the face of repression.

Now take those and invert them. Nonviolent campaigns tend to fail because they have a comparatively small group of supporters who are demographically similar, they can't get the opponent's supporters to defect, they never move beyond a single tactic that fails to seriously disrupt the regime's workings, or they collapse in the face of repression.[89]

Of these, the most common reason movements fail is probably the second one: because they cannot push the opponent's key groups of supporters to defect and demand change. Usually that's because the regime's supporters never lose faith in its ability to endure, or they cannot envision prospering in the society the movement is trying to create. For example, during the mass uprising in Syria, key groups—such as Alawites, middle-class Sunnis, Christians, and Kurds—maintained loyalty to dictator Bashar al-Assad, in part because of the fear of Islamist extremist groups who had begun infiltrating the ranks of the resistance and escalating the conflict into a violent one.[90] A regime's supporters may also stay loyal to it because powerful international allies have propped up the regime. In Syria, al-Assad has benefited from military and diplomatic support from Iran, Russia, and Hezbollah, whose interventions on his behalf have kept his regime alive. And the United States' continual support for repressive regimes in Egypt, Bahrain, and Saudi Arabia certainly helps those regimes to maintain support among key domestic constituencies.

Has civil resistance succeeded against corporate targets?

Yes, many times. Civil resistance campaigns have won countless victories using organized labor and consumer actions, including strikes, product and consumer boycotts, public shaming campaigns, sit-ins, demonstrations, die-ins, and many other techniques. Like governments, corporations rely on numerous groups that can be pressured to defect, including workers, consumers, contractors, distributors, transportation agents, investors, government regulators, and more. All these groups are vulnerable to pressure and disruption, which can affect corporate behavior.

One well-known successful civil resistance campaign against corporate targets in the United States was the 1965–1970 California farmworkers' movement, led by César Chávez and Dolores Huerta. The farmworkers forced grape vineyard owners and industry interests to increase wages, offer benefits, and eliminate workers' exposure to pesticides. The movement used a variety of tactics along the way, organizing work stoppages and strikes involving hundreds of thousands of laborers nationwide. It also organized a mass boycott against grapes alongside a public information campaign against the grape industry, which involved standing outside of grocery stores asking people not to buy grapes, and encouraging stores not to sell grapes. As the financial consequences began to pile up, grape owners appealed to the US government for support. The Nixon administration approved a subsidy to grape farms, which involved purchasing large quantities for shipment to US troops stationed overseas. Yet the movement scored a major win when, honoring the farmworkers' strike, truckers and longshoremen refused to ship those grapes to distributors. By 1970, the grape owners were forced to capitulate to the demands of the farmworkers.

Of course, in the United States, the power of organized labor has diminished since the 1970s. The US Bureau of Labor Statistics suggests that union membership has declined by half between 1983 and 2016, with fewer than 11% of American workers currently belonging to a labor union. States like Wisconsin have passed laws that curtail collective bargaining power. But movements have been able to mobilize to improve social responsibility practices among US corporations, with activists increasingly likely to confront corporations directly. Civil resistance campaigns have worked to pressure:

- Nestlé to adopt ethical marketing standards in baby formula, in a campaign that ran from 1977 to 1984 and is still ongoing in various stages.
- Brown University to divest from HEI Hotels & Resorts (which manages Hilton, Hyatt, and Westin) in 2010 because of unfair workplace practices for hotel and janitorial staff, including attempts to block the staff from collective organizing.
- Starkist, BumbleBee, and Chicken of the Sea to change their suppliers' fishing practices so that dolphins aren't killed while ships trawl for tuna.
- Marriott and other companies to improve worker conditions.
- PNC Bank to end its financing for mountaintop removal coal mining projects.

Around the world, workers and consumers have altered corporate behavior in many other contexts as well. In a study evaluating campaigns against corporate human rights abuses in Thailand, Brazil, Mexico, and Indonesia, it was clear that civil resistance campaigns had won significant concessions from corporations in all four countries.[91] These movements won for reasons much like those that help movements win against governments: when they organized sustained action with large-scale participation, they could push the opponents' supporters to turn away, and were able to extract concessions.

Of course some civil resistance campaigns against corporate targets fail. But they work more often than you might expect.

Has civil resistance succeeded against long-standing systems of oppression, like racism?

Civil resistance has seen some successes against long-standing systems of oppression, along with many defeats. Among the successes was the ending of chattel slavery of enslaved Africans and their descendants. That system was in place for centuries and was taken for granted as normal by millions of people, until it was ended by a decades-long, global abolitionist movement that relied heavily on civil resistance methods to create domestic and global coalitions to destroy this institution. Great Britain abolished slavery in response to both armed and unarmed revolts by enslaved populations themselves. In the US, abolition in 1865 followed a four-year Civil War between Northern and Southern states. But crucially, emancipation also followed decades of organizing and resistance by abolitionists. During the 1700s and 1800s, Black abolitionists innovated numerous alternative institutions—like the Underground Railroad, mutual aid, and compensation schemes for formerly enslaved people—and gave speeches and teach-ins, filed freedom suits and petitions, and deployed various forms of protest and economic noncooperation—to promote emancipation.

That said, systemic racism has endured. In the United States, various iterations of antiracism civil resistance campaigns have challenged the enduring manifestations of white supremacy, including the US civil rights movement, Black Lives Matter, and the Movement for Black Lives. These campaigns have educated Americans about systemic racism's persistence, changed laws, and transformed policing practices in many cities. While the US hasn't yet eliminated racism, these movements exposed its many forms to a much broader public than ever. As a result, these antiracism resistance campaigns have won over progressive groups, institutions, and political parties, forced them to reckon with white supremacy, and advanced racial justice as top priorities among such groups.[92]

And that's just one example of transformative, system-level campaigns. Since World War II, movements have successfully pressed for international human rights laws and conventions that condemn and criminalize state discrimination and violence against people based on race, ethnicity, and minority status. Large-scale organizing and resistance have reduced other violent cultural practices that used to be common around the globe, such as dueling, blood feuds, and female genital mutilation. Peace movements have made war much less popular than it was in prior centuries. While war hasn't been eliminated, national leaders can no longer engage in brazen conquest or imperial projects without significant political resistance and backlash.

Women have won freedom from the explicit subjugation and dehumanization they endured in many parts of the world for centuries. More than a century of feminist activism worldwide has challenged sexism and misogyny. From the suffragist movement to women's liberation, from the campaign against child marriage to women's rights to drive in Saudi Arabia, civil resistance campaigns have limited governments' ability to justify suppressing women—even in highly traditional societies.

What's more, for decades, the LGBTQ+ liberation movement has challenged discriminatory employment, housing, policing, and public health practices, by coming out and demanding equal rights for gender and sexual minorities. As a result, younger generations in many countries increasingly support the equal rights of gender and sexual minorities, in large part because of decades of effective organizing and resistance that have awakened many to their common humanity.

Civil resistance campaigns have effectively challenged other entrenched systems as well, taking on corruption in many different contexts, and scoring local wins in places as diverse as Kenya, Turkey, and Sicily.[93] Even the excesses of unrestrained capitalism and globalization face significant resistance. After decades of mobilization and resistance in the Global South, mass protests disrupted the World Trade Organization's (WTO) meetings in Seattle in 1999. That set of protests dramatized objections to how unevenly globalization enriches the few and impoverishes and harms millions of other workers around the world. Twelve years later, Occupy Wall Street put a similar spotlight on rising global inequality where a handful of people capture the vast majority of the world's wealth while others struggle. Movements in Europe, Latin America, and Asia have resisted the devastating effects of austerity policies, which cut funding for public programs like food assistance, public transportation, health care, basic income, and education—further enriching the wealthy while further impoverishing the poor.

And global inaction on climate change has prompted an explosion of civil resistance campaigns. Groups like Greenpeace, the Sunrise Movement, Fridays for Future, and Extinction Rebellion have emerged to demand urgent, systemic action to change the economic and social practices that threaten life on earth.

One of the most difficult challenges in overturning an oppressive system—where resources, power, and practices are entrenched and where people take the system for granted—is imagining realistic and constructive alternatives that people accept as better than the status quo. Climate denial is a pernicious barrier to global climate reform, for instance. Many believe—or behave as if they believe—that the fossil fuel–based economy is fine as it is; or that human behavior isn't what's causing the climate to warm; that nothing can slow down or reverse the shifting climate; or that shifting to green energy will be too economically costly. Powerful interests that benefit from the extraction, sale, distribution, and use of fossil fuels and other carbon-emitting industries have run their own campaigns to sell and reinforce those beliefs; those powerful groups and interests try to block progress toward creating viable alternatives, ridiculing the idea that they're needed or decrying the effort as useless.

But climate change is only one example. Many movements find it extremely difficult to help others imagine and create alternatives to any existing system, especially alternatives that would appeal to a broad coalition—and that becomes more difficult when the system is complex and self-reinforcing. As Slovenian philosopher Slavoj Žižek has said regarding the global economic system in particular, "It is easier to imagine the end of the world than the end of capitalism."[94]

To confront an oppressive system, it is also necessary to suggest alternatives that appeal to a broad enough coalition that it can overcome and defeat the opposition. This is precisely why the Sunrise Movement, which backs the Green New Deal, has suggested a wholesale reform of the economy, reinvesting from fossil fuels into green energy sources and providing a range of safeguards for those who may lose their jobs, careers, or wealth because of these changes.

Systems of oppression are often remarkably persistent, enduring, and difficult to change. But when people have challenged or eliminated oppressive systems in the past, there was usually a multigenerational civil resistance movement working to confront and dismantle the system—and replace it with a newly imagined reality.

Can civil resistance work in deeply divided societies?

Around the world, many societies are profoundly divided between two very different political camps, ferociously opposed to one another. In a 2018 national poll, 70% of Americans reported that the country was at least as politically divided as it was during the country's war in Vietnam, a time when masses of people took to the streets.[95]

But that's not necessarily a barrier. Many mass movements have succeeded in deeply divided societies. Either people rose up under authoritarian governments that controlled many different institutions, or people kicked out imperial or colonial powers in profoundly racist and unequal settings.

And yet deep social and political divisions can be hard for movements to overcome, and so these contexts often inform movements' strategies for how to create change. For instance, one of the most important success factors for civil resistance campaigns is the ability to bring in a broad range of supporters. Political scientist Ches Thurber has found that some groups have opted to avoid nonviolent resistance altogether—and taken up arms instead—when they concluded that ethnic or racial hatred against them was so severe that it would be impossible to broaden their support or win over security forces.[96] Of course, waging violent conflict only deepens these divides.

Deep polarization in a country can also lead to popular upheavals in which power moves back and forth between the two competing groups for years, with the victory of one side mobilizing the other side to rise up. Egypt experienced two subsequent popular upheavals—one overthrowing longtime dictator Hosni Mubarak, and another one several years later overthrowing his replacement, the newly elected Muslim Brotherhood candidate Mohammed Morsi. After that, the Muslim Brotherhood briefly revolted against Morsi's replacement, President Abdel Fattah al-Sisi, which ended with the Egyptian Army massacring nearly one thousand Muslim Brotherhood activists who were protesting in Rabaa. Similarly, Bolivia heaved back and forth between two sides with popular uprisings throughout the 2000s, 2010s, and the current decade. And a nonviolent uprising overcame a military dictatorship in Thailand in 1992, after which about six popular upheavals interrupted numerous subsequent governments there, until the military again took power in 2015.

Extreme political divides tend to intensify during periods of economic upheaval, such as the Great Depression of 1929 and during years leading up to the Great Recession of 2008. Longtime organizer and activist George Lakey argues that we can learn from some very different historical examples about the various ways societies can navigate out of deep political polarization. In Sweden and Norway, "democratic socialist movements pushed their economic elites off their pedestals and invented the egalitarian Nordic economic model," which in turn created "historically new levels of equality, individual freedom and shared abundance."[97]

How did this happen? He argues that Nordic activists first began to build their new society from the ground up. They did this by building co-ops and cultural groups that helped meet pressing needs. They then used this grassroots social and political base to appeal to business owners and economic elites, advancing a democratic socialist vision that solved pressing social problems while respecting citizens' desires to be treated fairly. For instance, they promised universal basic services, including healthcare and a guaranteed base income, instead of proposing services that would only help poor people. And finally, they built a movement of movements, a broad coalition that enabled them to challenge wealthy elites—who had a grip on elected politicians—through a series of successful nonviolent actions such as protests, strikes, marches, and pickets.[98] By 1935, Norway had achieved a historic agreement to destroy economic elites' monopoly on power, shifting power to a coalition of laborers and farmers, who aimed to expand public ownership over the country's means of production. As I mentioned earlier in this chapter, within the next decade, Norway also weathered the Nazi occupation of the country through a series of teacher strikes and solidarity activity, reflecting the society's unity and capacity for united and effective resistance.

Thus, civil resistance can indeed work in deeply divided societies. But it requires careful, patient planning if competing subcultures don't communicate or socialize across divides and have come to distrust and disdain one another—whether those are Democrats and Republicans in the United States or secularists and Islamists in Egypt.

How does civil resistance spread? What helps or hinders that spread?

Civil resistance does tend to spread, both within countries and across boundaries. Civil resistance campaigns tend to look back to, learn from, and build on, their own country's past protests and resistance. For instance, when American students from Parkland High School organized mass walkouts and marches to protest gun violence in March 2018, they reportedly learned from Black Lives Matter, the Women's March, and the protests against the Keystone XL Pipeline project by the Standing Rock Sioux. And protesters in one country often try to replicate the successes of nearby countries. For instance, in 2011, protesters in Egypt gained inspiration from activists in Tunisia, launching an Egyptian version of Tunisia's Dignity Revolution. Scholars call this "diffusion."[99]

But when activists in one country—no matter how close they feel, ethnically or religiously, to neighboring countries—assume that they can replicate their neighbors' efforts, they often fail. To explain why, political scientist Kurt Weyland points to the global wave of mostly violent revolutions in 1848. In France, revolutionaries overthrew the monarchy and established a republic. Inspired, revolutionaries in many other countries tried the same strategy—but were thwarted by better-prepared, better-resourced monarchs who were quite different kinds of opponents.[100] Having witnessed what had happened in France, these rulers could anticipate the revolutionaries' moves, crushing the uprisings and dividing its supporters.

Something similar may have happened in the Middle East over the past decade, especially for those countries whose populations rose up later in the Arab Spring.[101] For instance, Syria's ruler Bashar al-Assad, whose countrymen mobilized in March 2011, was better prepared than Tunisia's Ben Ali, against whom the regional wave of uprisings began in December 2010. You might call this the downside of diffusion.

Have governments of one country provoked civil resistance campaigns in other countries?

Decidedly not. But before I explain, let me first acknowledge that countries often try to meddle in the internal affairs of their adversaries. The United States has backed—or helped to orchestrate—violent coups to topple left-leaning regimes in places like Congo, Chile, and Iran. The US tried and failed to carry out coups in Cuba and Venezuela. And the US has fomented unrest and backed right-wing movements and insurgencies in many other countries, from the Contras in Nicaragua to armed militias associated with the Indonesian military during anti-communist mass killings of 1965–1966.

The US is not the only country that has dabbled in the dark arts of subversion. Iran has supported armed movements in Lebanon and Palestine to pester its arch-nemesis, Israel. Pakistan has turned a blind eye to jihadist groups who have attacked cities in India, including a series of deadly attacks by Lashkar-e-Taiba in Mumbai in 2008. In recent years, Russia has attempted to foment unrest in the US by amplifying disinformation about US elections, spreading polarizing information about Black Lives Matter, and amplifying white supremacist rhetoric. So major powers play these games often, and their efforts may indeed have important influences on toxic political discourse, patterns of social unrest, and political instability.

But civil resistance campaigns—which rely on organized, bottom-up, grassroots people power—cannot be effectively exported or imported by the US or any other country. This is important because many authoritarian leaders try to discredit people waging nonviolent struggle by arguing they're run by "outside agitators" or enemy governments. In reality, from 1900 to 2006, fewer than 10% of nonviolent revolutions received any direct material support from other governments. Among those that did, the aid didn't help much.[102] Why?

As we've discussed, nonviolent campaigns only succeed if they can assemble a massive number of people from very different parts of the population—which is impossible unless the movement grows from authentically local roots and grievances. Trust comes from genuinely knowing those involved; movements spread across social divisions only if local people have confidence that their concerns and hopes are widely shared. Ordinary people tend not to put their own lives on the line if they suspect that they are pawns in a geopolitical game.

While massive amounts of direct financial assistance to movements may not have helped civil resistance campaigns succeed in the past, the actions of outside governments can impact the dynamics of the conflict in other ways. Governments can use diplomatic leverage to pressure regimes to reform; pressure the other country to admit foreign journalists to cover the events; provide modest grants to support independent media, human rights attorneys, and other civil society groups within the country; offer moral support to the opposition through diplomatic pronouncements, press releases, and phone calls; and threaten to withdraw economic and security aid from regimes that refuse to respect human rights.[103]

More generally, one of the most effective ways that outsiders have supported nonviolent campaigns in the past has been through training workshops.[104] Between 1948 and 2003, a tremendous increase has taken place in international nongovernmental organizations (INGOs) that focus on nonviolence, such as the International Center on Nonviolent Conflict, Nonviolence International, and Peace Brigades International, which provide educational materials, training, and skills-building to nonviolent movements. Sociologist Selina Gallo-Cruz has found that these organizations' rise is correlated with the increase in nonviolent resistance campaigns worldwide. INGOs have helped civil resistance campaigns by training them, offering legal support, encouraging international media coverage, and protecting activists from state violence by personally accompanying them where they live and work.[105] And training workshops are often the first settings in which activists and organizers are able to meet to learn and strategize with one another, providing them an opportunity for longer-term capacity for coalition-building, organizing, planning, and mobilization.

So while direct support from outside governments may hurt civil resistance movements by making them appear less legitimate, that doesn't mean such movements must be entirely left to fend for themselves without any international assistance at all.

Can civil resistance work without at least some international support?

It depends on the movement's cause. Secessionist movements and anticolonial movements have often found international support— particularly diplomatic recognition—critical to their success. It's especially difficult for a territory to secede without international support; without global recognition of statehood, secession campaigns haven't actually won.[106] That's why movements in Catalonia, Western Sahara, Palestine, and Kosovo have had diplomatic efforts underway to support their local campaigns.[107]

Yet most campaigns, including those trying to overthrow dictatorships at home, may not find international support particularly useful. A foreign government's aid may actually undermine a civil resistance campaign's critical source of strength: mass participation. If ordinary people believe the campaign is a foreign power's puppet, they may stay away, considering it less legitimate than a genuinely homegrown movement. This is arguably part of what happened to the pro-democracy movement in Venezuela in 2019 and 2020. A diverse, inclusive movement to challenge the power of Nicolás Maduro began to shrink in size and diversity once the United States began to double down on economic sanctions against Maduro and his close associates, actively support opposition leader Juan Guaidó, and threaten armed intervention to install him.

But outside governments and INGOs can often indirectly support nonviolent activists and human rights defenders, as I mentioned above, as long as local movement leaders and participants remain the central driving force for the movement.[108]

Why were so many people caught off guard by the collapse of the Soviet Union—just as, twenty years later, they were surprised by the Arab uprisings?

Economist Timur Kuran argues that revolutions are inherently unpredictable.[109] Under authoritarian rulers, most people do not reveal their private thoughts and feelings for fear of persecution. Therefore, a regime may be wildly unpopular, but that's hard to see—either for the country's citizens themselves or for outside observers—because all of them keep their grievances concealed.

Kuran argues that at key moments, a single event can abruptly push that mass dissatisfaction to erupt into the open. That's what happened in Tunisia in 2010 when Mohammed Bouazizi, the humiliated fruit vendor, set himself on fire. It's what happened in the United States in August 2014 when a white police officer in Ferguson,

Missouri, fatally shot eighteen-year-old Michael Brown, an unarmed black man, and police left his body on the road for hours in the hot sun as his shocked and outraged family members and neighbors gathered nearby, leading the Black Lives Matter movement to expand into a nationwide uprising. And it's what happened in Puerto Rico in 2019 when a news outlet published leaked Telegram group chats between Puerto Rican governor Ricardo Rosselló and several Puerto Rican officials. The leaks revealed plans to smear political opponents and rivals, as well as sexist, homophobic, and derogatory remarks about victims of Hurricane Maria, while the citizenry was still suffering from a devastating economic crisis and widespread grief because of the inability to bury family members who had died during the hurricane.

A regime's legitimacy may erode slowly, over a long period of time, without anyone being bold enough to challenge it—until a single protester or a single defiant act encourages others to open up their own long-simmering resentment and rage, suddenly bringing masses of people into the street to call for the end.

But what triggers such events, and when? Do the regimes facing these explosions have anything structural in common? No one knows. Studies that have evaluated competing theories about such mass uprisings have found that none of them accurately predict when and where nonviolent campaigns will erupt.[110] Scholars are fairly good at predicting armed uprising, coups, or government collapse.[111] That's not true for nonviolent mass campaigns, which can happen almost anywhere for any reason. They often happen in places where scholars would expect it to be very difficult to mobilize dissent. And it's not at all clear what might make them spread and remain vibrant. People power movements simply depend so much on the local context—citizens' moods, experience with particular nonviolent methods, even the weather—that the usual forecasting tools and data structures can't identify generalizable causes. Or to put it differently, people who organize nonviolent uprisings often overcome adverse conditions in creative ways that defy expectations.[112]

This is why, in spite of all that we know about the fragility of authoritarian regimes, we are always surprised when people power movements emerge to successfully challenge them.

Are there situations where nonviolent resistance is impossible—or where violent resistance works better?

In some situations, neither nonviolent nor violent methods work very well. For instance, secessionist campaigns rarely succeed out-right, regardless of whether the campaigns are armed or unarmed. That's because, as mentioned above, other governments and supra-governmental bodies like the United Nations must agree to allow the new government to join the recognized list of countries in the world; they're generally loath to do so, because any decision to grant state-hood to one territory often emboldens other separatists. Spain's government opposed the Scottish Independence Referendum in 2014 when a significant minority of Scots voted to withdraw from the United Kingdom. Spain argued that, should Scotland succeed in becoming independent, the European Union (EU) should not accept it into the European Community. Spain has been beset by a couple of secession movements: the Basques and Catalonia. If Scotland voted to break away from the United Kingdom and was welcomed into the European Union, Spanish leaders reasoned, the Catalonian inde-pendence movement might demand the same.

Second, genocidal or totalitarian regimes like those imposed in the Americas by the Spanish Conquistadors; in the Caribbean and southern United States by slaveholding plantation owners; in Mosul under the Islamic State; or in various colonial contexts such as Belgian Congo or Japanese-occupied Manchuria; Nazi Germany under Hitler; or North Korea under Kim Jong-un are difficult to confront with any kind of resistance, violent or not. Yet, even in all of these contexts, people have defied the odds and resisted these regimes, covertly or in small-scale, everyday acts of defiance.[113] What's more, even in such extreme situations, a mass movement can deny the opponent the ability to commit the genocide; mass vi-olence requires willing agents to carry it out. In Tunisia in 2011, Ben Ali discovered that his troops were not willing to slaughter civilians in large numbers, even though he tried to order them to do so. Their refusal to carry out his orders is part of what finally motivated him to step down in January 2011.[114]

In sum, it's no easier to identify systems or structures that make nonviolent resistance unlikely to succeed than it is to identify moments when mass campaigns are likely to erupt.

But keep in mind the central point of this chapter: civil resistance succeeds or fails mainly based on encouraging massive numbers of people to participate, from all walks of life, and their ability to prompt the regime's supporters to defect. No single person facing down tanks and guns in individual courageous acts can bring about change all by herself. And nonviolent resistance does not always work, even when many people are using it together.

But in many cases, there are no better alternatives. Doing nothing may not be an option for people facing intolerable conditions. And taking up violence may be even more disastrous than nonviolent resistance.

Yet the belief that violence is an inevitable and necessary way to make change is remarkably persistent. Even many proponents of mass mobilization suspect that nonviolent resistance cannot work on its own—and that supplementing civil resistance with small amounts of strategic violence can help movements win. The opposite tends to be true. That issue is so important in influencing the fate of resistance campaigns that it deserves an entire chapter of its own.

3

CIVIL RESISTANCE AND VIOLENCE FROM WITHIN THE MOVEMENT

Violence and nonviolence are not mutually exclusive; it is the pre-dominance of the one or the other that labels a struggle.

—Nelson Mandela, 1999

Do civil resistance movements win more quickly and decisively if, on their fringes, some participants use violence? For centuries, movements have debated whether to take up arms. In the United States alone, that debate has roiled the abolition movement, the labor movement, the civil rights movement, the 1960s antiwar movement, and various other movements over the past fifty years. In the 1960s and 1970s, the American left split over whether even occasional violence was either wise or necessary—a split that was so divisive that liberal, progressive, and radical groups went their separate ways, reducing their effectiveness for decades.[1]

After the Battle of Seattle—a series of protests, blockades, and walkouts that disrupted the 1999 World Trade Organization (WTO) executive committee meetings in Seattle—the debate surged back into popular view. Labor, environmental, student, anarchist, and antiglobalization organizations had planned a series of protests, road blockades, human chains, and other methods of nonviolent civil disobedience to prevent trade negotiations from taking place among WTO leaders. Assembling tens of thousands of demonstrators, it was perhaps the largest antiglobalization event in US history at that time. Police responded with tear gas, stun grenades, and arrests of hundreds of protesters. Several hundred people engaged in vandalism, smashed windows and police cars, threw tear gas canisters and other projectiles at police, and engaged in street fighting. Ultimately the governor of Washington state deployed the National Guard to quell the protests. The trade negotiations were ultimately unsuccessful, in part due to varying reactions to the protests among the leaders in attendance. Although property destruction and street fighting were controversial among movement participants, activists largely saw the Battle of Seattle as a success, both because of its disruptive effects on the WTO's trade negotiations and the fact that it pushed antiglobalization into the national spotlight.

Twelve years later, in the wake of the 2008 global recession and the inspiring wave of uprisings in the Arab world, Occupy Wall Street resurrected the issue in the United States, Canada, and Europe. Creating tent cities in hundreds of locations around the world, activists brought economic inequality and economic justice back into the forefront of global consciousness. But as police forcibly evacuated tent cities in public parks, in city squares, and on college campuses, movement participants debated whether methods such as street fighting with police, destroying property, and using strategic violence against counterprotesters could help or hurt the movement's chances of eradicating income inequality and creating just alternatives to global capitalism.

More recently, we're seeing this debate in response to the growth of white nationalist, white supremacist, and neofascist groups across the Western world. Fascist ideology is extremely violent, exclusionary, and terrifyingly effective for leaders who want to capitalize on chaos and fear to attract adherents. Because of this existential threat, many antifascists say that they must contain and disrupt neofascist groups completely, including with physical assault.

Such debates aren't limited to the United States and Europe alone, of course. In 2019, Hong Kong's democratic movement held mass protests for months to protest a bill that threatened to extradite certain criminals to mainland China. When Hong Kong's leaders responded to the protests with a heavy hand, the movement expanded its demands to include the resignation of Hong Kong's chief executive, Carrie Lam, investigations of police brutality, the release of all imprisoned protesters, retraction of the government's mischaracterization of the protests as "riots," and the expansion of universal suffrage in Hong Kong's elections. These "five key demands" reflected growing fear that China's authoritarian system would eliminate the city's democratic rights. Millions of Hong Kong's residents have reportedly engaged in marches, protests, demonstrations, road blockades, and limited strikes. During some demonstrations and during an occupation of the University of Hong Kong in September 2019, some activists selectively attacked police and mainland Chinese citizens. Although the movement has no recognized leaders or official spokespeople, some activists have defended these attacks to journalists, arguing that they are justified in protecting themselves—and that their violence hasn't reduced the movement's public support.

Do such actions help or hurt a movement's cause? The question is delicate, controversial, and very political. Many movements face extreme oppression, enduring violence, arrests, and assassination from the regime's police and militaries. Extreme violence by the state—both direct violence and structural violence imposed by the militarily superior state—is often what's motivating the uprising in the first place. Many believe that they must fight back using arms, at least occasionally, to protect themselves and their families, or to resist with dignity. And some believe that violence might actually speed up victory by attracting public attention, conveying the movement's commitment and resolve, dramatizing the moment's urgency, or otherwise catapulting the movement into national or international view. Others have argued that the violent factions help nonviolent campaigns look more moderate in comparison, strengthening their bargaining positions.[2] A popular idea about the civil rights movement is that the rise of an armed Black Power movement made Martin Luther King Jr. more palatable to white Americans, creating space for moderate (but not radical) progress on civil rights.

These are all understandable and reasonable assumptions. When people are living under a government that's terrorizing them— whether because of the color of their skin, their ascribed ethnicity, language, religion, gender, sexuality, or political beliefs—they have the right to fight back to win the ability to govern themselves. International law protects that right in many circumstances. UN Resolution 3314 bans countries from invading others' territories and endorses the right of resistance movements to fight back with arms if necessary. Some people extend a similar logic to situations in which protesters are confronting police, security forces, or armed counterprotesters in the streets during mass demonstrations, by arguing that protesters have the right to defend themselves against state violence using arms if necessary.

People can choose whatever means they have at their disposal to liberate themselves from oppressive systems and regimes. But those who advocate using some violence to advance the goals of popular nonviolent movements often downplay the tactical risks and strategic consequences of this approach. In fact, the historical record reveals considerable costs and risks for doing so—as well as a timeless debate about whether such approaches are wise or whether nonviolent civil resistance is more powerful on its own. Most importantly, fringe violence often complicates the narrative of a movement both internally and externally. Movements that have to spend time defending tactical choices have a harder time keeping the public's focus on the overwhelming nature of the state's violence—and the legitimacy of the movement's claims.[3]

This chapter looks at the research into how fringe violence affects civil resistance movements' chances of achieving major political change. We'll look at common questions, including:

- What counts as violence?
- Is there no such thing as a truly nonviolent movement?
- Does some violence at the fringes reinforce and support nonviolent civil resistance campaigns?
- Does occasional violence help protect nonviolent activists?
- Are nonviolent civil resistance campaigns doomed once violence erupts?

What counts as violence?

Before we get started on the substance, let's review some key terms. Here, I'm using "violence" to mean an action or practice that physically harms or threatens to physically harm another person.[4]

Political scientists use the term "violent flanks" to refer to individuals or groups who use violence alongside an overwhelmingly nonviolent campaign. Violent flanks involve varying degrees of violence. There are two kinds of violent flanks: those that involve *armed violence*, in which people take up weapons designed to kill or maim others, from handguns to bows and arrows to rocket launchers; and *unarmed violence*, where individuals punch, kick, hit, or perhaps throw sticks or stones at those whom they oppose during what begins as a nonviolent protest. With unarmed violence, some people begin fighting the police or counterprotesters in the streets; rioting; or throwing rocks or improvised Molotov cocktails.[5] In many cases, unarmed violence is spontaneous or unintentional, and it remains fairly disorganized and marginal to the overall movement.

Those involved in movements sometimes refer to such acts as "diversity of tactics" or "black bloc tactics": combining nonviolent events with more physical confrontation that includes either random destruction of private property (e.g., smashing windows of businesses and homes) or more targeted destruction (e.g., blowing up bulldozers that threaten protected forests), rioting, street fighting with authorities or counterprotesters, or "punching Nazis."[6]

Fringe violence manifests in multiple ways within otherwise nonviolent campaigns. Typically it involves only a few individuals who start fights while the vast majority of the movement participants do not. The violence can be improvised and spontaneous, or it can be organized and planned. It can be incidental, meaning that it happens once or twice over the course of a movement, or it can become routine, part of a movement's standard repertoire. But when a movement drifts away from disciplined restraint and begins fighting regularly, the campaign can no longer be considered nonviolent.

Some may question my narrow definition of violence. When an individual throws a Molotov cocktail at a well-equipped army tank indiscriminately firing live bullets and tear gas, is throwing that incendiary bottle genuinely violent? Certainly those two weapons aren't evenly matched; the tank is far more immediately destructive than the Molotov cocktail that bounces off its armor. But the broader public generally interprets the weapons' intended effects the same way: both are intended to harm, maim, or destroy others, even if one does so on a more limited scale.

This is true even when the violence is committed in self-defense. That's because the public often has a hard time differentiating who is to blame for initiating the violence—protesters or police.[7] Regimes are often adept at exploiting this ambiguity—and convincing the public that the protesters are really a dangerous, radical fringe.

How common is it for organized armed groups to fight alongside nonviolent campaigns?

It is not the norm for armed wings to accompany mass nonviolent movements. It is quite rare among contemporary reformist campaigns, like those seeking labor rights or voting rights. And even among revolutionary movements, like those trying to topple governments or create newly independent countries, this practice is not universal. According to a database of nonviolent revolutionary campaigns between 1955 and 2018,[8] less than 40% had armed factions accompanying an ongoing nonviolent campaign.

Armed factions have often emerged when nonviolent movements begin to demobilize—often because of extreme government repression—and the more radical or extreme members who remained decided to escalate their methods to include armed action.[9] We can see this pattern in the case of Umkhonto we Sizwe (Spear of the Nation), which emerged as the armed wing of the African National Congress (ANC) established in 1961 after the Sharpeville Massacre in South Africa.

In other examples, violent flanks overtake nonviolent movements completely. This process occurred at the beginning of the period known as The Troubles in Northern Ireland. In the mid-1960s, a group called the Northern Irish Civil Rights Association (NICRA) had been pushing for equality among Catholics and Irish inhabitants of British-controlled Northern Ireland, where Catholics often experienced economic and political discrimination in favor of British Protestants living in the six counties. Inspired by the US civil rights movement, NICRA organized a series of mass demonstrations and actions demanding that Catholics and poor people in Northern Ireland have equal rights with British inhabitants of Northern Ireland.

But then an episode of extreme repression and counterprotest brought NICRA's movement to a crossroads. Activists from the Derry Housing Action Committee (DHAC) organized a peaceful march on October 8, 1968, in Derry, demanding voting rights and an end to housing discrimination for Catholics. The British home minister had banned the activists from marching through predominately Protestant neighborhoods, but the DHAC insisted on proceeding with the march, and NICRA agreed to back it despite its leaders' reservations about the possibility of a needless confrontation. Royal Ulster Constabulary (RUC) police forces assaulted the activists with clubs, and the activists and neighborhood youth responded with a series of riots that prompted more crackdowns, including police attacks, arrests, and further bans on demonstrations.

Loyalists planned provocative counterprotests as well. And during a series of peaceful marches in Derry in August 1969, British troops and Loyalist factions again began attacking the demonstrators. These events led to days of communal riots, during which youth groups representing Catholics and Protestant Loyalists began to attack one another. The RUC intervened by targeting Catholic participants, mobilizing a three-day urban insurrection known as the Battle of Bogside.

With little control over the events, NICRA began to fade into the background and the Provisional Irish Republican Army (PIRA) emerged as a key player, using armed attacks to resist British forces and their local collaborators and calling for the more extreme goal of reunification with Ireland. The PIRA attacked British forces, bombed Protestant and Loyalist properties, and assassinated political opponents. The British imposed a policy of internment, detaining suspected PIRA operatives without charge and using secret trials to reduce their public visibility and sympathy.

Meanwhile, NICRA activists demonstrated against internment in an infamous march in Derry on January 30, 1972. British Army troops fired on the march, killing fourteen demonstrators in an event that came to be known as Bloody Sunday. This effectively ended the nonviolent uprising in Northern Ireland and initiated the thirty-year period known as The Troubles. This case shows how extreme repression and countermobilization by loyalist groups caused riots and street fighting to escalate to full-blown armed struggle, overtaking the nonviolent movement.[10]

On a lesser scale, a similar radicalization process took place in the United States in 1969, when a national leftist student activist group called the Students for a Democratic Society (SDS) was holding its annual convention with the goal of setting an agenda for the year ahead. However, a faction called the Revolutionary Youth Movement (RYM) wanted to take SDS in a more militant direction against imperialism, capitalism, and racism. The RYM ultimately overtook SDS at the convention, expelling members and factions they deemed to be too conservative, and restyled the organization as the Weathermen. The Weathermen believed that real revolution would require violence to counter imperialism. The group began to conduct bombings around the United States, operating from clandestine safe houses around the country as the Weather Underground, before that group also demobilized in the late 1970s and early 1980s.

Has there ever been a purely nonviolent campaign—that is, one without unarmed violence like street fighting or riots?

Yes. There have been many.

Among mass civil resistance campaigns, such occasional eruptions of unarmed violence are more common than organized armed insurrections, but certainly not universal. According to data I collected with Christopher Shay,[11] more than 80% of large-scale, nonviolent uprisings attempting to overthrow dictatorships between 1945 and 2013 involved some minimal use of violence at some point, whether street fighting or some other improvised action.[12]

But nearly 20% of mass nonviolent campaigns totally rejected and avoided violence—including property destruction or street fighting. These included pro-democracy movements in Honduras (1944), Czechoslovakia (1989), Mongolia (1989), Georgia (2003), Thailand (2005 and 2013), Togo (2012), and dozens of other cases.

Unarmed violence is even rarer among mass campaigns pursuing political, social, or economic reforms rather than the overthrow of an existing system, such as the lunch counter sit-ins that helped to desegregate Nashville in 1960, a wave of protests in 2007 that led to land titling reform in India, and a 1995 teacher strike in Angola that led to wage increases. Among over twenty-five hundred large-scale reformist campaigns from 1955 to 2018, only 26% used violence, street fighting, or riots alongside primarily nonviolent action.[13]

And if we count the rate of unarmed violence in protest *events* rather than in overarching *campaigns*—which typically involve scores of events—unarmed violence is even less common. For instance, among the tens of thousands of protest events that took place during the summer of 2020 in the United States, over 97% were uniformly nonviolent. That's true even though police arrested thousands of protesters during that period and attacked and injured hundreds more—and even though armed counterprotesters tried at times to provoke, attack, or frighten demonstrators.[14]

What are some examples of campaigns that have involved unarmed violence?

The Polish Solidarity movement, which is often considered a hallmark of decades-long, disciplined nonviolent resistance, essentially started when Lech Walesa, then a young shipyard worker, walked up to his Communist Party–backed manager in an act of defiance and punched him in the nose.

During Hong Kong's pro-democracy campaign in 2019, the overwhelming majority of the pro-democracy movement protested, marched, demonstrated, engaged in strikes, and faced down police brutality without resorting to violence themselves. But a small minority of activists fought with police or attacked Chinese bystanders in spontaneous and improvised skirmishes.

We also saw instances of unarmed violence in Egypt during the January 25 Revolution in 2011. Inspired by the ongoing movement against Ben Ali in Tunisia, youth activists in Cairo began planning similar protests with the goal of ousting President Hosni Mubarak. Protests began on January 25 when a coalition of youth activists organized a secret march and occupation of Tahrir Square in the center of Cairo. The protests grew rapidly and, while initially led by young men, eventually grew to include incredible diversity, with Muslims and Christians, women, and the leaders of most major political and social groups, including the banned Muslim Brotherhood. Egyptian security forces attempted to suppress the protests in various ways, initially with riot police using batons, tear gas, and water cannons and later with paid vigilantes to attack people in the Tahrir Square encampment with clubs, knives, and guns. Youth activists engaged in self-defensive violence, skirmishing with vigilantes and police, and burning down numerous police stations, although the overwhelming majority of Egyptians remained nonviolent. On February 8 and 9, in a critical move, labor unions joined the movement with tens of thousands of workers striking in factories around Egypt, expressing both their support for the protesters in Tahrir Square and demands for higher wages and better working conditions. On February 11, under pressure from the military, Mubarak resigned and handed power over to the Supreme Council of the Armed Forces.

And at the University of California at Berkeley in February 2017, supporters of black bloc tactics declared victory after a group of antifascist (antifa) activists shut down alt-right figure Milo Yiannopolous's scheduled talk on campus. About 1,500 protesters had assembled in a main square of the UC-Berkeley campus and attempted to prevent entry to the building. Soon, about 150 Antifa demonstrators arrived on the scene. They physically attacked several supporters of Yiannopolous during televised interviews; tore down metal fences; hurled rocks, Molotov cocktails, and fireworks at police; and vandalized numerous nearby buildings. Six people were injured, and Yiannopolous's talk was canceled. The violence was widely condemned by national, state, and local authorities. But Antifa supporters celebrated the incident as a demonstration of how small acts of violence can be an effective complement to broad-based nonviolent movements to deprive fascists of their ability to gain sympathy and support.

Don't all nonviolent campaigns implicitly threaten violence?

Some skeptics argue that nonviolent civil resistance's real power is the latent threat of mass violence that people power engenders. In this view, when people rise up en masse, they are signaling that if they chose to take up arms, they could seriously damage a society—and that nonviolent action amounts to a warning: meet our demands or else.

There are three major problems with this logic. First is a lack of empirical support. If this logic were correct, we would expect to regularly see frustrated civil resistance movements transform into armed struggles. But empirical research suggests that this rarely happens. From 1945 to 2013, among 384 resistance campaigns aimed at overturning a government, just 13 (3.4%) escalated from sustained nonviolent resistance into armed conflicts.[15]

Among the 211 civil wars documented in our database, only 6.2% relied on nonviolent resistance for at least one year before escalating to violence. Those include Algeria—whose independence campaign against France escalated from a primarily nonviolent campaign into a civil war in 1954—Yemen's nationalist Arab movement in southern Yemen (1963), Guatemala's leftist struggle (1965), Northern Ireland's self-determination struggle (1969), El Salvador's leftist struggle (1980), Western Sahara's independence movement (1982), South Africa's anti-apartheid campaign (1984), the First Palestinian Intifada (1993), and a handful of other cases. The other 93.8% of armed conflicts started with few or no sustained attempts at civil resistance. So it's the exception rather than the rule.

Second, most people who participate in mass nonviolent civil resistance do not willingly join an organized armed uprising. Militant groups that launch armed struggle are rarely made up of the same people as those who organize nonviolent struggle. The rise of the Provisional Irish Republican Army in Northern Ireland, which I mentioned earlier, is a case in point. Seeing a political opening with the demise of NICRA, armed militants began advancing urban guerrilla struggle and advancing much more radical demands, including allowing Northern Ireland to secede from the United Kingdom and join the Republic of Ireland or full independence. Reactionary Protestant militias that wanted to remain part of the United Kingdom launched their own campaign of violence to counter the PIRA and its offshoots.

The Northern Ireland case illustrates the third point as well. In most cases where a nonviolent insurrection did become a civil war, governments and their armed supporters are the ones who typically do the most to escalate the conflict. This point follows the observation that government crackdowns often suppress or sideline nonviolent activism and embolden a small group of radicals to step into the vacuum and organize an armed counterresponse.

For instance, in Syria beginning in March 2011, unarmed dissidents protested nonviolently to topple President Bashar al-Assad's autocratic rule, install a democracy, and bring al-Assad and his security forces to justice for killing and torturing peaceful dissidents. In response, al-Assad waged a scorched-earth counterinsurgency campaign against unarmed demonstrators, strafing them with gunfire, sending in *shabiha* (pro-government militias) to kill and maim political opponents and their families, and rounding up, torturing, and killing tens of thousands of suspected political opponents. After al-Assad had been committing these atrocities against civilians for nine months, the civil resistance campaign essentially dissolved or went underground, replaced by the Free Syrian Army, Al

Qaeda–linked groups like Jabhat al-Nusra, the Islamic State in Iraq and Syria, and other armed groups that began to coalesce out of local militias. As the conflict escalated, al-Assad responded with even more indiscriminate violence, destroying homes and neighborhoods with artillery fire, dropping barrel bombs on top of crowded civilian areas, attacking cities like Ghouta with chemical weapons, and engaging in siege warfare against entire cities like Aleppo, Homs, and the Damascus suburbs of Darayya and Muadamiyat.

Fourth, authoritarians are usually the ones who suggest that any nonviolent protest is really a veiled threat of armed insurrection. They're trying to discredit and delegitimize their country's dissidents. By denouncing peaceful protesters as "extremists" or "terrorists," tyrants attempt to paint themselves as protectors of the people and to reinforce loyalty within their regime. Consider what happened in Turkey during the Gezi Park uprising in 2013. Activists had initially organized demonstrations to resist the government's plan to replace a popular public park with a parking lot. But when police attacked the demonstrators with brutal beatings, rubber bullets, tear gas, and arrests, the protests swelled into a massive uprising demanding Turkish president Recip Erdogan's resignation. Despite the fact that demonstrators remained peaceful while riot police maimed and killed Turkish civilians in the streets, Erdogan routinely denounced nonviolent activists involved in the Gezi Park uprising as terrorists and hooligans. The same dynamic played out in Russia, where President Vladimir Putin has faced numerous small pro-democracy mobilizations over the past ten years. In 2019, a group of pro-democracy activists was quickly rounded up during a protest and charged with crimes against the state under Russia's draconian Terrorism Laws. And in the United States, Donald Trump's administration has routinely accused liberal and left-leaning political opponents of engaging in violent rhetoric, warning that the country is on the brink of civil war despite the overwhelmingly peaceful nature of the left's political activities.

The message to governments facing nonviolent uprisings is simple: if you don't want a civil war, don't start one. But those in power know that mass nonviolent action threatens them more than violent unrest. That is precisely why autocrats go to such great lengths to label nonviolent activists as violent traitors—and to provoke nonviolent movements into violence.

Does some fringe violence help movements to succeed?

Some scholars have argued that some peripheral violence tends to help civil resistance campaigns. Others are more skeptical. Table 3-1 breaks down what the research has found about the tactical and strategic effects of fringe violence.

Table 3-1 Benefits and Drawbacks of Fringe Violence for a Civil Resistance Campaign

	Benefits of Fringe Violence	Drawbacks of Fringe Violence
Tactical (Immediate) Effects	Draws immediate media attention to the campaign. Causes police and security forces to expend more resources to try to control or contain the situation. Fighting back can sometimes prevent arrest, assault, or death. Can shut down or stop an event. Requires less coordination and agreement among campaign participants prior to an event; allows individual agency in the moment.	Usually distracts media from peaceful protests and participants. Escalates confrontation and results in preventable injuries or death. Can disproportionately harm or sideline marginalized groups or communities. Creates suspicion among onlookers about the movement's goals.
Strategic (Long-Term) Effects	Signals resolve. Signals capacity to disrupt. Generates awareness of a claim or injustice. Deepens bonds among radical participants. Increases fear and reduces morale among security forces. Reinforces an oppositional culture among participants, leading to longer-term commitment to a group and its goals.	Usually alienates potential allies and sympathizers. Signals chaos or intent to do harm to the opponent, bystanders, or both. Generates confusion about the claim or injustice and opens the movement up to charges of hypocrisy. Divides movement supporters and sidelines voices calling for nonviolent action. Reduces likelihood of defections.

Table 3-1 Continued

Benefits of Fringe Violence	Drawbacks of Fringe Violence
Makes more moderate elements of the movement appear appealing, opening bargaining opportunities for them. Gives individuals full autonomy, in keeping with principles of self-determination.	Reduces diversity of participants and supporters. Leads to more intense and indiscriminate repression. Keeps people away. Heightens the risk of armed escalation and civil war. Lowers the chance for democratic reform and heightens the risk of autocratic backsliding after the campaign is over.

First we look at the benefits, starting with the immediate impact of fringe violence. Violent incidents certainly draw instant media attention; sometimes they help a movement burst into the spotlight and make its claims to a broader audience. In fact, that's often what those involved say they were aiming at: intense media coverage of property damage, street fighting, and setting objects on fire. In a 1984 study of the civil rights movement, sociologist Herbert Haines argued that rioting and other militant activities raised the Black Power movement's profile, drawing more attention to its demands.[16] And after smashing windows, fighting with alt-right protesters, and hurling projectiles at police near Trump's inauguration ceremonies in Washington, DC, in 2017, one self-described anarchist defended his group's violent tactics by telling the *New York Times* that the protests had been successful because they got the television stations to cut away from the inauguration, even for a brief period.[17]

Some research suggests that riots and street fighting can disrupt what's happening on the street, forcing police and security forces to spend more time, resources, and energy responding to the violence.[18]

Supporters of fringe violence often argue that their actions help to defend and protect others. The opponent is so powerful and intransigent, the argument goes, that all tactics should be available to those resisting. For instance, during the 2017 Unite the Right Rally in Charlottesville, Virginia, armed fascist and white supremacist rally-goers attacked nonviolent protesters by punching them and beating them with sticks and other improvised weapons. To protect the protesters, a coalition of antifascist and socialist activists fought back, unarmed. They argued that disciplined nonviolent action was submitting to intolerable hatred.

The willingness to use violence to disrupt or shut down an event can work, short term, to temporarily deprive people of platforms or audiences.[19] Many contemporary antifascists draw inspiration from various antifascist actions in Europe during the twentieth century. For instance, British antifascists often confronted "black-shirt" English fascist groups who were speaking in public. The goal was to stop them from spreading their ideologies, bringing in new members, and growing in power and influence. Some of their techniques were fairly effective in shutting down Nazi parades and rallies. For example, contemporary antifascists often point to the Battle of Cable Street—a major confrontation between communist, socialist, anarchist, and Jewish groups; the London Metropolitan (Met) Police; and the British Union of Fascists (BUF) that occurred in East London in October 1936. Oswald Mosley, the leader of the BUF, planned to march several thousand black-shirt fascists through a neighborhood with a large Jewish population. Despite a popular outcry among East End residents, the British Home Secretary allowed the march to continue, and thousands of Met police mobilized to protect the fascists and keep public order. About twenty thousand socialists, communists, anarchists, and Jewish groups set up blockades and fought with thousands of Met police with sticks, table legs, and other improvised weapons. Neighborhood residents dumped garbage, refuse, and chamber pots onto the police below their balconies. The riots effectively prevented the march from proceeding, with the BUF dispersing instead. Antifascist groups in Britain continued to interrupt and attack Mosley on other occasions, ultimately preventing him and his group from expanding their political base. Contemporary antifascists also highlight the tactical effectiveness of partisan guerrilla movements that fought the Nazis throughout Europe during World War II to explain why antifascist movements in particular must use any means necessary to stop fascism.[20] Of calls for peaceful protest against neofascist movements today, one member of Antifa said, "That kind of argument can devolve into 'just sit on your hands and wait for it to pass.' And it doesn't."[21]

Another common argument is that violent flanks are necessary to protect nonviolent activists from a highly militarized police force, especially when the broader public is apathetic or indifferent to their suffering. In this view, activists—especially activists from marginalized communities—need to be able to use a variety of tactics to protect themselves. And so those who are willing to accept risk and rumble with the authorities should be allowed to do so. For instance, in the book *This Nonviolent Stuff'll Get You Killed*, activist Raymond Cobb (2014) argues that violence is often necessary to protect nonviolent activists from the worst abuses.[22] Those favoring fringe violence often point out that at the beginning of Dr. Martin Luther King Jr.'s career in the civil rights movement, he kept a loaded gun in the house and hired armed guards to protect his family from white supremacist vigilantes. Of course, Dr. King later disposed of his guns and armed guards, deciding that his leadership in the movement required a comprehensively nonviolent approach, come what may.

Next, allowing for fringe violence means that movements can proceed without advanced coordination or agreement about how participants will behave. Disciplined nonviolence involves a great deal of consensus, coordination, and training regarding the boundaries and limits of behavior. If movements do not adhere to disciplined nonviolence, the argument goes, then they do not have to invest in such arduous preparations, and individuals can decide for themselves whether to use nonviolent techniques or to fight back violently to protect themselves or others from overwhelming state violence.[23] This approach also satisfies those who criticize advocates of nonviolent resistance as overly dogmatic or dominating of others.

Allowing violence on the fringes may have longer-term value as well. First, some insist that only violence conveys true resolve and commitment to a cause.[24] A turn to violence shows that the movement is willing and able to hurt other people until demands are met. Violence also shows a willingness not to back down and to keep imposing pain on an opponent until a movement gets its way. As a result, some within the government will try to find a way out of the impasse, opting for negotiation to avoid years of instability and violence. Similarly, some scholars have also suggested that attacking police or security forces can frighten them and reduce their morale, making it more likely that they desert or mutiny.[25]

Violence may also draw attention to a grievance or injustice in ways that can have both short- and long-term political effects. For instance, Ryan Enos, Aaron Kaufman, and Melissa Sands have argued that riots can awaken observers to key injustices, motivating citizens to vote for politicians and policies that will respond to the movement's claims.[26] For instance, in 1991, a bystander videotaped four Los Angeles police officers assaulting Rodney King, an unarmed Black man, after pursuing him on a high-speed chase. This was an extraordinary sight in the years before mobile phones and the internet. In response, Los Angeles's South Central neighborhood, which was primarily Black, erupted into riots that lasted days, and were echoed in several other cities. Enos, Kaufman, and Sands find that in districts affected by the riots, white citizens have voted for more liberal politicians who support racial justice initiatives even several decades after the riots.[27] But this study does not compare the effects of riots to the effects of unambiguously peaceful protests against police brutality, which were also taking place nationwide. In fact, studies of the civil rights movement have found that nonviolent protests had similarly enduring effects in other numerous nationwide.[28]

Next, violent groups may create strong bonds among the people involved. In a study on militant labor activists, for example, Larry Isaac and his coauthors argued that once people have destroyed property, rioted, or fought in the streets on behalf of radical ideals, they remain committed to those ideals throughout their lives—often reaching leadership positions and encouraging others into lifelong activism.[29] In some cases, violent actions have had profound social and cultural effects, spreading a commitment to opposing the misuse of power. For instance, Howard Barrell, a former anti-apartheid activist in the African National Congress, argues that guerrilla attacks by the armed wing of the ANC emboldened those engaging in nonviolent action to be more disruptive, confrontational, and courageous.[30]

Some observers have claimed that fringe violence benefits civil resistance movements in more indirect ways as well. In particular, some argue that if the violent fringe comes across as militant and uncompromising, the nonviolent movement may seem less threatening and more reasonable to negotiate with.[31] Many people have interpreted the US civil rights movement this way, concluding that Martin Luther King Jr. gained leverage with John F. Kennedy and Lyndon B. Johnson in the early 1960s because those presidents recognized that if the federal government did not respond to King and other peaceful groups advocating for civil rights, they would have had to deal with Black militants advocating for more radical demands.

Strong ideological traditions lie behind these arguments. For instance, the anarchist tradition rejects as hopelessly corrupt any social hierarchies and authorities, "normal" approaches to politics like elections, judicial systems, and liberal economic policies. They see all these as valuing private property more than human life. They similarly reject civil resistance movements' attempts to control participants' conduct as what anarchist scholar David Graeber dismissively called "violent peace-police."[32] Ultimately anarchists reject political projects that they see as reformist or cooperative with hegemonic, violent, state-centric practices; they want to replace the status quo, end domination and subjugation of people, and achieve full equality, autonomy, and self-determination. Those inspired by anarchist traditions aren't alone. Many groups—including those focused on class or racial hierarchies—reject privileged groups' critiques of how marginalized groups can and should behave. For instance, given the United States' history of white supremacy and racism, some activists argue that calls for nonviolent discipline are both paternalistic and racist—the equivalent of white people telling Black people to be good.

Undeniably, fringe violence sometimes has short-term tactical benefits and often reinforces bonds of solidarity among radicals, who can attract the mainstream media's insatiable cameras. Fringe violence has caused enough chaos and instability to force universities, civic groups, and even extremist political parties, to cancel events. It can publicly dramatize anger, rage, hopelessness, autonomy, independence, and a total rejection of the status quo. And refusing to enforce nonviolent discipline can allow individuals to express or defend themselves however they want to.

But fringe violence also brings both tactical risks and serious long-term disadvantages. This is important, because all these short-term tactical and strategic advantages come with important trade-offs that proponents often obscure or ignore.

Do violent flanks undermine nonviolent campaigns?

As you can see in the right-hand column of Table 3-1, fringe violence can undermine otherwise nonviolent civil resistance campaigns in several ways, both tactically and strategically.

Let's look first at the tactical risks. Riots, street fighting, and people taking up arms—whether impulsively or in an organized fashion—almost always prompt security forces to respond immediately. And in these direct confrontations, security forces usually have the upper hand.[33] Whether by firing tear gas, rubber bullets, or live ammunition, security crackdowns almost always hurt not just the people involved in street-fighting or other violence but also some of the peaceful majority. In other words, lots of people can get hurt, arrested, or killed who did not consent to those risks.[34]

Second, although violence almost always brings media attention, that attention doesn't necessarily frame the movement in a sympathetic light. It typically shifts the spotlight away from the movement's core demands and onto the violence itself. Because of how the human brain works, when observers see violence or vandalism, they have a tough time understanding what exactly the protesters want. Observers tend to assume that violent people intend to harm others—and can't or won't consider whether the movement's cause is just.[35]

It's a bit easier to examine the long-term strategic effects of fringe violence—in part because we've got plenty of data to compare what happened after campaigns with and without violence at the edges. From 1900 to 2019, 65% of nonviolent campaigns without fringe violence succeeded in overthrowing regimes or winning self-determination. The reliance on nonviolent methods helped those movements keep masses of people from very different walks of life actively involved. By contrast, only 35% of nonviolent campaigns that included some fringe violence succeeded.

Why the gap? The reasons are numerous. First, fringe violence typically means fewer people get involved with the cause, and that the people who do get involved are more homogenous—which undermines the main advantage that comes with nonviolent civil resistance. In fact, on average, nonviolent campaigns with fringe violence had about 17% fewer people involved than nonviolent civil resistance campaigns that included no such violence.[36] Similarly, the emergence of violence in one year tends to lower movement turnout in the next.[37] These trends refer to studies on revolutionary movements in which large-scale violence occurred alongside otherwise nonviolent campaigns. But scholars who have studied reformist campaigns and protest events have come to the same conclusion across different national and cultural contexts. Using social media data on all documented protest events and state responses across twenty-four cities from five countries between 2014 and 2017, Zachary Steinert-Threlkeld, Jungseock Joo, and Alexander Chan (2019) found that protester violence tends to shrink crowd sizes at subsequent events.

Why? There are a few reasons. First, protester violence makes those protests physically riskier for everyone, not just those who are attacking. Of course, nonviolent action always carries risks. But protester violence ups that risk dramatically, always prompting security forces to respond with coercive tactics like firing tear gas and rubber bullets, beating people with billy clubs, mass arrests, and shooting live ammunition.[38]

Second, we know from historical studies that people tend to be more willing to put themselves in harm's way than to actively hurt others.[39] When it appears that a mass movement has devolved into street fighting, attacks against opponents and their bystanders, and harsher counterresponse from repressive forces, that pushes many away people who just don't want to be associated with violence. This is especially true if potential protesters begin to think that the movement is falling into disarray or chaos.

Third, protester violence tends to drive out a crucial group: women.[40] This is not because women are inherently more peaceful or afraid of danger. As we saw in Chapter 2, women often participate in mass movements at great personal risk, despite overwhelming repression against the movements. Having women actively involved and right out front can make a difference in whether civil resistance movements succeed. But movements that embrace or adopt violence tend to alienate women. What's more, they keep out other marginalized individuals or groups, who often feel they are more likely to be targeted and harmed when security forces crack down on street fighting.[41] As scholar and activist Stephen Zunes has put it, generally movements have to choose between fringe violence and diverse participation.[42] It's hard to have both.

Next, even when fringe violence does not drive out any of a movement's supporters, it can alienate potential supporters—making it much harder for the movement to grow. In May 2016, political scientists Jordi Muñoz and Eva Anduiza were halfway through conducting a survey on popular support for Spain's anti-austerity group M-15, otherwise known as the *indignados*, when a street riot broke out among some radical groups associated with the movement. Muñoz and Anduiza were therefore able to compare public attitudes toward the movement before and after the riot. They found that the riot reduced support for the *indignados* by about 12 percentage points from the pre-riot average. These levels of support depended on respondents' predispositions toward the movement and its claims. Hard-core supporters tended to remain firm in their support, no matter what the movement did. But among people who considered themselves neutral, weakly supportive, or opposed to the movement, support dropped significantly. In other words, even a little fringe violence limited the movement's ability to expand support beyond its most committed base.

Psychologists and sociologists have similarly surveyed individual attitudes toward violent and nonviolent activism in lab settings. In 2014, psychologists Emma Thomas and Winnifred Louis published a study examining the Australian public's attitudes toward anti-fracking and anti-whaling movements. Using an experimental survey, they found that the public responded positively to nonviolent collective action—perceiving it as legitimate and effective—far more than to group violence.[43] A broader study by psychologists Seyed Nima Orazani and Bernhard Leidner analyzed American attitudes toward twenty-three movements with varying ideologies and claims, including women's rights, anti-whaling, anti-abortion, gun control, and more.[44] They found that, across the board, a commitment to nonviolence enhanced Americans' support for and willingness to get involved in the movement. The authors argue that movements relying on nonviolent methods come across as having greater moral conviction, which elicits sympathy and respect—and that nonviolent action makes any harsh government response look starkly unjust. They also find that Americans believed that nonviolent action could actually succeed. Since people like to side with winners, they were therefore more willing to either get involved or to sympathize with the action's goals.

These patterns aren't limited to the US alone. Adelman, Orazani, and Leidner (2017) replicated these findings in Iran and Bahrain, suggesting that in many different kinds of social and political worlds, disciplined nonviolence increases both public support and willingness to get involved.[45] And in a study based in Malaysia, psychologists Hema Preya Selvanathan and Brian Lickel conducted surveys in November 2016—before and after a day of mass action against corruption.[46] They found that when Malaysians observed nonviolent protests, they became more willing to support the movement and its claims. But if they had a more threatening perception of the protests—for instance, if they perceived the anticorruption demonstrations as violent, chaotic, or unsafe—their support for the movement and its claims tended to fall.

Another recent study shows that public attitudes toward fringe violence depend somewhat on the movement's demands. Sociologists Brent Simpson, Rob Willer, and Matthew Feinberg similarly conducted a series of internet-based survey experiments in the US about respondents' attitudes toward antiracist and white nationalist protesters, checking if attitudes varied when either group used nonviolent or violent methods.[47] They found that people tend to view antiracist groups that attack white nationalists as unreasonable, and that such violence reduces support for antiracists and increases it for white nationalists. Oddly enough, popular perceptions of white nationalist groups don't change when they're violent. The authors speculate that this is because white nationalist groups are already deeply unpopular—and that Americans expect them to be violent, given their antagonistic attitudes. This finding points to a fairly intuitive (if maddeningly unfair) political reality for progressive groups. Precisely because their legitimacy comes from their opposition to violent or harmful systems, the public holds them to a higher moral standard in their own conduct.

Beyond experimental studies, there is some solid historical evidence showing that disciplined nonviolent resistance favorably shapes public opinion of a movement, at least in the US case. Political scientist Omar Wasow looked at how civil rights protests affected public opinion during the 1960s. His research finds that nonviolent protests in a particular district resulted in higher support for civil rights, pushing civil rights to the top of public concerns in opinion polls. By contrast, more violent protests led more people to consider law and order the most important public issue. It's no accident that after 1965, as violent protests became more common, favorable public opinion shifted away from civil rights and toward the police response. The movement stopped expanding its appeal among crucial pillars of support, and that shift translated into electoral outcomes. Wasow found that support for law and order was highly correlated with votes for Republican leadership, suggesting that different protest types have had lasting political effects in the United States. This finding is reinforced by another recent study by political scientist Shom Mazumder, who found that people living in electoral districts where nonviolent sit-ins had taken place during the civil rights movement were likelier than others to support affirmative action and identify as Democrats several generations later.[48]

These findings are broadly consistent with another statistically sophisticated study by economist Emiliano Huet-Vaughn, who used instrumental variable techniques to determine how violence shaped the different outcomes of French labor disputes.[49] He finds that violence and property destruction tend to reduce the probability that labor groups will win concessions. Fringe violence, in other words, is counterproductive.

Another reason why fringe violence can reduce the chances of success for nonviolent campaigns is that it makes security forces less likely to defect. Although street fighting can diminish the morale of police and troops in highly unpopular regimes, in more entrenched and politically powerful systems, it can embolden and unify police and troops. And as we saw in the section about pillars of support, that can be a real impediment to making broad-scale change.[50]

Next, while some people claim that violence on the fringes helps to protect peaceful activists from the state's brutal response, it typically does the opposite. Protester violence often gives government forces license to crack down on all protesters and regime opponents more intensely and indiscriminately. In a global study, Elizabeth Thompkins finds that nonviolent movements that erupt with violence on the fringes are more likely to be targeted with more indiscriminate repression.[51] In another global comparative study, political scientist Sabine Carey similarly found that lethal repression—in other words, killing the opposition—tends to happen after riots and guerrilla violence. By contrast, governments tend to respond to protests, strikes, and boycotts with much more limited and less fatal responses.[52] These findings are reinforced by more recent cross-national research by political scientists Zachary Steinert-Threlkeld, Jungseock Joo, and Alexander Chan, who found that across twenty-four social movements in five countries between 2014 and 2017, governments always responded to protester violence with more violence.[53] Political scientists Yonatan Lupu and Geoffrey Wallace found that citizens in India, Argentina, and Israel tended to support human rights violations against those who committed violence—but generally believe that governments should respect the human rights of nonviolent protesters.[54] This is consistent with separate findings from political scientists Courtney Conrad and Will Moore who found that government human rights abuses—like torture—tend to persist during periods of violent dissent, but they tend to diminish when dissidents rely on nonviolent resistance.[55]

The scholarly consensus, then, is that governments that attack otherwise nonviolent movements are more likely to get away with it if some protesters are violent themselves—even if the fringe violence is of the unarmed variety. Most oppressive or autocratic regimes accuse their opposition of being thugs, murderers, and traitors no matter what they do. But bystanders and other citizens are more likely to believe the government if even a small number of activists commit violence. In Israel, for example, the government has used several Palestinian and Islamist groups' militancy as a pretext for mass crackdowns against unarmed Palestinian activists. The violent acts of a few have pushed both Israeli leadership and citizens slowly but decisively to the right, as ordinary people increasingly want security and safety. The fear of Palestinian violence has now all but destroyed any hope of a two-state solution, even though over the years the vast majority of Palestinian self-determination activism has been nonviolent.

Of course, movements that seriously challenge the status quo always face government repression. But that doesn't necessarily doom a movement. So long as the civil resistance campaign can keep masses of people actively involved, can win more sympathy from outsiders, and can begin to chip away at the pillars of support, it has a better chance of surviving—and winning. Movements without fringe violence are much more likely to do all three.

Understandably, when movements face attacks, arrests, persecution, crackdowns, and long-standing discrimination, participants begin to debate whether to escalate to armed struggle. Escalating repression does make it difficult for movement leaders to continue arguing for nonviolent discipline.

But those who argue in favor of fringe violence rarely acknowledge that in doing so, they are shutting others out of the movement—perhaps permanently. And they often ignore the fact that not everyone supports their violence. Those calling for using "any means necessary" against an overpowering adversary rarely acknowledge that by doing so they are shutting others out of the discussion—or even placing them in harm's way.[56]

Effective resistance appears to require a disciplined and uncompromising denial of what the opponent wants. Strategically speaking, fringe violence tends to move the movement's struggle onto the government's territory, losing the advantage of disciplined nonviolent resistance.[57] The more oppressive the opponent, the more the resistance must refuse to play the opponent's game—even though, paradoxically, it becomes more difficult for resistance leaders to make the case for nonviolent action.

So let's review the evidence. The emerging consensus in research studies is that fringe violence tends to drive supporters away from the movement, even if everyone else remains nonviolent. It tends to repel potential allies, increase government repression, and discourage those supporting the regime from defecting. Given these patterns, it's no surprise that such movements with violence at their fringes tend to suffer defeat more often than they succeed. And it's also no surprise that regimes try to infiltrate social movements to push the movements toward violence. In the United States, that's what the FBI tried against various leftist and anarchist groups during the 2011 Occupy Wall Street movement—and during its controversial COINTELPRO program, which infiltrated and divided the Black Power movement, the American Indian movement, Puerto Rican independence groups, and various other new leftist movements during the 1960s and 1970s. Various government and corporate groups also tried infiltrating the labor movement in the early twentieth century. Governments and corporations try to weaken social movements by planting provocateurs who push violence—which tells you that the powerful know violence will help them. Effective resistance movements work hard not to cooperate—intentionally or unintentionally—with the opponent. That includes rejecting behavior that the opponent wants them to embrace.

Such conclusions underscore a tough political trade-off for movements. If organizers decide that civil resistance is the most effective way forward, they can attempt to train members to adopt nonviolent discipline and reject coalition partners who engage in street fighting, limited violence, and improvised vandalism. However, maintaining nonviolent discipline requires some degree of enforcement within the movement. And this often elicits criticism from among the movement's most ardent supporters, who may accuse movement leadership of policing participants' behavior—and reinforcing simplistic narratives that try to sort out "good" protestors from "bad" ones.

Alternatively, movements can avoid constraining the activities of their adherents, prioritizing the protection of individuals' rights to resist according to their own circumstances, contexts, and consciences—and hoping that the disruptive and creative power unleashed will benefit the movement. Yet, accepting an unlimited range of tactics opens up the movement to greater risk of crackdowns, public condemnation, and numerous other political setbacks that are ultimately difficult to surmount. In other words, allowing for fringe violence often elicits greater criticism from both within *and* outside the movement, from would-be participants, sympathizers, and potential allies.

Regardless of the evidence and trade-offs, ultimately it's always up to movements themselves to resolve this debate—not powerholders, and not self-appointed critics who are sitting on the sidelines.

Does violence always hurt a civil resistance movement in the long term—or can it help in some situations?

On average, fringe violence does not help civil resistance campaigns succeed in the long term. That's true even if you account for things like a country's wealth, demography, and level of democracy versus autocracy.[58]

There are some guiding principles that seem to apply generally, according to the survey data cited above. Most onlookers favor non-violent movements over violent ones. They are especially sympathetic to movements when the government's violence in response appears to be an overreaction to what the movement has done. Unarmed action is also more likely to gain supporters from across the social, economic, and political spectrum.

There is an important exception to these trends. Some research suggests that deep societal divisions—such as race, ethnicity, class, and other cleavages—can make it harder for marginalized people to gain supporters even when they maintain nonviolent discipline on their own. For instance, some survey experiments have found that in the United States, white respondents tend not to sympathize with African American protesters—no matter how they protest, violently or not.[59] Something similar is going on in Israel and Palestine, where the animosity between Israeli Jews and Palestinians—not to mention the United States' unconditional support of Israel—makes it difficult, if not impossible, for Palestinian civil resistance to succeed in winning self-determination. In both the United States and Israel-Palestine, most people in privileged groups generally approve of police or military violence against protesters from marginalized populations. That's yet another glimpse into how hard it is for such groups to succeed without active participation and support from the majority.[60] That said, there is little evidence that protester violence—or organized armed action—has helped such movements build their base of supporters and overcome these power asymmetries either.

Of course, what's considered unacceptable levels of violence varies in different contexts. Sometimes, but not always, onlookers may be tolerant of vandals who show up alongside an otherwise exciting mass movement. In Egypt in 2011, for instance, in seemingly spontaneous acts of defiance against the much-hated police, dissidents burned down numerous police stations near Tahrir Square. That didn't repel would-be allies; in fact, it seemed to draw even more people into participating in the January 25 Revolution. At that uprising's peak, the Egyptian Army sided with the people rather than either the corrupt police or their erstwhile commander in chief, Hosni Mubarak.

Similarly, in Hong Kong, recent surveys suggest that the youth-led movement remains popular even though some have fought back against police brutality, sometimes with weapons. But as in Egypt, this is because the Hong Kong police are so widely unpopular, so deeply despised, that any acts of defiance against them are rewarded with public sympathy—although not necessarily by public participation. Protester violence tends to be popular only among those who already sympathize with the movement—while pushing others away.[61]

But that doesn't mean such acts are essential for a movement and its ultimate aims. For organizers, whether an act counts as nonviolent is less important than whether onlookers—active supporters, passive supporters, and neutral parties—view the movement's tactics as wise, legitimate, proportionate, and consistent with the overall goal. So a key question for many movements is whether its participants' actions tend to expand its power by broadening the base and bringing in more people from diverse groups—or whether their tactics start to push people away.

How do violent flanks affect countries in the longer term?

Movements with fringe violence sometimes succeed in spite of them. But the political dynamics unleashed in the process are often difficult to control in the longer term. Violence is deeply polarizing, and polarization tends to encourage still more violent escalation. For example, historically, revolutionary nonviolent campaigns where fringe violence emerges have been more likely to lead to civil war, even years after the conflict is supposed to have subsided.[62] What's more, when a revolutionary movement involves fringe violence, the country is more likely to have authoritarian institutions after the conflict is over.[63]

How often do provocateurs succeed in provoking fringe violence?

At their peak, civil resistance movements live or die by bringing in masses of people from many parts of society—which makes them more vulnerable to infiltration than small, clandestine groups whose founding members are known to one another.[64] A paradox of civil resistance is that its greatest source of strength—people power—is also its greatest vulnerability when it comes to provocateurs.

Provocateurs are infiltrators—usually paid by and acting on be-half of the adversary—who pretend to be activists. They sometimes work their way into organizing or leadership groups to gather in-formation on movement plans and activities, assess movement weaknesses, and foment paranoia, personality conflicts, and divi-sion to weaken the movement.

Governments have used such provocateurs to infiltrate, sabo-tage, and undermine movements for centuries. Russian secret po-lice infiltrated anti-tsarist movements, including the Bolsheviks, before the Russian Revolution to sow dissension and suspicion.[65] The Republic of New Africa, a Detroit-based Black radical group, was undermined and disbanded in large part due to infiltra-tion during the FBI's COINTELPRO program.[66] An undercover New York detective helped open the Bronx chapter of the Black Panthers. Malcolm X's bodyguard, who attempted to resuscitate him when he was shot, was also an undercover officer.[67] More recently, police departments have sent undercover personnel to protests by progressive organizations like Black Lives Matter, gaining access to text messages and other private information. In another sinister development, Russian agents set up fake social media accounts disguised as Black Lives Matter sites to heighten tensions within the United States. One such Facebook account called Blacktivist attracted five hundred thousand followers, and featured divisive material meant to further outrage and polarize sympathizers, supporters, and opponents.[68]

At other times, provocateurs and plainclothes police may simply show up at public gatherings and encourage violent conflict with po-lice, bystanders, or counterprotesters, aiming to disrupt the event and force the movement to explain or defend itself. Their ultimate aim, of course, is to banish public sympathy and support for the movement while giving the government justification for heavy-handed tactics such as beatings, mass arrests, or lethal coercion. A secondary aim is to divide the movement, often through accusations that those who insist on nonviolent discipline are not radical enough.

Because fringe violence can be so deeply divisive and polarizing, that governments often try to nudge movements toward violence shouldn't be surprising. As activist Steve Chase wrote in 2017, "There is simply no documented case that I know of where a paid undercover government or corporate agent has encouraged activists to engage in strategic civil resistance tactics and maintain their non-violent discipline doing it. They do not see such movement actions as being in their interest."[69]

Why do some nonviolent campaigns adopt, embrace, or tolerate violent flanks?

Movements tend to lose nonviolent discipline under a few circumstances.[70] First, when police and security forces stop staying on the sidelines and start attacking, beating, or shooting participants, various people associated with the movement start questioning whether nonviolent methods are working—and whether the opponent is just too brutal to fight through nonviolent action.

Many civil resistance campaigners who argue in favor of at least some violence justify it as a last resort. But they're often conflating "peaceful methods" with protests alone—or, more often, with negotiations, lawsuits, or reforms of how elections are run. This argument ignores the fact that nonviolent resistance methods include far more than protest. In Chapter 1, we read about the broader array of nonviolent methods that are available to movements seeking change, such as stay-at-homes, noncooperation, and other lower-risk methods that can be very effective. Although it's difficult to measure, most movements that allow or turn to violence have not considered or tried many of these other nonviolent actions first. As academic Michael Walzer put it in 2001,

> It is not so easy to reach the last resort. To get there, one must indeed try everything (which is a lot of things)—and not just once, as if a political party or movement might organize a single demonstration, fail to win immediate victory, and claim that it is now justified in moving on to murder. . . . It is by no means clear when they run out of options. . . . What exactly did they try when they were trying everything?[71]

Importantly, not every movement facing brutal repression automatically turns to violence. Earlier, I mentioned a number of revolutionary campaigns—in Honduras (1944), Czechoslovakia (1989), Mongolia (1989), Georgia (2003), Thailand (2005 and 2013), and Togo (2012)—where movements responded to government repression with a high degree of nonviolent discipline. There are thousands of other campaigns seeking nonrevolutionary reformist goals that have done the same. As political scientist Wendy Pearlman has shown, many movements have maintained nonviolent discipline and stood up against repression when they had strong organizational cohesion, widespread agreement about nonviolent strategy, and a clear collective vision for the future.[72] However, without a strong organizational structure, movement leadership can have a hard time convincing everyone involved to stick to nonviolent action in the face of repression.

Second, and somewhat ironically, movements also tend to lose nonviolent discipline when the state begins to make concessions.[73] This is because concessions tend to divide the movement into moderates and radicals—those who are willing to accept some concessions short of full success, and those who are only willing to accept total victory. When such divisions emerge, radical groups are often tempted to escalate to violence to spoil any negotiations between moderates and their adversaries, to distinguish themselves from the moderates, and to outbid them for recruits and support.[74]

Finally, nonviolent discipline is more likely to break down when movements rely exclusively on concentrated street actions, such as protests or sit-ins, which increase opportunities for direct confrontations between protesters and police. Strikes and other forms of noncooperation are slightly less likely than protests or sit-ins to lead to protester violence, in part because security forces aren't likely to attack them directly, and partly because they're harder for provocateurs to infiltrate.[75]

So what have we learned? In sum, fringe violence may sometimes achieve some short-term *process* goals like media attention; the perception of self-defense; a bond among a radical, militant core; or catharsis after blowing off steam. It liberates people from hierarchical systems and allows participants to avoid the problem of over-policing within the movement, which can reinforce the problematic power relationships that the movement is fighting against. But movements that do not adhere to nonviolent discipline often find that fringe violence has undermined their longer-term *strategic* goals, like building an increasingly large and diverse movement, encouraging outsiders to support the movement's goals, and winning over defectors from various pillars of support. Nonviolent campaigns with fringe violence may occasionally win a battle, but they tend to lose the war.

Okay, so how can nonviolent campaigns prevent or limit fringe violence?

The surest way to minimize the political effects of a violent few is to significantly outnumber them with nonviolent masses. This allows a movement to maintain momentum and signal that the vast majority of those involved are unarmed civilians. Of course, this can be challenging if fringe violence starts to reduce a movement's popularity and leads its supporters to stay home.

Many civil resistance movements plan their methods in a way that reduces the chances that provocateurs could steal the scene. For instance, in moments of deep grief or fear—for instance, if the government has recently escalated its brutality or terror tactics— movement leaders have called off large-scale public protests in favor of fasts, planning sessions, or silent marches. Silent marches can demonstrate mass participation while encouraging discipline and channeling rage and grief into a solemn public display. This reduces the chances for improvised or inadvertent violence. A silent march makes it incredibly clear who is sticking to the movement's plan and who is not. Political scientist Jonathan Pinckney has found that methods like strikes and other forms of noncooperation can help those involved maintain nonviolent discipline at times when the government is likely to escalate. Relying more on protests and sit-ins, on the other hand, may make direct confrontations with police more likely—increasing the chance of further repression, unplanned fisticuffs, or more intense forms of violence.[76]

When confrontations are inevitable, movements have spent days or weeks training activists and participants how to deescalate conflict nonviolently. Some movements have even required that anyone who wants to attend go through nonviolent direct action trainings first, thus building trust among members, preparing people who are about to take risky action, and ensuring they fully know and anticipate the risks. During the civil rights movement, Black activists associated with the Student Nonviolent Coordinating Committee (SNCC) role-played maintaining nonviolent discipline in the face of attacks privately, in advance, in church basements in

Nashville and beyond. Video footage shows that they rehearsed in staged but realistic situations, such as having white men use derogatory language toward Black women sitting at lunch counters. They practiced managing their own fear and anger, not so that they would appear "respectable" but so that they could successfully carry out their missions to sit in at the lunch counters until they were arrested, continue their nonviolent occupations of jails and bail hearing rooms, and return to the lunch counters to sit in again.

Releasing and publicizing shared guidelines or boundaries in advance of an action can be a helpful way to make sure participants know the risks and still commit themselves to maintaining nonviolent discipline. By helping people feel that they are knowledgeable about, in control of, and committed to various forms of resistance without violence, movements protect themselves against impulsive violence and make it much more likely that they can maintain nonviolent discipline against the odds.

Guidelines like these have an honorable history, having successfully helped large movements prepare to maintain discipline in extremely trying conditions. Under British colonialism in South Asia, a movement emerged among Pashtuns to resist British colonial rule in what is now Pakistan. The leader of the movement, Badshah Khan, recruited a hundred thousand people into a "nonviolent army." Members of the movement took a solemn oath to fight against British colonial rule using Gandhian techniques of mass noncooperation and constructive program.

In 1965, leaders of the Congress of Racial Equality (CORE), one of the major groups involved in the US civil rights movement, developed and distributed rules and guidelines for participants in CORE actions and activities. Among the rules: when violently attacked, CORE members could not retaliate in word or action.

Other movements have undertaken similar commitments, many of which were widely shared among the population as a whole. For instance, during the 1968 Prague Spring, after the Soviets militarily occupied Czechoslovakia rather than allow it to become a democracy, dissidents circulated a set of guidelines known as the "Ten Commandments" to encourage noncooperation with Soviet troops.[77] Just six days after the Soviet invasion, on August 26, 1968, the newspaper *Vecerni Prah* published the guidelines:

When a Soviet soldier comes to you, YOU:

1. Don't know
2. Don't care
3. Don't tell
4. Don't have
5. Don't know how to
6. Don't give
7. Can't do
8. Don't sell
9. Don't show
10. Do nothing

More recently, during the 2019 Smile Revolution that deposed the Algerian dictator Abdelaziz Bouteflika, Algerian writer Lazhari Labter published eighteen commandments for the "pacifist and civilized marcher."[78] They are:

1) I will walk peacefully and quietly,
2) I will behave in a dignified and civilized manner,
3) I will bring water and vinegar [to counteract the effects of tear gas],
4) I will not respond to any provocation,
5) I will isolate provocateurs and turn them into the police,
6) I will not throw a single stone,
7) I will not break a single window,
8) I will not use profanity,
9) I will not lay a finger on people or their property,
10) I will smile at the policeman and the gendarme,
11) I will offer a rose to the woman,
12) I will share my water with those who are thirsty,
13) I will watch over the old, women, and children,
14) I will walk with determination,
15) I will fight against the odds,
16) I will be a worthy heir to the Novemberists [Algerian independence rebels who launched a rebellion against French colonization in November 1954],

17) After the march, I will clean up the streets and the squares,
18) To the world watching me, I will provide a lesson and serve as an example, because I know that Liberty awaits me at the end of the road and will welcome me into her open arms.

When there's violence on a movement's fringes, some leaders have found it useful to open a dialogue with the groups involved. For instance, veteran Portland, Oregon, peace activist, and scholar Tom Hastings has contacted groups that accept and endorse violent tactics before a planned peaceful action, and to ask them to stay away from the otherwise "family-friendly" event unless they can respect and abide by the publicized nonviolent code of conduct, in which case they are very welcome. At times, he reports, they listen to his reasoning and agree to stand down or to maintain nonviolent discipline for the duration of the event.[79]

As I mention above, recent research also suggests that movements are vulnerable to developing fringe violence when their opponents make concessions or capitulate to one or more of their demands. Such situations can create or heighten divisions between moderates and radicals within the movement. Movements can prepare for and potentially prevent this tendency by anticipating it and developing core movement principles that emphasize unity over short-term strategic gains.[80]

Of course, some people do come to large demonstrations intent on committing violence. To be ready for this, some movements assign trained peacekeepers in advance, putting them in charge of monitoring potential escalation—either by police and security forces or by willfully provocative participants. Such peacekeepers are often trained in conflict resolution and conflict management, and can deescalate or defuse the situation immediately. If that fails, they can help move everyone else to safety, or can use a method called "interpositioning." This is a technique where a large number of people stand between provocateurs and their targets to keep them apart, creating a human barrier. Sometimes a smaller group then surrounds the provocateurs and quickly moves them away from the scene. In Serbia in 2000, when hundreds of thousands of Serbians were protesting Slobodan Milošević's attempt to steal an election, student organizers paid taxi drivers to station themselves near major protests. Movement peacekeepers would walk provocateurs out of the crowd and ask them to get in the taxi, after which the drivers would drop them off far from the events.

At times, movements are not able to use methods like these. But they may be able to minimize the *political* effects of these violent flanks by using news releases or public statements to denounce the violence, distance the movement from the perpetrators, or simply refocus the narrative once again on the movement's core claims. This works best when the movement clarifies explicitly that it is a nonviolent one.

Sometimes, though, movement leaders can't afford to condemn or denounce those who use violence. For instance, in the United States, activists fighting for racial justice would pay a political price for denouncing those who fight for racial justice by rioting or taking up more militant means. Martin Luther King Jr. would not denounce people who rioted to protest police brutality. Even though he thought riots weren't strategically helpful, he understood that exposing cracks within the civil rights movement would be even more strategically harmful to its overall aims. Moreover, doing so may have reduced his political power among his core supporters. And it could expose weaknesses in the movement coalition that the authorities could further exploit. Regardless, being sidetracked by spurious claims—that a nonviolent movement stands for violence because of the actions of a few—gives oxygen to propaganda that helps the state.

That's part of the reason why leaders of many nonviolent movements are often silent about violent groups with a common cause. Yes, the leaders know that violence will probably hurt them politically with the broader public. But those leaders also know that their supporters are counting on them to speak for everyone in the broader movement—and that if they denounce those who are violent, they'll be amplifying critiques of the movement, and they'll be seen as betraying their own. That damages both the leaders'—and the movement's—moral standing.

Thus, even more important than tactical discipline may be narrative discipline: the ability of a movement to maintain clarity and focus on its core demands, the urgency and legitimacy of its claims, its vision of tomorrow, its ever-widening basis of support, and its progress toward these goals. Rather than being distracted by defending, or denouncing, the actions of a few people or debating

the morality of various methods of resistance, controlling the narrative of the movement by the movement is essential to its impact
and success.[81]

How can movements stay united when there are genuine disagreements about whether violence is acceptable?

Sometimes they don't. Many movements split bitterly between those
dedicated to nonviolent discipline and those committed to pursuing
their aims by any means necessary. Some movements do avoid those
splits, but they don't fall into general patterns; each approach is particular to its own circumstances. Sometimes, movement leaders
have used internal shaming mechanisms to try to punish anyone
using violence in the movement's name. For instance, Gandhi sometimes called off nationwide noncooperation campaigns after riots,
claiming the need for collective reflection and atonement before
Indians were fully prepared to wage an effective struggle against
British imperialism. And César Chávez and other leaders of the
California Farmworkers Movement would fast as a way to shame
movement participants who were agitating for or using violence in
the movement's name. Because of Chávez's considerable moral authority within the movement, these actions persuaded his more militant comrades to fall in line.

But these techniques work for movements united behind a ca-
pable and charismatic leader or group of leaders—which isn't
true of many movements today. And keeping people dedicated to
nonviolent discipline gets harder as the state escalates its violence
against protesters to beatings, killings, torture, and even massacres.
Under these shocking conditions, it is understandable for any remaining idealistic hope to sour into disillusionment and despair.
Some movements allay that tendency by training and preparing
participants for a long, difficult struggle. The movements ensure that
those involved know the risks and grasp that nonviolent struggle,
like armed struggle, often involves sacrifices and small, hard-won
victories along the way. And they provide numerous opportunities
to share in the grief and pain of crushing losses, though healing
gatherings, artistic expression, and the creation of new techniques
of struggle, such as the Chilean women who danced alone to

symbolize the loss of their loved ones to Pinochet's torture and execution chambers,

So how can civil resistance organizers mobilize large numbers of newly awakened people who are willing to get actively involved in a movement that can make real social and political change—when thousands upon thousands of them believe that real change requires violence?

Here's something to keep in mind: as scholar-activist Michael Nagler points out, movements must not abandon their struggles for justice just because of fringe violence, even among large groups. Yes, dealing with violent groups can be challenging—alienating some of the public, and at times straining coalitions. But if people power movements abandon the struggle, they're giving in, just as if they gave up in the face of harsh policing. They're amplifying the setbacks that those violent few have inflicted, rather than managing and overcoming them like any other challenge on the way to success.[82]

Can movements that start violently transform into civil resistance campaigns—and succeed?

Yes. From 1946 to 2013, about 4% of armed uprisings eventually became nonviolent civil resistance movements—and some were victorious. That happened in Nepal in 2006 after a grinding ten-year civil war between a monarchical government and a Maoist insurgency.[83] In 2005, a mass civil resistance movement rose up to depose the government and shut down the insurgency, resulting in the end of the war and the toppling of the dictatorship in 2006. In South Africa in 1994, legal apartheid came to an end not because of the ANC's decades-long armed struggle, but rather because of nonviolent economic disruption that included Black townships boycotting white businesses over ten years; marches, demonstrations, and strikes; and organizers around the world coordinating international economic pressure through such tools as divestments and sanctions. In both East Timor and West Papua, Pacific islands that had been colonized by other nations, armed independence movements were overtaken by civil resistance campaigns. Timor won independence from Indonesia in 2000, while the West Papua movement is still struggling against Indonesian rule as of this writing. I could name another dozen examples. Laying down arms and replacing them with civil resistance has indeed led to victory for many armed groups.

Is fringe violence inevitable?

In 1962, President John F. Kennedy said, "Those who make peaceful revolution impossible will make violent revolution inevitable."

When movements have tolerated or even embraced the violence on their edges, those involved have often argued that violence couldn't be avoided. When vast numbers of untrained, outraged people face widespread repression, when large crowds confront police and security forces' provocations or attacks—the argument goes—how could anyone expect disciplined nonviolent action in response? Activists who take up arms often justify that decision by saying there was no other choice, given the level of repression—in Bashar al-Assad's Syria, for instance, which brutalized civilians involved in nonviolent resistance as well as civilians living in proximity to armed rebel groups since 2011. In some cases, nonviolent activists have thanked the local fighters who took up arms to defend them against al-Assad's security forces loyalist militia.

But here's what such activists don't argue: that violence by those local fighters will help them win politically.

Scholar John Braithwaite has argued that in many cases, while violent flanks may not be ideal, movements can't prevent them from emerging. Therefore, he argues, nonviolent movements should consider coordinating with those violent fringe groups to maximize political pressure against the regime.[84] Similarly, in a 2019 *Washington Post* op-ed, historian Paul Adler argued that the 1999 Battle of Seattle, during which small groups of activists engaged in street fighting and vandalism alongside others who were using nonviolent direct action, showed progressives that they can pursue different tactics—and still cooperate and coordinate to pursue their shared goals.[85]

But is that true? When governments have a hard time dealing with civil resistance, it's because they don't have an effective response to massive numbers of citizens refusing to cooperate with the regime: when they refuse to ride and pay for the city buses; when they stay away from the mines or factories or shops and freeze all business; when they bang their pots and pans so loud and long that nothing else can get done; when they build underground universities, distribute illegal newspapers, and form shadow governments that make the government's claims to legitimacy seem hollow and irrelevant in day-to-day life.

Most governments would have an easier time dealing with a chaotic street fight—they can arrest and assault their way out of that with few political penalties—than with an effectively waged mass nonviolent campaign.

Fringe violence makes all of that far less effective. Violence drives away supporters and shrinks a movement to its most dedicated core—who aren't numerous enough to shut down a government. Violence tends to repel potential allies and discourage possible defectors from the government's elite supporters. This tends to hurt a movement's chance of success—even (or especially) when the regime is attacking, arresting, and otherwise repressing the movement.

But violence does still more harm in the longer term. Historical studies suggest that fringe violence increases the risk that a country will slide into authoritarianism. In extreme cases, the presence of violent groups alongside nonviolent civil resistance eventually results in civil conflict and war. [86]

So how can a movement respond to a regime's violence and repression? Let's look at that in the next chapter.

4

CIVIL RESISTANCE AND VIOLENCE AGAINST THE MOVEMENT

There are opportunities even in the most difficult moments.
—Wangari Maathai, 2006

Can civil resistance defeat a truly brutal opponent? Many people believe that the answer is no—and that only violence can overturn a tyrant who's willing to turn to mass slaughter, imprisonment, torture, and other immoral and inhumane means to stay in power. They argue that where nonviolent civil resistance campaigns succeeded, it was only because the opponent was not willing or able to use massive violence against them. And they point to failed campaigns and say that nonviolent action could never have succeeded because the opponent was so brutal—as if taking up arms against that tyrant's military might would have kept dissidents safer. That's a common argument about, say, the 1989 Chinese student protests in Tiananmen Square, in which pro-democracy activists were brutally crushed by the Chinese Army. And it's a standard argument about, more recently, the 2011 nonviolent uprisings in Syria, which escalated into a multiyear civil war in which hundreds of thousands have died and millions have been forced out of their country. Another popular argument is that Gandhi's Indian independence movement only succeeded in the end because Indians were facing the British crown, not Hitler's Germany.

Although it is true that fear of government brutality often deters people from rising up—and that intense repression has crushed many attempts at resistance—the historical record shows that the opposite is also true. As we explore in this chapter, although it is more difficult in the context of extreme repression, civil resistance is neither impossible nor wholly ineffective in such circumstances. We examine the most common ways tyrants have tried to crush nonviolent resistance campaigns, and we look at how such people power movements have responded to these setbacks—and even prevailed in spite of them.

What is repression?

I'll use the word "repression" to refer to when governments or their agents (militaries, internal security services, paramilitaries, or police) use coercive force to influence behavior. Different governments use repression in different ways, varying in:

- Scope, or how many people are affected.
- Intensity, or which kinds of coercion the government uses, whether that's arrest, harassment, and persecution; mass killing or genocide; torture, arbitrary political imprisonment, extrajudicial killing, or other human rights abuses.
- Lethality, or whether the state kills people through disappearances, extrajudicial killings, or executions; or whether the state uses nonlethal repression, such as detentions, harassment, intimidation, job losses, land seizure or home demolition, and forcibly dispersing crowds with tear gas, beatings, and mass arrests.
- Duration, meaning whether the coercion involves short-term or longer-term efforts against a particular social, political, ethnic, or racial group.

Governments claim monopolies on the legitimate use of force—and that claim to a legitimate monopoly is a basic difference between, say, police and vigilantes. Because many citizens accept this monopoly, an oppressive government can exercise repression without using direct coercion at all, simply by making clear what it *could* do if it so chose. For that reason, political scientists Emily Ritter and Courtenay Conrad have argued that even though a government may not be actively repressing its citizens on any given day, it still might be a highly repressive state.[1]

Can people even attempt nonviolent civil resistance campaigns against brutal tyrants?

Yes. In fact, increased state brutality is one of the main reasons people rise up in the first place, as political scientist Jay Ulfelder and I found.[2] Because we were curious about why nonviolent uprisings occur in some countries but not others, we assembled a dataset using a list of indicators that we imagined might have an influence. Those included a country's level of democracy or autocracy, population size, record of human rights abuses, recent experience with labor strikes, youth population, ethnic fractionalization or polarization, government instability, poverty, history of civil conflict, global economic integration, and whether the region—or the world—was seeing a wave of resistance. As mentioned in Chapter 2, it was very difficult to find any variables that consistently influenced the onset of nonviolent uprisings, which are inherently unpredictable.

But here's what was noticeable: the most consistent and influential predictor of nonviolent uprising was a country's human rights record. Countries with *worse* records had a higher chance of witnessing a mass nonviolent uprising than countries with relatively better records. This may sound counterintuitive, but it reveals a powerful point: human rights violations—like arbitrary imprisonment, torture, extrajudicial killings, and disappearances—can convince people in many different parts of society that the government's behavior is so illegitimate and threatening that they have no other choice but to act. People often cross the barrier of fear to rise up in very repressive places.

How common is repression against nonviolent campaigns?

That depends on how much the campaign threatens the opponent. When dissidents don't threaten the status quo in a serious way, governments commonly ignore them or give in to a few of their demands.[3] Governments generally interpret mass protests and demonstrations as popular attempts to blow off steam—or as minor events that don't represent a serious political threat.

But when mass nonviolent campaigns are challenging major social, political, economic, or cultural institutions or systems, governments very commonly respond with repression. In fact, violent repression against unarmed dissidents who have the goal of shaking things up seriously is so common that political scientist Christian Davenport calls it the "law of coercive responsiveness."[4]

Let's quantify that. Of the nonviolent revolutions between 1900 and 2019, regimes responded with lethal repression 88% of the time (and 94% of the time against violent revolutions). When a civil resistance campaign is trying to overturn the government, unseat an authoritarian regime, or declare territorial independence, their adversaries almost universally respond with human rights abuses: disappearances, arbitrary detention, torture, and extrajudicial killing. Yet government-led mass killings—perhaps the most extreme form of repression—are relatively rare against nonviolent uprisings.

In other words, governments facing unarmed revolutionary challenges most commonly combat them with brute force. But how widespread, how devastating, and how intense that response is—in other words, the repression's degree, scope, and intensity—all vary. And that variation is based in part on the characteristics of the resistance itself.

How does repression affect nonviolent campaigns?

As is true with many of civil resistance's dynamics, repression's effects are unpredictable. Scholars generally agree that extreme repression or "smart" repression—which means highly sophisticated, selective repression—can make things difficult for mass movements. However, scholars also agree that brutal incidents can actually set off, rather than end, a nonviolent campaign against overwhelmingly oppressive systems. Think of the 1955 lynching and mutilation of fourteen-year-old Emmett Till in Mississippi.

After his body was recovered, Till's mother insisted on an open casket at the funeral, putting the horrific atrocity on display. A wave of outrage, support, and sympathy pushed thousands more to get involved in or support the US civil rights movement. The same could be true of the killing of George Floyd, Ahmaud Arbery, and Breonna Taylor, whose killings set off the largest and broadest mass mobilization for Black lives in US history during the summer of 2020.

As noted above, a relatively sudden increase in repression—or an episode of violence that shocks a nation into rebellion against an oppressive system—is consistently associated with the beginning of mass nonviolent uprisings.[5] But two things strongly influence how movements weather repression: first, the movement's organizational cohesion, and second, the political status of the group the movement represents.

What are those two things, exactly? By "organizational cohesion," I mean how well the movement's organizers or organizing coalition keep people unified, through a shared and accepted plan of action, a collective idea of what the movement is trying to create, and some degree of organizational continuity that allows the movement to keep moving even if one or more leaders is arrested or killed. By "political status," I mean the degree to which the government sees that group as essential to its own political survival.

Let's look at each of these in a bit more detail.

Organizational cohesion

Some research suggests that strong organization is the most important factor in helping civil resistance campaigns survive repression. In her book on the Palestinian national movement, political scientist Wendy Pearlman argues that the presence or absence or organizational cohesion best explains why the movement has shifted between nonviolent and violent methods over time.[6] Let's look at how organizational cohesion in the face of repression affected two distinct phases of the Palestinian independence movement: the First and Second Intifadas.

The First Intifada began in 1987 when Palestinians from all walks of life rose up in response to an incident in which an Israeli Defense Force (IDF) truck collided with a passenger car, killing four Palestinian workers. Palestinians were outraged by the incident, which they interpreted as deliberate collective punishment for the recent killing of a Jewish person in Gaza. The uprising began in Jabalia Refugee Camp in the Gaza Strip, which had been home to three of the four people killed in the car crash, but quickly spread to many villages and cities within Gaza and the West Bank.

A clear leadership of grassroots and civil society groups coalesced. From 1987 to 1991, Palestinian communities and grassroots groups formed a broad-based coalition, called the Unified National Leadership of the Uprising (UNLU), which pressed for Palestinian independence, self-determination, and freedom from violence by Israeli military personnel. Largely organized by women's community groups, the UNLU expressed a formal commitment to avoid lethal violence and engaged in significant outreach in local communities to persuade Palestinians to maintain nonviolent action even when Israeli military personnel were using lethal force, arguing that resorting to violence would undermine the legitimacy of the Intifada in the eyes of sympathetic Israelis and potential international allies.[7] Hundreds of thousands of Palestinians participated in work stoppages, strikes, protests, boycotts of Israeli civil administration institutions, and nonviolent demonstrations.

Although news media tended to focus on rock-throwing by Palestinian youth as the iconic image of the First Intifada, the IDF's own records identified 98% of Palestinian demonstrations as nonviolent.[8] Yet the Israeli military cracked down, assaulting Palestinian activists with live ammunition, beatings, home demolitions, the destruction of olive trees, and detention without trial. Over 1,200 Palestinians were killed during the uprising, with many more injured or imprisoned. Over 150 Israeli civilians and soldiers were also killed, largely by militant groups that were operating outside of the UNLU's control. But because of the UNLU's agreed-on leadership, collective vision, narrative discipline, and clear internal norms and rules that kept the movement united, Palestinians relied overwhelmingly on nonviolent methods—such as mass demonstrations, tax refusals, road blockades, boycotts of Israeli products, and strikes in Israeli settlements—no matter how repressive the Israeli state's response was. The images of unarmed Palestinians confronting Israeli tanks and uniformed personnel in their villages shifted international and Israeli public opinion toward recognizing the rights of Palestinians. A group of IDF personnel began to refuse service in the Palestinian Territories. Called "refuseniks," this key group of defectors led to an even further shift in Israeli public opinion regarding a need to recognize the basic aspirations of Palestinian self-determination. These events led to talks in Madrid and Oslo, resulting in a historic agreement in 1994 that established the Palestinian Authority, which granted significant autonomy to Palestinians to govern the West Bank and Gaza Strip, and led to partial IDF withdrawals from both regions. In the accords, the Palestine Liberation Organization (PLO), represented by Yasir Arafat, also recognized Israel's right to exist.[9]

Yet the unity and organizational cohesion that animated the First Intifada did not last. During and after the Oslo Accords, Hamas—a militant Islamist Palestinian group—increased its attacks against Israelis from small-scale killings in 1988 to deadlier suicide bombings in 1993. This wave of terror foreshadowed an overall shift to violent struggle among Palestinian militant groups from 2000 to 2004—a period known as the Second Intifada.

Let's look at how fragmentation—the opposite of organizational cohesion—affected this phase of the conflict, starting with the emergence of Hamas. Hamas cast itself as a militant, Islamist alternative to the more secular, leftist PLO, which it saw as too accommodating of Israel's right to exist. In Hamas' charter, written in 1988, the group vowed to destroy Israel. As the Oslo Accords came into effect, in 1993 and 1994 the group unleashed a wave of suicide terror, hoping to derail the peace process and to polarize the Israeli public. Although Hamas's terrorism had the desired effect of polarizing the Israeli public, it mainly did so by empowering hardliners within Israel, such as the hawkish leader Ariel Sharon. The escalation of violence toward Israeli civilians—killed by suicide bombings while they were eating in cafés or riding the bus to work—also silenced the Israeli peace movement, which found it increasingly difficult to push Israel to maintain its commitments to grant Palestinian autonomy while the public reeled with grief and outrage.

But in 2000, the Second Intifada began, provoked by a visit to the Temple Mount in Jerusalem—an Islamic holy site—by Ariel Sharon, the belligerent Israeli defense minister. When Palestinians in Jerusalem spontaneously protested this controversial appearance, the Israeli military fired tear gas at, beat, and killed the protesters. In response, Palestinian militant groups—Hamas, Palestinian Islamic Jihad (PIJ), the Popular Front for the Liberation of Palestine (PFLP), and Al Aqsa Martyrs Brigades—began to target Israelis with a much more intense wave of suicide attacks, resulting in about one thousand Israeli deaths. During this phase of the struggle, militant Palestinian groups competed with one another for recruits and popular support from among their constituents, leading to a dynamic known as "outbidding."[10] The Israeli government responded with gunfire, tank and helicopter attacks, targeted assassinations, home demolitions, mass arrests, and military occupations, resulting in thousands of Palestinian deaths.

What were the results of the Second Intifada? Israel ultimately subdued the wave of terrorism using overwhelming repression. The Israeli government demolished homes of the families of suspected suicide bombers, imprisoned thousands of Palestinian political opponents, and began building a concrete barrier between Israel and Palestinian territories in Gaza and the West Bank, leading to numerous small-scale border disputes as the barrier cut through villages and separated Palestinian families from their olive trees—a major source of subsistence in Palestine. The IDF withdrew from the Gaza Strip in 2005, leaving Hamas to win elections there in 2006 and then to drive out its secular competitors in a low-grade civil war in 2007. Hamas has controlled the Gaza Strip since, while Fatah (the PLO) controls the West Bank, leaving Palestinian political leadership fragmented and impotent. Within Israel, public support for hawkish political candidates increased. Since 2001, Israeli politics has been dominated by right-wing parties, which rely on overwhelming military responses to Palestinian resistance—nonviolent or violent—while expanding Jewish settlements within Palestinian territories, imposing a blockade on the Gaza Strip, and refusing to provide meaningful concessions to Palestinian leaders whenever there are attempts to resume the peace process. Today, the cause of Palestinian independence seems further out of reach that it was in the early 1990s.

So, the First Intifada and Second Intifada followed two different trajectories—one primarily nonviolent, and the other primarily violent. Pearlman argues that Israeli state repression was just as intense during the nonviolent phase of the First Intifada as it was during the Second.[11] But the First Intifada produced meaningful progress toward a two-state solution, while the Second Intifada did not. Why? Pearlman argues that the First Intifada featured a much more cohesive campaign, with an agreed-on coalition leadership structure, large-scale popular participation, and a sense of shared legitimacy regarding the cause and the appropriate methods to achieve it. The Second Intifada began somewhat spontaneously from an organizational perspective—triggered by frustration with an unsuccessful peace process in 2000 and the provocative actions of then–defense minister Ariel Sharon—and did not involve a coordinated structure rooted in grassroots organizations. As a result, the Second Intifada featured a much higher level of infighting among militant organizations, with no coordinated leadership among them. Moreover, the Second Intifada did not involve large-scale popular participation among Palestinians in the same way that the First Intifada did. The escalation of armed resistance during the Second Intifada was itself a sign that each rival militant group sought greater attention and public support from among Palestinians.[12] In sum, Pearlman's study of the Palestinian national movement suggests that movements can make significant progress in the face of brutality when they remain united and organized. But when movements are largely improvised, repression can lead to rapid escalation—particularly when armed militant groups are already in the mix.

More recent studies confirm Pearlman's insights in other contexts as well. In a study of forty-six mass killings between 1989 and 2011, political scientists Jonathan Sutton, Charles Butcher, and Isak Svensson[13] examined quantitative data about the effects of government killings on the outcomes of nonviolent demonstrations. They found that even when the government kills more than one hundred people during unarmed demonstrations, movements can still succeed in the long run if they are part of a well-organized campaign. And social scientists Clifford Bob and Sharon Nepstad found that movements can survive their leaders' assassinations—if they are well organized and have clear plans in place to continue the struggle.[14] When the leader has developed an administrative structure, a succession plan, and a relatively united and cohesive organization, a movement is more likely to survive the loss of a figurehead or leader.

Of course, some research suggests that newly emerging nonviolent opposition movements can have more difficulty facing down highly sophisticated repressive regimes—especially those with genocidal ambitions and willing executioners. For instance, political scientist Christopher Sullivan examined a national archive of original documents detailing the Guatemalan security forces' systematic dismantling of the country's nonviolent leftist opposition between the 1960s and 1975 before it could coalesce into an effective nonviolent resistance campaign.[15] During this period, US-trained army, police, and paramilitaries (or "death squads") disappeared, murdered, tortured, and massacred high-profile union organizers, intellectuals, students, Indigenous leaders, Catholic clergy, and other suspected oppositionists in large numbers. These efforts forced remaining opposition groups underground; many leftists who survived this period of extreme brutality largely abandoned nonviolent resistance and turned instead to guerrilla warfare, with small-scale bombings and hit-and-run attacks in cities and insurgency in the countryside. The Guatemalan dictatorship responded with scorched-earth counterinsurgency tactics, including genocide against Mayan people suspected of being anti-state.[16]

This example of extreme government brutality against unarmed civilians offers chilling insight into how some would-be dissidents are killed before they even start to organize a coalition, build a participation base, and mobilize mass nonviolent resistance.

But remember that such brutality is risky for governments too— they always face the possibility of alienating their own supporters through such actions.[17] Regime repression against unarmed demonstrators can often backfire by creating moral outrage, drawing in more supporters, building outsiders' support for the movement, and pushing security forces to defect.[18] Faced with a mass nonviolent uprising, governments cannot always keep the loyalty of their subordinates.

A movement's political status

So when have regimes gotten away with brutality toward nonviolent protesters? That seems to depend in part on whether the people who are resisting have the numerical, economic, or social power to create change on their own.

Political scientist Ralph Summy[19] argues that repression is more likely to backfire when the government's survival relies squarely on citizen obedience—which is what happens when people in the majority group refuse to accept the government's behavior. For instance, in Serbia in 2000, three years of student-led resistance finally unseated dictator Slobodan Milošević. But the Milošević government couldn't survive without the relatively homogenous Serb population; attacking peaceful opposition protesters would have been repression against a "nonthreatening in-group," which would have been deeply unpopular in the country.

Sometimes, in military occupations, the occupying force similarly relies on the local population's cooperation. For instance, Nazi Germany's occupations of Norway and Denmark depended on people in those countries continuing to support the war effort— working in factories, keeping the railroads running, providing them food from local farms, keeping children in schools, and so on. Most people in Norway and Denmark refused to work or cooperate with occupying forces—shutting down railroads, refusing to teach, not going to jobs in arms factories, putting sugar in fuel tanks, and using various other methods of subversion to prevent the Germans from carrying out these tasks themselves. Mass repression to compel obedience would have been counterproductive and costly, and so the Nazis attempted to use more selective forms of repression, targeting suspected ringleaders of opposition groups rather than the population as a whole.

But when a government decides it can rule without a minority group's obedience—usually a racial or ethnic group, or a group living in rural or distant areas—it can sometimes crack down violently without political backlash. For example, the Communist Party of China does not need the Tibetan population's obedience to maintain its one-party rule. Tibet is located in China's western frontier, away from densely populated urban areas, and the Tibetan population is extremely small compared to China's overall population. And so the Chinese government has completely suppressed any meaningful resistance there, maintaining heavy surveillance of the area for perceived threats to stability, blocking internet access to information about protests or communication with Tibetan exiles, and quickly rounding up and executing Tibetan monks or youth activists at the first hint of resistance.

In situations like Tibet's, minority activists have attempted to "extend the nonviolent battlefield,"[20] as Maria Stephan described it, meaning building relationships with powerful third parties who adopt the struggle as their own. Tibetan independence activists have tried to do this by forging relationships with people whom the Chinese government does need to stay in power. Tibetan activists and exiles have worked with various Western governments and agencies to try to pressure China for its human rights violations. When the Olympics were held in Beijing in 2008, Tibetan independence activists used that as an opportunity to draw international attention to the Chinese government's crackdowns in Tibet by staging protests at Chinese embassies around the world and, in some cases, calling on countries to boycott the Beijing Olympics. Despite the widespread coverage and objections from human rights groups and governments worldwide, most states were unwilling to boycott the Olympics for fear of alienating China—a global economic powerhouse. Only one world leader—the prime minister of Poland—boycotted the Opening Ceremonies of the Olympic Games in 2008 in protest of Chinese violence in Tibet. Unfortunately for Tibetan independence, very few mainland Chinese support their cause—even among those who value human rights and liberal values. Nor has international pressure been meaningful or consistent enough to push China to change its approach. Under President Trump, the United States invited the head of Tibet's government in exile to the White House and issued condemnations of China's policies regarding Tibet—symbolic moves that did not necessarily bring the Tibetan population closer to independence. These steps reflected the Trump administration's "tough on China" stance, rather than a genuine interest in helping Tibetans realize their aspirations of greater autonomy or independence.

But others have more successfully expanded the nonviolent battlefield. For instance, in 1975 East Timor was a tiny island with a population of under six hundred thousand. It had been a Portuguese colony from the sixteenth century until 1975, when it was invaded, annexed, and occupied by neighboring Indonesia, the world's largest Muslim country, with a population of over 130 million. A Timorese self-determination movement fought back—but Indonesian forces crushed the armed rebellion, slaughtering up to half the island's population through a scorched-earth counterinsurgency campaign. Unable to fight Indonesia's military might, East Timorese activists forged relationships with mainland Indonesian students who already supported human rights. Those students then helped to organize a global solidarity group called the East Timor Action Network (ETAN). This network effectively lobbied various governments—including the United States—to stop sending Indonesia military aid that would support the occupation of East Timor. A widely publicized massacre of a funeral party in Dili in 1991 drew international outrage and condemnation of Indonesia. As international opinion grew to favor East Timorese independence, Indonesian forces withdrew, but not completely. Then in 1997, Asia was hit by a financial crisis that destroyed the value of the rupiah, Indonesia's currency, leading President Suharto to approach international institutions for financial aid. This became a source of leverage for ETAN and the international bodies it was trying to pressure. International financial institutions like the International Monetary Fund and powerful nations like the United States forced Suharto to agree to a Timorese independence referendum as a condition of being bailed out. In a 1999 UN-backed referendum, the Timorese population voted overwhelmingly in favor of independence. Because Indonesian troops and militias continued to treat Timorese people brutally, a UN peacekeeping mission was deployed to the island during the tumultuous and violent transition to independence, which was completed in 2002.

East Timor's path to independence was long and bloody. But it illustrates how an apparently powerless minority group's civil resistance campaign can win—even if its oppressor does not need their obedience. Expanding the nonviolent battlefield—involving majority groups and influential or powerful outsiders—can make an enormous difference, even when the majority population supports the government's repression. As Mary Elizabeth King, a veteran of the US civil rights movement, once put it to me, "Oppressed people should always be the ones deciding the terms of their own liberation. But movements of the oppressed should always include members of the oppressor class."[21]

In sum, repression can crush and disperse a civil resistance movement, at least temporarily. Or it can backfire and end up expanding the movement dramatically. Which path it takes depends in part on how organized the movement's leadership is, who's involved, and whether those people effectively reach out to supporters outside their group to build meaningful leverage over the opponent's pillars of support.

How risky is civil resistance?

Nonviolent movements that truly challenge the status quo are very risky. When a movement challenges a powerful opponent by violating legal and institutional norms, making their dissent from the status quo impossible to ignore, that opponent almost always responds with violent repression. Beyond physical risk, there are other kinds of risks—such as the loss of reputation, the risk of shaming, and the risks of losing a job, healthcare, housing, and child custody.

But of course, the level of risk varies according to who you are, what you do, when, and in what larger context. For instance, if you're participating in a mass demonstration while elsewhere a violent resistance movement is attacking the regime, you may be more at risk of violent crackdowns by the state if the regime is poised to treat all challenges in the same way. That depends in part on the opponent, of course; is the regime, corporation, or other power structure willing and able to send in police, militias, or thugs with guns to brutally dislodge your group from a major town square, or whatever it might be?

But to what are we comparing that risk? For some people, nonviolent resistance is no riskier than going along with the status quo, because they already feel endangered by the regime. And if resistance is the only option, then nonviolent resistance is much less risky than taking up arms against the regime. Controlling for a wide variety of factors, nonviolent campaigns aimed at dislodging a power structure between 1946 and 2013 suffered remarkably fewer fatalities than their armed counterparts. The average armed insurrection during that period suffered more than 2,800 deaths per year, whereas the average unarmed revolution suffered about 105 deaths per year.[22]

And there are ways to wage civil resistance campaigns that account for the risks of those involved. Nonviolent resistance is always riskier for people who are already marginalized or discriminated against. As we've discussed, security forces are prepared to brutalize these populations and are less likely to defect. That's why "expanded battlefield" alliances with people in positions of power can be so important for such groups, helping them to amplify their own power and leverage. For example, during the US civil rights movement, Black organizers knew that racist police in the South would enthusiastically carry out orders to abuse peaceful protesters; winning defections from them wasn't in the cards. And behind the official police forces were white supremacist groups and the Ku Klux Klan, deeply involved in the legal power structure, and quite active in terrorizing Black community leaders above and beyond police violence. That's one reason civil rights leaders focused instead on targeting local business owners and showed their economic power by boycotting segregated businesses, violated segregation norms by sitting in at lunch counters and in "whites only" areas, invited broadcast news outlets to observe their disciplined protests and marches locally and nationally, and assembled legal and financial assistance for those jailed during these campaigns. The resulting economic and political crisis forced white community leaders to the table, won nationwide (if not local) support for desegregation and integration, won federal policies criminalizing Jim Crow laws, and enshrined racial equality as a central goal in the Democratic Party's platform for the past fifty years.[23]

How often does a regime respond to nonviolent campaigns with mass killings?

Social scientists tend to define "mass killings" as episodes of state violence in which at least one thousand unarmed civilians are killed. This can include large-scale killings at several demonstrations or killings that accumulate over the course of a movement. Evan Perkoski and I found that during the period 1955–2013, about 23%— or nearly one in four—nonviolent revolutions aimed at overturning a regime endured mass killings at some point.[24] That's an extraordinary level of lethal repression—and strongly suggests that those involved in the movement felt that daily life under the status quo was brutal enough to risk death.

But again, the question is: compared to what? Compared with obedience, perhaps, civil resistance is risky. But it's less risky than armed resistance. Governments launched mass killings against about 70% of violent resistance campaigns, slaughtering civilians they suspected to be supporting armed insurgents. The state is far more likely to respond to armed insurrection with overwhelming violence.

How do civil resistance campaigns respond to repression?

We can break down the answer to this question into several responses, each of which we look at in more depth. First are the movements that have prepared for repression, and that respond quickly by shifting from methods that gather many people in one place to dispersed methods that are less easy to attack. Second, some movements try to maintain their momentum by publicizing the violence and calling on others to join or support the movement. Third, others retreat, regroup, and reconfigure their strategy. Fourth, some react by escalating to violence themselves, either impulsively or by explicitly deciding to wage organized armed struggle. A final campaign response to a brutal crackdown is disunity and disarray.

Some movements respond to crackdowns by quickly switching tactics

Some movements recognize early on that the regime will respond with violence. That helps them prepare to switch quickly from tactics in which masses of people gather in one place to tactics that keep people spread out. For instance, in December 2018, people began rising up in Sudan in response to a sharp increase in bread prices. The Sudanese government responded with disproportionate force, using tear gas, live ammunition, and rubber bullets against protesters, killing dozens. Outraged, the population began to protest across the country, demanding the resignation of President Omar al-Bashir, whose brutal dictatorship had been in power for thirty years. Over the next few months, a broad-based coalition of oppositionists, including workers; women's groups; trade associations of doctors, lawyers, and other professionals; and students began to coordinate mobilization. The Sudanese Professionals Association (SPA) became a key organization coordinating these efforts and communicating about movement plans and strategies throughout the country. Tactical innovations abounded, including the appearance of "Bucket

Man"—a Sudanese youth who attended demonstrations and used buckets to cover tear gas containers before they could emit their toxic gas and disable protesters.

The movement achieved a major breakthrough on April 11, 2019, when some Sudanese military officers deposed al-Bashir, declared themselves a Transitional Military Council (TMC), and called on Sudanese people to stop demonstrating. In response, thousands of Sudanese people continued to protest, demanding that the civilian opposition have a role in the transitional process toward democracy. Toward the end of April, several TMC leaders resigned as a concession to the movement's demands, but the TMC remained in power. Sudanese people continued to resist, including at a sit-in outside the regime's military headquarters in Khartoum, to demand democratic guarantees and more seats for civilians at the negotiating table. On June 3, security forces stormed a protest camp in Khartoum, killing over one hundred people, raping seventy others, dumping bodies in the Nile River, and attacking wounded civilians recovering in hospitals. The massacre in Khartoum was intended to break the spirit of resistance among the Sudanese opposition members. But instead, the SPA called for people to maintain strict nonviolent discipline and to engage in full-blown civil disobedience, refusing to go into work, shutting down streets and shops, and preparing for a three-day general strike. The strike took place from June 9 to June 11, during which time schools and universities emptied; utilities workers shut off electricity and heat; oil and gas stations, banks, stores, and transportation services closed; newspapers stopped printing; and all nonessential medical offices closed. The strike cleared the streets, literally taking participants out of the line of fire, while also pressuring the TMC both economically and politically to meet the demands of the SPA. By June 12, the TMC announced that it would resume talks with the SPA, and that over a dozen perpetrators of the Khartoum Massacre had been arrested.

Sudan's revolutionaries—like many before and since—sensed that different nonviolent methods carry a variety of risks and have varying political effects. Methods that involve people physically dispersing tend to be harder to attack with brutality than methods that are physically concentrated. Moreover, methods in which people commit transgressive acts—methods of commission—can be riskier than methods where people refuse to meet expectations—methods

Table 4-1 Nonviolent Methods and Associated Risk Levels

	Commission		Omission
Dispersion (people spread out rather than gathering together)	Coordinated and dispersed flash mobs, development of alternative markets, political boycotts, stay-at-home demonstrations, divestments, embargoes, developing alternative institutions, singing illegal songs, overloading administrative systems, and more.		Coordinated electricity shut-offs, stay-at-home strikes, reporting in sick; and more.
Concentration (gathered together)	Sit-ins, nonviolent occupations, marches, demonstrations, rallies, teach-ins, reverse strikes, seeking imprisonment, turning one's back, etc.		Silence, go-slow demonstrations, walk-outs, etc.
Risk level	Highest	High	Medium Lowest

of omission. By shifting between high- and low-risk methods, movements can maneuver in the context of repression.

I've grouped these methods in Table 4-1.

Take Chile under President Augusto Pinochet, a general who'd led a military coup that overthrew the elected government of socialist Salvador Allende in 1973. As happened under US-backed right-wing dictatorships throughout Latin America, Pinochet often responded to political opposition with torture and disappearances. Visible mass protest was highly risky. Pinochet tried to co-opt folk music to reinforce his legitimacy among rural populations, declaring a traditional folk song and dance, *la cueca*, to be Chile's national song. The regime paid men and women to perform the dance together during patriotic parades and rallies. But in 1978, in celebration of International Women's Day, Chilean women began to dance *la cueca* alone in public, holding photos of their disappeared loved ones in an act of extraordinary courage and defiance. Some women began doing this regularly, even in front of the Presidential Palace. Women also began to sew tapestries, called *arpilleras*, commemorating loved ones whom Pinochet's regime had disappeared. Women also organized survival groups as an important parallel institution, including *arpillera* workshops, communal kitchens, and coordination of wholesale buying of food at lower prices. The Catholic Church in Santiago provided space for these groups to meet and plan, with the pro-democracy group Vicariate of Solidarity supplying fabric and helping the women to sell their tapestries abroad. In 1983, Chileans began to signal their discontent toward Pinochet by banging pots and pans out of their windows—a simple act with its roots in previous eras of Chilean resistance that quickly spread throughout neighborhoods and city blocks and showed the widespread rejection of Pinochet's policies and brutality.

Because these groups were building power and expressing discontent without openly gathering in the streets, Pinochet couldn't focus his usual tactics—arresting opponents, disappearing suspected organizers—against what appeared to be every kitchen in entire Santiago neighborhoods. After years of semi-coordinated actions—pots-and-pans protests, symbolic solo dancing of *la cueca*, underground organizing, and labor action—in 1988 Pinochet launched a bid to renew his legitimacy by holding a referendum on whether he should serve an additional eight years as president. Opposition leaders and grassroots groups seized the opportunity. They formed a coalition that organized canvassing efforts, rallies, and campaign slogans to coordinate "No" votes, and trained poll watchers to obtain an independently verifiable vote count to make sure that Pinochet would acknowledge the results if he lost. The coalition was extremely successful on all counts, getting 7 million Chileans to vote "No," from Antofagasta to Santiago—carrying nearly 56% of the vote. When it was clear that Pinochet had lost, the military chose to back not the president but the people, and supported some constitutional reforms and an election to replace the president. In 1989, Chileans adopted the reformed constitution and held an election, after which Pinochet stepped down.[25]

Some movements focus on tactics that minimize the repression's damage

Second, some movements keep their momentum by responding carefully and tactically to the particular problems that repression inflicts. For instance, the movement may find creative approaches that can help free members from detention, as we've seen in earlier chapters. These movements may document and raise the visibility of human rights abuses to help counter regime propaganda that accuses the movement's supporters of treason, terrorism, or other major crimes; this works especially effectively if the movement has already developed clear messaging on these points. And movements often work carefully to persuade those involved not to react to violence with violence—since reacting violently can bring terrible repercussions, including losing public support and making security forces more likely to obey orders to repress the movement, as discussed in Chapter 3. Staying nonviolent keeps the movement on higher moral ground, attracts a wider swath of public supporters, and helps weaken the loyalties of the regime's supporters.

Some movements retreat temporarily to regroup and plan their next moves

Tactical retreats are sensible when public action—however dispersed—is just too risky, but the movement is well organized and well equipped enough to focus on building its parallel institutions, such as alternative schools, media, social welfare programs, and everyday forms of resistance. Consider Syria, where in 2011 the nonviolent revolution collapsed into a multiyear civil war involving thousands of armed groups, powerful international players, and a brutal government using its full military might to destroy its own citizens so that it could stay in power. There, as of this writing, overt civil resistance is simply too dangerous. However, people associated with the Syrian Local Nonviolent Coordinating Committees have continued to serve the immediate needs of people living under siege or constant threat of mass violence, by helping to mediate ceasefires, assisting with humanitarian evacuations, providing food and medical assistance, and documenting human rights abuses. Groups of Syrian women have also attempted to broker ceasefires, initiate international peace processes, and envision a postwar Syria in which people can pursue accountability and justice for the crimes committed during the war.

Some movements escalate to violence

Sometimes civil resistance movements stumble into violence through improvisation. In Hong Kong in 2019, protesters who used fringe violence say they were motivated to respond to police brutality, although the protesters' escalation was largely improvised. Other times, movements make an explicit decision to wage organized armed struggle, as happened within the African National Congress (ANC) in the wake of the Sharpeville Massacre. On March 21, 1960, thousands of Black protesters assembled outside a police station in Sharpeville, South Africa, to protest the racist pass laws, which required Black South Africans to carry identity books with them in an attempt to reinforce racial segregation and limit the movements of Black people outside of their townships. In response to the protests, police opened fire to disperse the crowd, ultimately killing 69 people and wounding over 150 others. Twenty-nine children were among the casualties; many people were shot in the back as they tried to flee the massacre. Several weeks later, the South African government banned the ANC—the main political entity pushing for equality among Black and white South Africans.

Armed groups commonly explain that they turned to violence because intense state repression made nonviolent or peaceful actions impossible. In the wake of Sharpeville and the government's repression against the ANC more broadly, ANC leaders concluded that armed struggle was both justified and necessary to counter such a violent, racist regime.[26] The ANC developed an armed wing, Umkhonto we Sizwe (Spear of the Nation), to attack the regime through urban guerrilla warfare and sabotage. Notably, however, nonviolent resistance continued as well, with mass consumer boycotts, demonstrations, protests, and strikes pressuring the apartheid regime, as we discussed in more detail in Chapters 1 and 2.

Some movements disintegrate

Sometimes a brutal crackdown pushes a civil resistance campaign to collapse into disarray and disunity. This is especially likely when crackdowns happen during the early stages of mass mobilization, where people mobilize spontaneously and try to improvise or build an organizational structure along the way.[27] Recall the Sutton, Butcher, and Svensson study, mentioned earlier, which evaluated how crackdowns affected civil resistance campaigns' success rates.[28] Among forty-six cases of one-sided regime violence against unarmed protests from 1989 to 2011, the authors found that none of the demonstrations subsequently led to change except when they were integrated into a broader campaign of nonviolent resistance. Among those that were, one-sided violence backfired in about half of the cases. And just under half of those campaigns ultimately succeeded in achieving their goals despite facing massive regime violence.

Would the Indian Salt March have been nonviolent if they had been fighting against Hitler rather than the British Empire?

This is a common question, so I want to carefully examine several flawed assumptions that motivate it. The first is the idea that the British Empire ran a benevolent colonial system in India and elsewhere. The second is that Hitler's regime faced no nonviolent resistance and crushed what little it did. Let's look at each one of these ideas in a some more detail.

First, it is important to remember how brutal British colonialism was. The British Empire waged numerous savage wars to keep hold of its colonies in the Caribbean, Africa, and Asia, including modern-day India, Pakistan, and Bangladesh, which at the time were known collectively as British India. The empire inflicted shocking cruelty, including large-scale massacres. Gandhi's campaigns were attacked in waves of violence so severe that they prompted Indians into full-scale mass rebellion. For instance, in 1919, British colonial military forces massacred hundreds of nonviolent protesters gathered in Amritsar, a city in the Indian state of Punjab. Thousands of Indians had gathered to celebrate the Hindu and Sikh holy day of Baisakhi and peacefully protest the recent arrest and deportation of two pro-independence leaders—Satyapal and Saifuddin Kitchlew—who had been arrested a few days earlier. Anticipating a large-scale insurrection, the acting brigadier general sent in British Indian Army troops and ordered them to open fire into the crowds. Hundreds were killed, and over one thousand were injured. In response, J. P. Thompson, the British Raj's chief secretary of Punjab, recorded the following in his diary: "while it 'seems to have been a bloody business' 200-300 killed in a garden . . . probably it will be justified by [the] result.'"[29]

That nonchalant phrasing suggests that the colonial administration was used to dominate the region through violence. Indeed, the massacre at Amritsar was not exceptional in India. In 1930, Gandhi led the movement in the Salt March, during which thousands of his followers marched with him to the Indian Ocean and began illegally making salt, in defiance of British colonial laws outlawing autonomous production of salt. Upon arriving, the British colonial administration arrested Gandhi along with about sixty thousand other Indians. The country erupted in mass civil disobedience in response. Indian poet and nationalist Sarojini Naidu led thousands of people in a march to the Dharasana Salt Works, about 150 miles north of Bombay. When the marchers arrived, colonial troops armed with metal-tipped clubs beat and killed some activists and wounded hundreds more.

In general, British citizens in England accepted the fact that their government used military force to suppress anticolonial revolts, although there were some dissenters. The government depicted colonial rebels as "savages" who used still more brutal violence against their colonial rulers and their families. Because of racist ideas about the rights of white Europeans to subjugate others—as well as the fact that British soldiers were wounded and killed in these wars—Britain's citizens accepted that picture. But the public mood began to change when journalists began to report grisly details of the massacres against Indians waging nonviolent struggle. Through reporting, it became clear that those treated as rebels were unarmed children, women, and men—some of whose families had fought with the British against Germany during World War I and into World War II.

Now let's examine the second fallacy in the hypothetical question that titles this section: the assertion that Hitler would have crushed nonviolent resistance to his rule. In fact, across Nazi-occupied Europe, people were indeed challenging the Nazis through both violent and nonviolent resistance. But it was the nonviolent resistance that Hitler understood to be a particularly puzzling threat. Hitler and his generals were privately troubled about how to defeat the unarmed resistance that had become ubiquitous throughout Nazi-occupied territories. In occupied Norway and Denmark, people resisted through various means, including pouring sugar into the fuel tanks of Nazi vehicles, circulating underground press with information about how to resist, gathering intelligence and passing it along to resistance groups, stealing weapons, organizing limited strikes and stay-at-homes, refusing to cooperate with orders to alter school curriculum, feigning ignorance about directions or workers' identities, and sabotaging munitions factories. In Denmark, train conductors stopped showing up for work, delaying Germans' plans to use Danish trains to continue its conquests until they could install their own conductors. Underground resistance newspapers circulated throughout the country, advocating different forms of sabotage of German military vehicles and munitions, as well as outright resistance through daily work stoppages. Coordinated go-slows—occurring for two minutes during the noontime hour—were common as a symbolic demonstration of Danes' continued defiance of Nazi rule. When word came through that the Nazis were preparing to arrest and deport the country's Jews to extermination camps, thousands of Danes hid their Jewish neighbors, smuggled them to the coast, and ferried them across the sea to asylum in Sweden, saving over seven thousand Jewish lives.[30] All of these actions required extensive planning, organization, secrecy—and the widespread involvement of ordinary Danes.

The strategist Basel Liddell Hart noted that "[The Nazis] were experts in violence, and had been trained to deal with opponents who used that method. But other forms of resistance baffled them—and all the more in proportion as the methods were subtle and concealed."[31] Hitler said to his advisor Alfred Rosenberg in July 1943, "Ruling people in the conquered regions is, I might say, of course a psychological problem. One cannot rule by force alone."[32] And Hitler had written separately, "In the long run, government systems are not held together by the pressure of force, but rather by the belief in the quality and the truthfulness with which they represent and promote the interests of the people."[33]

It's true that once he had consolidated power, there were no coordinated, widespread attempts to resist Hitler through either nonviolent or violent resistance within Nazi Germany itself. But there were meaningful pockets of nonviolent resistance that showed that such resistance was both possible and, in some cases, moderately effective. In a particularly harrowing episode, a student group calling itself the White Rose ran an underground campaign between June 1942 and February 1943 calling for the downfall of Hitler and the Nazis, the end of the war and militarism, and a return to democracy. The group printed and distributed six leaflets—a deeply dangerous effort in Hitler's totalitarian state. After a janitor at the University of Munich discovered the effort, the students and their co-conspirators were caught and executed. But they'd cracked the image of social unanimity, enthusiasm, and consent for Hitler's regime that the Nazis had tried to paint, an image that had discouraged resistance.

News of the White Rose and the execution of these young dissidents spread throughout Germany, demoralizing ordinary Germans while encouraging other shows of noncooperation. For instance, a mysterious "Executive Committee" began mailing personal messages to Nazi Party supporters, warning that they would pay for their complicity in Nazi crimes as soon as the war ended. In his diary, the Prussian aristocrat Friederich Reck-Malleczewen notes that news of the White Rose and its aftermath deeply affected the Nazi sympathizers in his town:

> the ghosts of the dead have already begun their work, and already the effects are felt in the systematic demoralization of the Nazi ruling structure. For weeks now, the lower echelons of hierarchy, district officials, township leaders, and bastions of the regime generally have been making gestures, meant to be noticed, of disillusionment with the Nazis.[34]

Reck-Malleczewen, a secret opponent of Hitler throughout his reign, took these developments to indicate that the regime's popular support was closer to collapse than he had realized. But not soon enough for him; Reck-Malleczewen was arrested in October 1944, taken to Dachau, and executed three months later.

Some Germans had more luck resisting Nazi programs. In Berlin in February–March 1943, a group of about one hundred aristocratic German women assembled outside of the Gestapo offices on the Rosenstraße to demand the return of their Jewish husbands, who had been detained and scheduled for deportation to concentration camps. Even though Gestapo officers threatened them with machine guns and ordered them to go home, the women set up an encampment. The question of how to disperse the women rose to the highest echelons of the Nazi Party, with senior leaders divided over the potential political fallout of a massacre of scores of German women in Berlin following a recent demoralizing defeat at Stalingrad and other internal acts of resistance against the Nazis. The party was confronted with a dilemma: slaughter a group of Aryan women who were displaying courage and matrimonial fidelity, or quietly return their Jewish husbands, even if temporarily. Ultimately, Josef Goebbels ordered all of the men released, and he ordered them not to continue wearing the Star of David to avoid confusion. This was a remarkable and effective show of defiance under totalitarianism.[35]

In addition to these collective acts of nonviolent resistance were effective individual efforts to subvert Nazi plans. German industrialist Oskar Schindler saved about twelve hundred Jews from extermination camps by employing them in his munitions factory, bribing Nazi officers in exchange for their lives. Similarly, Berthold Beitz, a German oil industrialist, saved some eight hundred Jews from extermination by giving them work permits, even though many of them were incapacitated from sickness or injury. The Israeli government keeps a record of non-Jews who risked their lives to help Jews escape or to survive extermination camps during the Holocaust. Called "Righteous among the Nations," the designation is reserved for people who took grave risks, provided substantial or repeated assistance, and expected nothing in return. Over twenty-seven thousand people are on the list—among them, over six hundred lived in Nazi Germany.

To sum up: people resisting British colonialism were fighting against a brutal and violent colonial system. Gandhi's experimental methods of satyagraha were forged in this oppressive environment, which brutally punished acts of defiance far out of the public eye within Britain. It was precisely this brutality that convinced millions of people in British India to join the struggle for independence—which, in turn, ultimately led to Indian independence and the partition in 1947. Moreover, nonviolent resistance under the Nazis was not only present, but also effective in some instances. If such resistance failed to bring down the Nazi regime, it nevertheless saved thousands of lives and contributed to the flagging morale of Nazi supporters within Germany. The suggestion that Gandhi only used civil resistance because he was fighting the British rather than the Germans neglects the trajectory of nonviolent resistance in both places.

Is armed resistance required to fight genocidal regimes?

Resistance of any kind is incredibly difficult under genocidal regimes. Governments intent on destroying entire peoples are often willing to kill all armed or unarmed opposition and anyone associated with them, whether that association is real or imagined. When governments and their structures of power are built on racist or ethnocentric divisions, that tendency can be even worse. Genocidal governments and their supporters in Guatemala, Rwanda, Bosnia, Indonesia, Cambodia, and elsewhere focused only on eliminating people in the targeted group, whether their victims were armed or unarmed, resisting the regime or not.

Yet state-led mass killings, including genocides, are most common during wars.[36] During World War II, when armed groups or partisans assassinated Nazi officers or attacked Nazi military convoys in Poland, Yugoslavia, or Belarus, the Nazis slaughtered entire families or villages during unspeakable reprisals.[37] The same dynamics have played out in many other wartime settings, where states wage war against civilians to punish insurgent attacks. In other words, armed movements operating in wartime contexts are more likely to face genocidal violence than those that are unarmed.[38]

But whenever there's armed resistance to a genocidal regime, there's probably unarmed resistance alongside it. After conquering Poland in 1940, for instance, the Nazis moved over four hundred thousand Jews into a ghetto in Warsaw and confined them inside without enough food or other necessities. For the next few years, its occupants resisted in a wide variety of ways, despite brutality and routine deportations to concentration camps. They created new schools, prayer groups, press and documentation centers, and lending libraries. They smuggled out individuals who could "pass" as non-Jews to work with the Polish resistance. They established orphanages and food smuggling routes to redistribute rations and ensure collective survival. They even organized their own symphony orchestra. By building these alternative institutions, those imprisoned in the Warsaw ghetto insisted on living with dignity, keeping up Jewish traditions and cultural practices, and defiantly resisting oppression even as the Nazis began to transfer thousands of them to concentration and extermination camps.

In April 1943, the night before the entire ghetto was to be transported to forced labor or extermination camps, the Jewish resistance launched an armed revolt with support from the Polish resistance living outside of the ghetto. They killed some Nazi troops over the multiweek uprising before the Nazis burned the ghetto to the ground. While a handful of Jews escaped, over ten thousand were killed during the uprising itself; the remaining Warsaw Jews were sent to concentration camps or death camps, where they were murdered. Marek Edelman, the former head of the Polish Jewish Combat Organization, was one of the few survivors of the uprising. He explained the rationale for rising up in armed resistance: "We knew perfectly well that we had no chance of winning. We fought simply not to allow the Germans alone to pick the time and place of our deaths."[39]

Most genocides have been highly organized, involving killing on an industrial scale. This means that mass killings often take place within detention camps where people are marked for mass extermination. Within such settings, all kinds of resistance have taken place, despite the risks. Political prisoners and detainees selected for killing on the basis of their ethnicity, race, sexuality, or physical impairments have nevertheless resisted, with or without arms. During the Holocaust, those imprisoned in ghettos and extermination camps took up arms—smuggled or stolen—to fight back repeatedly. One of the most successful revolts came in Sobibór, located in Nazi-occupied Poland, where in 1943 Polish-Jewish prisoners and Soviet-Jewish prisoners of war scheduled for the gas chambers led a mass escape, beginning with the killing of eleven prison guards, the seizure of the camp armory, and an escape across minefields surrounding the camp into the forests. Of the hundreds who participated in the uprising, half were recaptured. Fifty-eight survived. But other camps saw nonviolent resistance, including in Mauthausen where one hundred unarmed Soviet prisoners rushed the gates. Historian and British intelligence veteran M. R. D. Foot claims that about thirty got out, and one got away.[40]

So yes, nonviolent resistance has occurred under genocidal regimes, although it has often been suicidal. Like those using armed resistance, those who resist nonviolently may not have immediately brought down the regime. However, they did withdraw their cooperation and support, and in some cases disrupted or otherwise influenced the course of the genocide, if only temporarily. Of course, as I've mentioned throughout this chapter and this book, many people resisted the Nazis nonviolently throughout occupied Europe.[41] In fact, nonviolent resistance during genocides elsewhere has helped save countless lives. Whether the resisters survived or not, their efforts profoundly affected the psyches and morale of witnesses, those who heard about their efforts, and the tyrants they opposed.[42]

While societies often celebrate the triumphs of armed resistance against genocidal or totalitarian rule, countless episodes of nonviolent resistance usually accompany it—and require as much planning, discipline, skill, and courage as violence.

How have campaigns responded when pro-government militias, death squads, or other armed nongovernment groups attack violently?

Many mass movements must respond not only to government violence, but to violence by counterprotesters, militia groups, or even vigilante death squads. That's what happened to movements trying to unseat right-wing regimes in El Salvador from 1979 to 1992, in Guatemala from 1960 to 1996, and elsewhere. In all of these cases, US-trained groups used terror, torture, sexual violence, and other forms of shocking brutality to try to terrorize leftist groups into submission. In other situations, organized criminal groups, including narcotraffickers, have repressed communities near them, functioning as a terrorist state. And during civil wars, civilian-led movements for peace often contend with a large number of armed groups. For instance, in the US South during Reconstruction and Jim Crow, Black people were terrorized by the Ku Klux Klan, which conspired with local and state police and lawmakers to dispossess Black people of land, wealth, political office, and voting rights.

Such situations undoubtedly make civil resistance harder. When a movement is fighting against a government, the public can fairly easily understand which social sectors support and sustain its power—businesses, religious hierarchies, military families, civil service, or whatever it might be. As a result, the movement can more easily identify which groups need to be persuaded that loyalty to the opponent is not in their interests. That's much harder with nongovernmental militias or armed groups. It's not always easy to find out who's supporting them—the government, foreign governments, wealthy business elites, war profiteers, religious institutions, or others—how to influence those groups, or how to make it costly for them to keep supporting the status quo. This is especially difficult when an armed group does not intend to govern, but only wants to profit from the conflict.

Despite these strategic challenges, some communities have found ways to resist such armed groups by discovering their interests and attempting to nudge them into behavior that is easier for the community to live with.[43] Let's look at some examples to see how.

Colombia's civil war, which lasted from 1964 to 2006, left 220,000 people dead. One of the primary combatants was the left-wing Revolutionary Armed Forces of Colombia (FARC). FARC operated largely in rural areas, where many civilians lived in small villages. In addition to the Colombian military, right-wing paramilitary groups formed to attack the FARC and dislodge its bases and sources of support. Caught in the crossfire, beginning in the 1980s, some community organizations began to band together to declare their areas "peace villages," committed to nonviolence and noncooperation with any armed groups.[44] These peace villages often negotiated with the various guerrilla and pro-government militia groups that they would leave the village alone, or pass through without harming anyone. Many of these peace villages remained surprisingly above the fray for the duration of the war. Political scientist Oliver Kaplan looked into why some communities were able to do this effectively, and his argument boiled down to some familiar factors. First, cooperation seemed most effective when longestablished community organizations were well respected by local people, leading to organizational cohesion and reinforcing trust within the communities and among armed combatants. Second, communities that were broadly committed to nonviolence were much better at maintaining discipline, prioritizing effective dialogue and negotiation, and preventing the escalating of conflict despite potential provocations.[45]

Another unlikely example of nonviolent resistance against armed groups comes from Mosul, Iraq, where ordinary people found ways to resist the Islamic State, or IS, nonviolently. When IS first conquered Mosul in 2014, the group declared an Islamic Caliphate and quickly executed anyone suspected of organizing resistance against their mandates. Overt public displays of defiance became somewhat less common as a result. However, they did not fade away completely, and many Iraqis adopted everyday forms of resistance. A 2018 survey of over a thousand residents of Mosul, which IS occupied and governed with an iron fist from 2014 to 2017, revealed that over 80% of respondents had engaged in some form of nonviolent resistance against IS rule.[46] For instance, citizens would refuse to follow IS's rules about praying at specific times of day, and they ignored bans on smoking cigarettes or drinking alcohol, listening to music, growing beards (for men), or appearing in public without facial coverings (for women). Although only 6% reported doing such things publicly, almost 22% reported that they'd done such risky things as displaying anti-IS symbols and slogans, occupying public spaces where IS had forbidden gatherings, and insulting or berating IS members for their brutality. Fully 62% of survey respondents had refused to cooperate with IS rule, doing such things as withdrawing from IS-led schools and universities, refusing to pay taxes, and establishing alternative schools. In sum, even under the brutal rule of IS, people found ways to defy what they saw as illegitimate power.[47]

When does repression against an unarmed movement backfire?

Sometimes, instead of shutting down civil resistance, government repression instead attracts outsiders' outrage—boosting the movement's support. In fact, repression often backfires.[48] Consider these familiar examples:

- In September 1978, as Iranians gathered in Tehran for a religious festival in Jaleh Square, the Iranian military opened fire and massacred almost ninety people, injuring hundreds more. The Jaleh Square massacre came to be known as Black Friday. As newspaper coverage of the massacre spread throughout Iran, outraged Iranians joined the revolution in the tens of thousands, including petroleum workers who went on strike in October 1978. Many in the Shah's security forces defected—and by February 1979, Shah Reza Pahlavi was forced to flee to Egypt.

- In 1991, Indonesian forces massacred about 250 East Timorese civilians at a funeral for independence activist Sebastião Gomes. In addition to killing Timorese civilians, Indonesian troops and police also assaulted several Western journalists who had attempted to stand between the troops and the civilians, including American reporter Amy Goodman. A British journalist smuggled video footage of the massacres out of the country; widespread news coverage of the massacre led to an international outcry against the Indonesian occupation of the island. That gave a boost to a decade-long international solidarity campaign, which ended when East Timor reclaimed its independence.

- In December 1987, four Gazan youth were killed by an Israeli military truck that collided with their car on their way to work. When news of the deaths spread and Gazans began to protest the next day, IDF forces fired into the crowd, killing seventeen-year-old Mohammed Hatem Abu Sisi. From there, thousands of Palestinians began rising up in protests and marches throughout the West Bank and Gaza Strip. As the IDF responded with lethal violence, the killings shocked the conscience of the Israeli public as well as supporters of Israel, such as the United States. Hundreds of Israeli soldiers refused to serve in the occupied territories, and an Israeli peace movement began to strengthen its political influence within Israel. Under President George H. W. Bush, the United States encouraged Israel to pursue a peace process with the Palestinian Authority. Despite opposition from far-right groups within Israel, Israeli prime minister Yitzhak Rabin signed an accord with PLO leader Yasir Arafat, which signaled unprecedented progress toward Palestinian self-determination.

Notice how in all three examples, press coverage was essential in bringing the story of the repression to a broader public.[49] This is instructive. Scholars Brian Martin and David Hess argue that backfire is more likely to occur if, before the repression, the movement is prepared with a plan to counter the regime's censorship and propaganda.[50] Once the incident occurs, they argue that movements should quickly get the word out to relevant audiences, such as through video footage, press releases, and consistent communication. In doing so, the movement shows the repression as unjust, unfair, excessive, or disproportional.

Of course, that's not enough to guarantee that the violence will backfire. But well-organized, nonviolent movements that plan for repression are better equipped to flip the incident to their long-term benefit than movements caught off guard.

How do civil resistance campaigns deal with fear among participants and potential participants who are vulnerable to repression?

To engage in mass nonviolent resistance requires courage—precisely because it is dangerous. Courage means taking action despite fear, even when knowing how much there is to fear. And most civil resistance campaigns that are challenging entrenched power try to help those involved master their fear. That means campaign organizers help those who intend to join the movement fully understand the dangers and risks. Being able to acknowledge fear where it exist can be helpful. Many campaigns attempt to prepare their participants in advance, through training, education, and physical and spiritual preparation. Gandhi's satyagraha was years in the making, in part because he and the Indian independence movement leadership believed that Indians had to prepare spiritually to undertake a long and dangerous struggle that would involve considerable sacrifice. The US civil rights movement held church-basement trainings in responding calmly and courageously to repression, with friends and fellow activists acting the part of violent hecklers and club-wielding police. Other movements develop rapid response capabilities, preparing ways to extract arrested participants from detention, mobilize effective first aid and medical care, and explain and demonstrate safety techniques for various forms of attack—tear gas, rubber bullets, fire hoses, and so on. Sometimes organizers brief potential participants about what might be coming and how to handle it.

In the US civil rights movement, activists would sometimes carry toothbrushes and chapstick to help deflate fear of being detained.[51] During Occupy Wall Street, activists would write phone numbers of legal contacts or other support networks on their hands or arms so that they could not be confiscated during arrest. During the 2011 nonviolent uprising in Syria, when activists were working to destabilize Bashar al-Assad's regime, activists spread knowledge about how to avoid certain forms of torture while in detention, such as by trimming their own fingernails to keep them short.

During demonstrations and protests themselves, movements have tried to overcome fear by maintaining a festive atmosphere through dance, music, and street performance. They have trained participants in conflict de-escalation and possible escape routes should violence ensue. Increasingly, movements have shared advance information with how to avoid major injuries—for example, by encouraging people to carry their own water bottles, scarves, first aid kits, and other household materials for flushing tear gas or pepper spray from eyes or treat minor wounds; bring umbrellas, construction cones, or buckets to protect against tear gas canisters; wear masks to avoid facial recognition software and exposure to COVID-19; and wear helmets to avoid head injuries, to name a few examples.

Because many of the worst kinds of abuse happen in incarceration, movements often prepare to get vulnerable people out of detention as soon as possible. While preparations vary from one situation to the next, this often involves organizing legal assistance in advance, or preparing groups that will launch direct actions at police stations or detention centers, such as rallies or sit-ins demanding the immediate release of prisoners. Many civil resistance movements facing a dangerous or entrenched regime encourage members to attend to their own well-being, seeking emotional, psychological, or spiritual assistance; some movements offer such support themselves or refer people to resources outside the movement.

But we know from many different studies of collective action that people do feel safety in numbers, and training and preparation has given people more confidence. When movements stay organized, stay together, keep abuse out in the open, and document it, they help participants counter fear.

Can civil resistance movements prevent or reduce atrocities?

Again, it depends on the circumstances. In contexts where autocratic regimes have seen groups of people as less than human, and were able to exercise total control over populations, organized civil resistance campaigns have had a hard time preventing atrocities. This is especially true in cases where there were few widely known examples of civil resistance for people to use to inform a strategy.

For instance, in the sixteenth century, when the Spanish empire was colonizing the Americas, Europeans brought with them goals of territorial conquest, ideologies of racism, policies of extermination or enslavement, and smallpox and other diseases. Disease alone claimed the lives of some 90% of Indigenous peoples—a catastrophic depopulation that undermined any effective efforts at outnumbering the conquistadors and colonists who followed them.[52] It is hard to imagine that Indigenous populations could have effectively used civil resistance to prevent or reduce these atrocities. Yet several people tried. Guaman Poma de Ayala, a Quechuan Peruvian nobleman, traveled throughout the Americas to document violence committed against Native Americans by European imperialists. He sent an 1,189-page hand-illustrated letter of atrocities to Spain's King Phillip III, in a personal appeal to end the barbarism. Phillip never saw the book; it was discovered in the early 1900s in a Danish archive.[53] Some Europeans objected too. Bartolomé de las Casas, a Spanish clergyman, objected to the enslavement of Indians in the Caribbean on moral grounds, writing futile personal appeals to Prince Phillip II of Spain to put an end to the barbaric slaughter and subjugation of Native Americans.

For similar reasons, civil resistance was also very difficult to organize among people who were enslaved on plantations in the Caribbean and the US South throughout the seventeenth to nineteenth centuries. Applying systems of total control, familial dislocation, and terror, plantation owners made it very difficult for enslaved people to communicate with one another or coordinate effective resistance. During the nineteenth century in the United States, the abolition movement did develop a number of resistance strategies that helped tens of thousands of enslaved people to escape, such as the storied Underground Railroad organized and traveled by Harriet Tubman and others. Certainly protests, petitions, rallies, and abolitionist newspapers, novels, and other materials galvanized the movement in the United States to end slavery—although the Civil War interrupted and diminished the momentum of many nonviolent strategies. And there were some effective examples wherein enslaved people withheld their labor to demand improved working conditions—a method that was particularly effective in Jamaica, where enslaved people outnumbered plantation owners and white inhabitants by a ten-to-one margin. Coordinated work stoppages led to numerous concessions, but a widespread revolt ultimately led British troops to massacre suspected ringleaders—a massacre that so shocked the British public that it ultimately led the British government to abolish slavery in 1832. So in this instance, rather than preventing or reducing an atrocity, mass mobilization—and the visible brutality used to maintain the system of slavery in the face of resistance—propelled the movement to victory.

In more recent times, with good preparation and contemporary examples of nonviolent action to draw upon for inspiration, some civil resistance movements have been able to prevent or reduce what might otherwise have been mass slaughters. As we saw earlier in this chapter, sophisticated resistance networks successfully moved thousands of Danish and Norwegian Jews to safety in Sweden during the Holocaust. Individual Germans and others under Nazi rule, from industrialists to German aristocrats, saved some Jews from certain death as well. Of course, the Nazi extermination was an exceptional case, so it is difficult to generalize from it. But if people can act courageously in such extremes, what's possible in other circumstances?

More generally, Evan Perkoski and I studied post–World War II revolutions and found that, when compared to armed resistance, nonviolent resistance significantly reduces chance of mass killings.[54] In fact, from 1955 to 2013, armed struggle is the most robust predictor of government-led mass killings, both in the short and longer terms. This is because mass atrocities require willing executioners: security forces or militias willing to kill large numbers of people over months or years. Nonviolent resistance campaigns make that harder, because they often create ambivalence among security forces who do not want to kill peaceful civilians and instead defect, disobey, or shirk orders. As a result, nonviolent resistance itself reduces (although does not eliminate) the chance of mass killings.

Can the international community prevent atrocities against nonviolent movements?

Scholars have not come to a consensus on this question. To some extent, it depends on how the international community tries to intervene—through military intervention, diplomatic pressure, economic sanctions, or direct assistance to movements fighting against the regime.

Some research finds that international interventions—such as humanitarian military interventions—have stopped genocide, ethnic cleansing, or mass atrocities in the past.[55] Other research finds that interventions do not necessarily end mass killings, although they can help to keep the peace after armed conflict ends. But very rarely has the international community used military intervention to prevent mass atrocities against *nonviolent* uprisings. The exception is East Timor, when after the 1999 independence referendum, the United Nations kept a peacekeeping mission there to try to protect civilians from Indonesian reprisals and oversee the transition to independence. Aside from that case, most international military interventions have only stepped in to prevent or stop mass atrocities during "hot" wars, like those in Bosnia in 1993–1995, Kosovo in 1999, and Libya in 2011 when Muammar Gaddafi promised to slaughter political opponents and armed insurgents alike.

Besides multilateral military interventions, powerful nations can help slow or prevent mass killings on their own, particularly when they are allies or patrons of the offending regime. For instance, in 1986, after twenty-one years in which US-backed president Ferdinand Marcos ruled as a dictator in the Philippines, Marcos was facing down the millions-strong People Power movement that was demanding his immediate resignation. He had also lost the support of powerful domestic pillars, such as much of his army and the Catholic Church. Although Marcos had declared martial law and was keen to hold onto power at any cost, US president Ronald Reagan's administration reached out to Marcos to make it clear that the United States would not defend him if his regime attacked the protesting crowds. With US support withdrawn, Marcos fled to Hawaii, making way for a transition to democracy.[56]

Still, allies don't withdraw support unless a nonviolent movement is already pressuring the regime. The United States didn't abandon

Marcos until it was clear his regime was doomed. The People Power movement paved the way for Marcos' fall, and losing a powerful ally's support was the nail in the coffin of his reign.

More often, civil resistance campaigns have to figure out how to win even with the powerful ally—or even patron—still backing the regime. That's what happened in Iran in 1979, where the movement toppled the brutal Shah, even though he still had the backing of the US government.

Sometimes international nongovernmental organizations (INGOs)—like Nonviolent Peaceforce or Peace Brigades International—can support or even protect civil resistance movements from a regime's violent repression.[57] Movement activists who know they are in danger often ask such organizations for unarmed bodyguards. Sometimes called "nonviolent accompaniment" or "unarmed civilian peacekeeping," this practice involves trained civilians using nonviolent methods to protect other civilians from violence; they do so by accompanying them in their normal lives. Simply having this guarantee of international attention at the activist's side can sometimes keep militias, security forces, or assassins from attacking. Unarmed civilian peacekeeping can also help communities move ahead in building peace, sometimes by mediating between the movement and security forces or other armed actors who have threatened them. Other groups that offer such services include Christian Peacemakers Teams, the American Friends Service Committee, and Global Witness. Research suggests governments are much less likely to target human rights defenders when impartial outsiders are accompanying them.[58]

Do sanctions against brutal regimes help protect civilians waging nonviolent struggle?

The jury is out on sanctions as well. Maria Stephan and I found that international sanctions—like banning doing business with the regime, embargoing certain goods or products, or rescinding invitations to important events like the G8 meetings—have had no systematic influence on whether nonviolent campaigns succeed.[59] However, that may be because governments tend to use sanctions only when they already have very little influence with the target regime. At that point, sanctions may hurt the regime economically, but that does not necessarily translate into influencing its behavior. Therefore, in the short term, when a government imposes sanctions against a regime, that's unlikely to prevent the regime from committing atrocities against dissenters and marginalized minorities—unless the sanctions actually prevent companies from selling the regime the weapons it needs to attack. That said, many foreign policy experts feel that sanctions are just as important symbolically as they are practically. Governments use sanctions to emphasize their dismay or discontent with another state, refusing to let abuses and atrocities go unpunished.

For instance, the United States imposed sanctions on Bashar al-Assad and the Syrian regime when it began cracking down on unarmed civilians during the 2011 uprising. These involved freezing assets of al-Assad and his inner circle, prohibiting business with Syrian firms, and prohibiting new investment in Syria by US citizens. But the United States had so little diplomatic leverage with the Syrian government in the first place that these efforts made little difference. The Syrian government was much more concerned about staying on the good side of its patrons Iran and Russia. But the US government reasoned that it was important to respond to al-Assad's brutality, even if the sanctions were largely symbolic.

In sum, civil resistance campaigns that threaten the powerful often face violent attacks. Being targeted with massive repression—widespread disappearances, imprisonment, torture, and killings—can hurt campaigns; purposely provoking repression is very risky and even dangerous. But limited amounts of repression—security forces opening fire on a protest, or even assassinations of key leaders—don't necessarily doom a campaign, especially if movement organizers have planned their responses. Nonviolent campaigns with an array of tactics prepared tend to be more effective than those which rely on demonstrations alone. They're certainly more effective than violent campaigns or campaigns that combine armed and unarmed methods—even under extremely brutal conditions. Movements can often make strategic choices that prepare them for repression and that can counter its worst political effects.

The next chapter explores the aftermath of civil resistance—how countries fare politically, socially, and economically after experiencing a nonviolent revolution. It also reviews some troubling recent trends in the success rates of nonviolent resistance over the past decade, and lays out some propositions for how movements can endure, adapt, and prevail even after the global pandemic recedes.

5

THE FUTURE
OF CIVIL RESISTANCE

Peace will not come out of a clash of arms but out of justice lived and done by unarmed nations in the face of odds.

—Mohandas Gandhi

Today, you may feel that we live in a particularly disruptive time in world history. [1] That is true in many ways, but it's the *kind* of disruption that is truly unique to our time. Contrary to conventional views, more people today turn to nonviolent civil resistance than to violence as a way to remedy dire circumstances—and this has become increasingly true over the past fifty years.

According to comprehensive data on revolutionary campaigns—nonviolent and violent—627 mass campaigns sought to overthrow dictatorships or achieve independence from 1900 to 2019. Although liberation movements are often depicted as gun-wielding rebels, fewer than half of these campaigns involved organized armed resistance. Rather, 303 were armed guerrilla or insurgent campaigns, while 324 relied overwhelmingly on nonviolent civil resistance.

Of course, the distribution has changed over time. Armed struggle used to be the primary way movements fought for change. But as Figure 5-1 shows, since the 1970s, violent insurgencies have declined in incidence, while nonviolent resistance campaigns have increased rapidly. By the year 2020, nonviolent resistance campaigns had become the most common approach to contentious action worldwide. Amazingly, there have been more nonviolent revolutions over the past two decades alone than during the entire twentieth century.

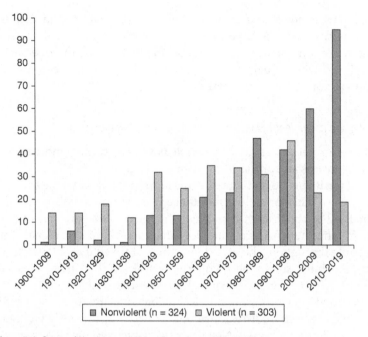

Figure 5-1 Onsets of Nonviolent and Violent Revolutions, 1900–2019

Trends from the last decade—from 2010 to 2019—are particularly staggering. Not only was it the decade with the most nonviolent resistance recorded since 1900, but also it included the launch of ninety-six nonviolent revolutions. Fifteen of these began in 2019 alone, and twenty-three others were continuing as 2019 came to a close. That's nearly double the number seen during the previous record-breaking decade: fifty-eight during the 2000–2009 period.

Yet many of the movements that have developed since 2010—from the Arab uprisings in Egypt, Yemen, and Syria to pro-democracy movements in India, Hong Kong, and the United States—have faced a surprising number of challenges. And with the sudden arrival of the coronavirus pandemic in winter 2020, many of these movements abruptly stopped mobilizing, either to regroup, innovate new techniques of dispersed resistance, or in some cases, fade away altogether.

In this chapter, we explore what these trends mean for the future of civil resistance. I address the skepticism that nonviolent resistance campaigns only initiate more chaos in a country, that nonviolent campaigns never lead to meaningful transformation, and that authoritarian regimes have become better at effectively suppressing nonviolent resistance. And we conclude that despite these setbacks, civil resistance remains a viable and transformative force for people power now and in the future.

Why are nonviolent revolutions becoming more common?

There are a few reasons why people have been turning more to civil resistance as an approach to creating change.

First, it may be that more people around the world have adopted the view that nonviolent resistance is a legitimate and successful method of creating change. After the Indian independence movement and the popularization of Mahatma Gandhi as a global icon, people throughout the world have picked up civil resistance as an approach to use in their own struggles—from the United States to South Africa, from Czechoslovakia to Tunisia, and beyond.

Second, new information technology has made it easier for people to access information about events that previously went unreported or suppressed. News is now available online—on phones and computers—and easily shared via newspapers, social media, private chatrooms, and more. That means people in Mongolia can theoretically read about, become inspired by, and learn from the activities of people in Malawi. Because civil resistance is an increasingly common and effective method of struggle, news outlets and scholars may be more interested in the phenomenon. Moreover, people have access to different channels of communication, bypassing formal gatekeepers to communicate among others they perceive as likeminded. Elites can no longer control information as easily as in previous eras, suggesting that news and information featuring ordinary people may be easier to find today.

Third, the market for violence is drying up. This is most strikingly obvious with regard to the decline in state support for armed groups, which largely subsided with the collapse of the Soviet Union. The shift in the global balance of power functionally ended the practice of the United States and Russia competing with one another by arming and financing proxies—a competitive dynamic that fueled dozens of rebel groups in Asia, Africa, and Latin America over the course of the Cold War.

Fourth, in the post–World War II era, a significant number of people have come to value and expect the protection of human rights, fairness, and the elimination of violence.[2] This normative shift may have generated more popular interest in demanding these rights, as well as greater interest in civil resistance as a way to advocate for them.[3] In our time, the dangers and risks of armed struggle have become much more visible than in the past. While the horrors of war are visible to all, realistic alternatives are likewise more widely accessible. Selina Gallo-Cruz argues that the post–Cold War period has featured a growth in international nongovernmental organizations (INGOs)—such as the International Center on Nonviolent Conflict, Nonviolence International, and the Center for Applied Nonviolent Action Studies (CANVAS)—whose presence has coincided with the rise in nonviolent resistance around the world.[4]

Perhaps more troublingly, however, people around the world may think that mass mobilization against oppression is more necessary now. Over the past decade, more and more democratic governments have faltered and reverted into authoritarianism.[5] In recent years, democratic backsliding in Poland, Hungary, Turkey, Brazil, Egypt, India, and the United States has provoked mass anti-authoritarian movements in these countries and many others. With the advent of the Trump presidency, many people in the United States have begun to embrace theory and knowledge of civil resistance—and to put these insights into action at home. The past four years have featured unprecedented levels of mobilization within the United States, including a pro-democracy movement prepared to defend democracy through mass nonviolent resistance in the event that Trump would refuse to leave office if he lost the 2020 election to Joe Biden.[6]

The faltering state of democracy around the world has shaken popular confidence that established institutions are willing or able to manage urgent policy challenges, like climate change, public health, and rising inequality. Throughout much of the world, youth populations are growing, creating demographic pressure for jobs, education, and opportunity. Record numbers of highly educated young people are unemployed in some places. Their popular expectations of economic justice and opportunity are poorly served by economies that remain weakened after the Great Recession of 2008—despite accelerating wealth for the 1%—even before the coronavirus pandemic wreaked havoc on the global economy.

Is civil resistance becoming more effective over time?

We don't know the answer to that yet, since no one has examined the effectiveness of civil resistance as a technique across all kinds of different social movements. But among revolutionary movements, at least, we do have some data to compare success rates over time.

As I mention in the introduction, over 50% of nonviolent revolutions succeeded from 1900 to 2019. Success rates for revolutionary nonviolent campaigns hovered around or improved upon that average from the 1960s until about 2010. But there have been important shifts over time. From a low point in the 1940s, civil resistance campaigns steadily increased in their effectiveness each decade until about 2010. Since then, success rates for all revolutions have declined, as Figure 5-2 shows.

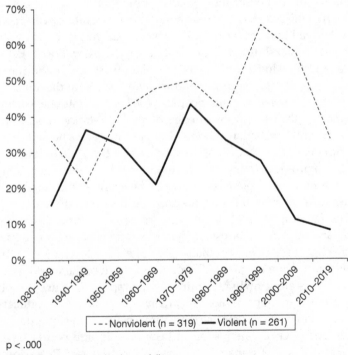

Figure 5-2 Success Rates of Revolutions by Decade, 1930–2019

In fact, less than 34% of nonviolent revolutions succeeded in the past decade, whereas less than 9% of violent ones did. Nonviolent resistance still outperformed violent resistance by a three-to-one margin. In other words, civil resistance improved its *relative* rate of success, compared with civil war. Armed confrontation has become less and less successful, a downward trend that has been underway since the 1970s. Even so, over the past decade, nonviolent revolutions also became less successful—a startling and new reversal compared with the upward trend of the previous sixty years.

The past ten years therefore present a troubling paradox: just as civil resistance became the most common approach for revolutionary campaigns to challenging regimes, it also grew less effective in the short term.

Why did civil resistance campaigns begin to decline in their effectiveness after 2010?

The most tempting explanation for the decline in effectiveness of nonviolent revolutions points to the changing nature of the global context in which these campaigns are operating.

First, ongoing movements may be facing more difficult regimes— ones that have prevailed over repeated domestic crises by shoring up local allies and supporters, imprisoning prominent opposition members, or provoking people's movements into using violence. Some have sought to delegitimize protesters by spreading rumors they are backed by foreign or imperial conspiracies; others have relied on powerful international supporters to provide the regime with diplomatic, and sometimes military, cover. Several regimes— like those in Iran, Venezuela, Turkey, Syria, Belarus, India, Hong Kong, China, and Russia—have proved especially resilient to challenges from below. There is no doubt that activists operating in such contexts are facing down difficult and intransigent foes.

But this explanation only makes sense in hindsight. It doesn't help us to predict which of these countries will see an uprising successfully topple an entrenched regime next. Many states—such as Sudan—have been considered resilient to domestic challengers up until the moment that a mass movement finally erupted and broke through. Then observers claim that the regimes were weak and overdue to crumble. Throughout history, many erstwhile stable autocratic regimes—like Chile under Pinochet, East Germany under Honecker, Egypt under Mubarak, and communist Poland—succumbed ultimately to nonviolent movements whose skillful mobilization often took years to develop.

Second, contemporary governments may be learning and adapting to nonviolent challenges from below. Several decades ago, the sudden onset of a mass nonviolent uprising was considered a surprise for many authoritarian regimes, which struggled to find ways to suppress uprisings without emboldening their citizens to support the movements. Back then, states may have underestimated the potential of people power to pose significant threats to their rule. Today, it is more widely understood that mass nonviolent campaigns are genuinely threatening to existing power holders. Moreover, civil resistance has become so ubiquitous that states have had more practice developing and standardizing more politically savvy approaches to repression—what many scholars call "smart repression."[7] One prominent suppression strategy is to infiltrate movements and divide them from the inside out. By doing this, the authorities can provoke nonviolent movements into using more militant tactics, including violence, before the movement has established a broad base of popular support and staying power. Radical escalation can discourage allies and moderates from joining, or complicate the movement's narrative discipline.

Third, growing domestic and global resistance to perceived US imperialism have led the United States to retreat from the global scene as a superpower intent on promoting its brand of liberal democracy abroad. This retreat arguably began in 2009, after disastrous wars in Afghanistan and Iraq had discredited the George W. Bush Administration's approach to fight against terrorism by exporting electoral systems through military invasion and nation-building. Although many have been rightly critical of the United States' pro-democracy agenda as a form of neo-imperialism, the post–World War II liberal international order established by the United States and other leading Western nations coincided with the expansion of human rights regimes that opened space for political dissent in many countries around the world. Political scientist Daniel Ritter has argued that in the post–Cold War world, authoritarian regimes were increasingly susceptible to nonviolent challenges from below because they needed to maintain the semblance of respect for human rights to appease their democratic allies and patrons.[8] In the context of the 2011 revolution in Egypt, for instance, the Egyptian military was attuned to the scrutiny of the United States, upon whose foreign assistance the country was highly dependent. In recent years, without the United States pushing liberal democracy as a model around the globe—and without powerful champions of human rights with real leverage or enforcement capacity over autocratic regimes—such regimes could get away with using greater brutality toward nonviolent dissidents.

That argument may have some merit. But it also has three key problems. First, the argument overestimates the degree to which the United States has ever been a genuine champion of democracy and human rights around the world. After all, the United States has a long history of helping to install right-wing autocrats after World War II—including Shah Reza Pahlavi in Iran, General Joseph-Désiré Mobutu in Congo, General Augusto Pinochet in Chile, and others who came to power through US-backed coups.

Second, the argument overstates the degree to which democratic patrons effectively pressure their autocratic allies to bend to their wishes regarding their own domestic political crises. For instance, during the Arab uprisings, hundreds of thousands of people began to protest against the Khalifa monarchy in Bahrain in 2011 to demand democracy. But US president Barack Obama issued a muted response, encouraging protesters to remain peaceful and encouraging the Bahraini government to observe human rights. Those words were not backed by meaningful pressure by the United States against Bahrain's government—an important military ally in the region. Instead, the United States was concerned about maintaining access to important strategic naval bases in Bahrain, which it maintained through an agreement with the monarchy. Demanding that the government reform or step down would have angered the monarchy and threatened this alliance.

Third, the argument neglects the fact that, historically, nonviolent resistance campaigns tend to be much more reliant on their ability to build and wield effective power through mass participation and the creation of defections among security forces and economic elites than on the behavior of fickle foreign governments.[9]

Ultimately, the global environment has not changed so much that civil resistance campaigns have faced altogether new types of opponents. Instead, I argue that the key reasons why nonviolent campaigns have declined in their effectiveness relates to features of the campaigns themselves.

First, recall that the single most important indicator of success is size. In recent years, civil resistance campaigns have become somewhat smaller on average than those we've seen in the past (Figure 5-3).

Remember the 3.5% rule we discussed in Chapter 2? Historically, campaigns in the 1980s, 1990s, and 2000s came closer to achieving it than campaigns today. In the 1980s, the average nonviolent campaign included about 2% of the population in the country where it was underway. In the 1990s, the average campaign size included a staggering 2.7% of a country's population. But since 2010, the average peak participation has declined to less than 1.3%.

During this period, we certainly have seen large-scale demonstrations around the world. In Venezuela, millions of people joined marches and demonstrations against President Nicolás Maduro in 2017 and 2019. In the United States, the 2017 Women's March on Washington drew well over four million people nationwide (about 1.8% of the US population). These events made for dramatic images and extensive news coverage. But surprisingly, at their peaks, they were actually smaller than successful movements of the late 1980s and 1990s, which tended to mobilize even larger proportions of the population. This is a crucial change, because mass uprisings are more

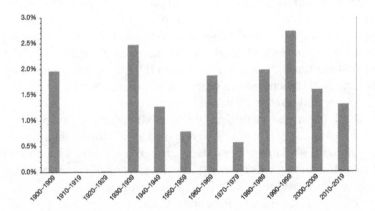

Figure 5-3 Average Peak Participation in Nonviolent Revolutions by Decade, 1900–2019 (n = 321)

likely to succeed when they include larger proportions representing more diverse corners of the nation's population.

Second, a related and counterintuitive development is that contemporary movements tend to overrely on mass demonstrations without developing and organizing other techniques of mass noncooperation—like general strikes and mass civil disobedience—that are more potent methods for imposing economic and political life.

Demonstrations and protests are what most people associate with civil resistance, leading many communities to mobilize such events before they have developed a broad coalition or a strategy for transformation. Protests may be easier to organize or improvise on short notice, as assembling large-scale participation in the digital age does not always require a large coalitional infrastructure with advanced planning and communication. But methods like mass demonstrations are not always the most effective in applying pressure to elites, particularly when they are not sustained over time. Other techniques of noncooperation, like general strikes and stay-at-homes, can be much more disruptive to economic life, and thus often eliciting more immediate concessions.[10] Quiet, behind-the-scenes planning and organizing gives movements the ability to mobilize powerfully over the long term, and to coordinate and sequence tactics to build participation, leverage, and power. With many contemporary movements' focus on leaderless resistance, such capacities can be out of reach, ultimately reducing their chances of success.

The reliance on public demonstrations and marches may well be related to a third important factor. Recent movements have increasingly relied on digital activism and organizing—via social media in particular—which has strengths and liabilities. On the one hand, digital activism makes today's movements very good at assembling mass numbers on short notice. It allows people to share their grievances broadly, reaching thousands or even millions of people, while creating toolkits and messaging documents to enhance narrative discipline, popularize movement slogans and images, and create viral content. Digital organizing enables people to communicate and organize through outlets not controlled by mainstream institutions or governments, which allows people within movements to tell their own stories. But movements that rely on digital platforms may also be less equipped to channel those numbers into effective organizations that can plan, negotiate, establish shared goals, build on past victories, and sustain their ability to disrupt a regime. In addition, the dark side of easier communication via the internet is easier surveillance, and easier countermobilization. Those in power can harness digital technologies to surveil, single out, and suppress dissidents, or simply interrupt communications and contest movement narratives. Autocrats have increasingly exploited digital technologies to spread misinformation, propaganda, and counter-messaging, while also calling on their own loyal supporters to rally on behalf of power holders.

Next, contemporary civil resistance movements may also be less effective than in the past because they increasingly embrace or tolerate fringes that become violent (Figure 5-4). As we saw in Chapter 3, fringe violence can undermine many of the supports that movements need to succeed—including diverse participation and the ability to create defections.

Even when the overwhelming majority of activists remain nonviolent, civil resistance movements that mix some violence—including street fighting with police or counterprotesters—tend to be less successful than such movements that remain disciplined in rejecting violence.[11] That's because governments tend to increase indiscriminate repression against movement participants and sympathizers without allowing the movement to paint their participants as

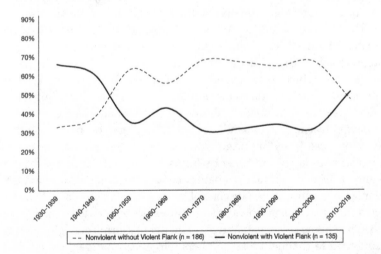

Figure 5-4 Nonviolent Revolutions with and without Violent Flanks by Decade, 1930–2019 (n = 321)

innocent victims of this brutality. Entrenched regimes can cast violent skirmishes as threats to public order. In fact, as we saw in Chapter 3, governments often infiltrate movements to provoke them into adopting violence at the margins in order to justify heavy-handed tactics to subdue movements. What powerholders really fear is resilient, nonviolent rebellion from below—a mass mobilization that exposes the lie that their power is invincible, and that lays bare the fragility of their own supporters' loyalties.

Finally, the decline in revolutionary effectiveness may also be driven in part by governments developing more sophisticated techniques of repression. Perhaps seeing the unreliability of brute-force coercion in disrupting civil resistance campaigns, in the past decade authoritarian leaders have also established a savvier playbook by which to suppress domestic challengers—including nongovernmental organizations (NGOs), opposition leaders, reformist campaigns, and revolutions alike.

What is smart repression, and how are movements adapting to it?

"Smart repression" involves a set of coercive tactics that governments use to suppress dissent without activating backfire.[12] As we discussed in Chapter 4, "backfire" is the process that unfolds when people see government repression as morally outrageous and throw their support behind the resistance movement.[13]

To avoid activating backfire, governments have developed techniques of repression that delegitimize movements in the eyes of the public, thereby diminishing the movement's capacity to mobilize a larger base of supporters, create defections, maintain discipline, or sustain the capacity to plan and strategize. Many regimes have adopted smart repression tactics, and they appear to be working from the same general playbook, too. Let's look at its key elements.

First, leaders under pressure try to blame foreigners and outsiders for their own political troubles. Vladimir Putin has routinely accused Western governments of deliberately stoking domestic dissent to threaten his grip on power at home, as well as in countries within countries within his sphere of influence. Similarly, when faced with the Gezi Park protests in summer 2013, Turkish premier Reycip Erdogan quickly blamed outsiders for the unrest, citing an international conspiracy against Turkish interests. And Nicolás Maduro's government in Venezuela responded to protests in 2019 by expelling American diplomats, citing evidence that the US government had conspired to support a coup against his government.

Related to this strategy is a second narrative approach, which involves attempts to label domestic opponents as terrorists, traitors, or coup plotters.[14] In Syria in 2011, Bashar al-Assad routinely referred to peaceful demonstrators as "terrorists" to drum up fears of violence and sectarian divisions before the start of the Syrian civil war in late 2011. In 2014, a Russian website called "traitor. net" encouraged users to "suggest a traitor" and listed names of people thought to oppose Putin's regime.[15] In Turkey, Erdogan referred to the 2013 Gezi Park demonstrators as left-wing "extremist" groups, prosecuting several protesters under Turkey's harsh anti-terrorism laws. In the United States, Donald Trump has referred to whistleblowers as members of a conspiratorial "deep state" and has called peaceful protesters demanding justice in the face of police brutality "radical leftists" and "paid professionals" in an attempt to discredit their grievances.

Next, at times, authoritarian regimes have attempted to co-opt opposition groups by making legislative reforms, such as allowing them to compete in elections or appointing opposition leaders to administrative posts.[16] Separating regime challengers into largely ineffective, disunited opposition parties allows the regime to divide and rule while keeping a watchful eye on skillful challengers, as has occurred in Belarus, Azerbaijan, and Uzbekistan, among other places.[17]

In some cases, authoritarian leaders attempt to protect themselves from domestic crises by paying off—or punishing—their inner circle. As we learned in Chapter 2, most people power movements succeed because key political elites, security forces, economic elites, business elites, civilian bureaucrats, and other power brokers conclude that continuing to support the authoritarian leader is no longer in their own personal interest and they effectively withdraw their cooperation from the regime. From the perspective of the leader, then, the key is to pay loyalists well and visibly punish defectors.[18] This may explain why oil-rich countries are less susceptible to such uprisings; their large reserves of sovereign wealth allow them to effectively buy off regime elites in times of crisis, thereby insulating themselves against the possibility that such elites will estimate greater returns from defection.[19] It also explains why President Trump vilified whistleblowers, Democrats, and some Republican senators, like Mitt Romney, for daring to contradict his narrative that his 2019 impeachment was based on a "hoax."

Another commonly used method is to countermobilize the authoritarian's own supporters, by paying loyalists to hold patriotic parades, setting up encampments, or turning out in progovernment marches.[20] This was a common method used by Bashar al-Assad during the early days of the Syrian uprising, where tens of thousands of pro-government demonstrators gathered in Damascus to bolster the regime's claim to legitimacy. Often such attempts come in the forms of pseudo–civil society organizations, like the youth movement Nashi (Ours) in Russia. During his time in power, Hugo Chávez established the so-called Bolivarian Circles, or progovernment grassroots neighborhood organizations, in the slums of Venezuela.[21] In contemporary authoritarian regimes, Weidmann and Rød find that one in seven protests are pro-regime.[22] Some autocrats may also establish government-owned NGOs (GONGOs), which reinforce and amplify the government's propaganda.

In many contexts, authoritarian leaders have been accused of planting plainclothes police as agents provocateurs, who would stoke violence against the authorities and create confusion in the context of otherwise peaceful demonstrations.[23] Such behavior essentially frames the movement for whatever chaos ensues, allowing the regime to justify more extensive crackdowns, lending credibility to propaganda claiming that protesters are really violent extremists, and diminishing participation. Such methods are particularly hard to verify, since it is often difficult to distinguish between provocateurs and ordinary protesters reacting to the heat of the moment. But as we saw in Chapter 3, the US government has used these techniques in the past to disrupt and undermine the reputations of leftist movements, particularly among Black-led organizations.

Because of the fear that regular security forces may not always be loyal in carrying out orders to suppress activists, many authoritarian regimes delegate their worst abuses by mobilizing vigilantes and armed gangs to repress and harass protesters. In Syria, once it became clear that al-Assad's military was not uniformly willing to repress unarmed activists, he began to dispatch armed gangs, or *shabiha*, to capture, beat up, or kill opposition leaders. In Ukraine,

dictator Viktor Yanukovich attempted a similar method in response to political opposition in 2014, relying on plainclothes police
officers and pro-government groups to intimidate, beat, and murder
activists, including one extreme case in which a Ukrainian activist
was kidnapped and crucified. And when Egyptian president Hosni
Mubarak became aware that some army units were not uniformly
loyal in 2011, his regime sent a group of armed vigilantes on camel-
back to break up encampments in Tahrir Square. Such methods give
regimes plausible deniability while also ensuring that those doing
the harassment are willing executioners. In some cases, regimes
rely on outside forces—as with Saudi troops in Bahrain or Iranian
Revolutionary Guard operatives in Syria—to avoid the possibility
that the troops begin to sympathize with the protesters.

Many authoritarian regimes have also mastered the arts of censorship, spin, and surveillance. China is the most obvious example,
where the government censors a significant amount of foreign news
and information while relying on state-controlled servers to control
and streamline communication throughout the country.[24] Moreover,
the Chinese government pays loyalist bloggers and social media
influencers to write posts and comments on critical websites, effectively
overwhelming these sites with massive amounts of pro-government
propaganda. In Sudan in 2011, Omar al-Bashir's government strategically used social media to manipulate activists and dissidents—in one
instance entrapping protesters who signed up to attend a fake protest that the regime manufactured.[25] Russia, Iran, and China intercept
communications through the internet or cell phones, quickly arresting
activists before planned protests even begin.

In the meantime, authoritarian regimes attempt to keep out foreign journalists and suppress domestic press freedom, effectively
discouraging independent reporting of domestic affairs. Removing
potential witnesses reduces morale among activists, who may view
actions in a closed information environment as futile. It may also embolden security forces to engage in higher levels of abuse, since they
sense that they can commit such acts with impunity. Other regimes
have barred international observers from monitoring elections, such
as Egypt, Russia, and Zimbabwe.[26]

In many instances, authoritarian governments use pseudo-
legitimate laws and practices to reinforce their grip on power. In
Russia, for example, authorities shut down human rights offices

accused of using pirated software or failing health inspections, and in China, the government has closed for "repairs" roads where protesters might march. Following the 2011 uprising in Egypt, the transitional government expelled nineteen Western NGOs from the country under the pretext of foreign subversion. And several years ago, Russia's highest court ruled as constitutional a law requiring that NGOs that receive funding from foreign entities must be designated as "foreign agents," restricting the degree of autonomy that they possess as well as the range of activities they are allowed to pursue. The Russian government has also driven out large Western foundations that have provided support to genuine pro-democracy and human rights organizations, further shrinking the space for civil society to operate. Moreover, Russia, Venezuela, Iran, and Kazakhstan have reformed electoral laws to favor incumbents or make it virtually impossible for opposition leaders to compete or even participate in the elections.[27]

Finally, authoritarian leaders have assembled a coalition of like-minded allies with whom to share information on how to suppress dissent. In 2005 and 2006, the Chinese government gave the governments of Belarus and Turkmenistan internet blocking and filtering technology to prevent outside information from flowing into those countries.[28] China and Russia vetoed a UN Security Council Resolution on Burma ahead of the defeated 2007 Saffron Revolution—the first time the two countries had both vetoed a resolution since 1989. China and Russia have consistently vetoed resolutions since then, striking down resolutions they saw as undermining sovereignty in Sudan, Kosovo, and Syria. Moreover, the Shanghai Cooperation Organization, Commonwealth of Independent States, and African Union have all developed their own "independent" electoral monitoring groups that have approved elections widely thought to be fraudulent, while attempting to restrict the autonomy of international election observer missions so that host governments have greater oversight over monitoring.[29] It is clear, therefore, that not only have these governments learned effective ways to dismantle opposition movements, but also they cooperate with one another in doing so. And even without necessarily cooperating with one another outright, leaders with authoritarian tendencies all over the world—such as Rodrigo Duterte in the Philippines, Narendra Modi in India, Jair Bolsonaro in Brazil, and Donald Trump in the United States—have emulated all of these practices in their dealings with their own domestic opponents.[30]

If you're worried about the playbook for smart repression falling into the wrong hands, it's too late. It already has. Now it's up to movements to innovate creative new strategies to recognize the playbook when they see it, adapt, and respond effectively.

Given these recent advances in the authoritarian playbook, does civil resistance have a future in challenging entrenched power in autocratic regimes?

The authoritarian playbook I just described is formidable and intimidating. But there are at least four reasons for cautious optimism.

First, none of the measures in the authoritarian playbook is fool-proof. For example, in the mid- to late 2000s, Egypt engaged in bi-lateral talks with Russia, China, and other countries throughout the Gulf region in an effort to protect the regime against do-mestic challengers. And Omar al-Bashir had withstood numerous challenges from below, exploiting ethnic divisions and the specter of genocide to maintain a decades-long grip on power. Yet people power movements removed Hosni Mubarak in Egypt and Omar al-Bashir in Sudan—two men whom many thought would die in office—as surely as they did in the Philippines, Iran, Poland, and Serbia in earlier decades.

Second, research shows that generalized repression is not neces-sarily a reliable deterrent to collective action. Instead, many revolu-tionary nonviolent campaigns throughout history emerged within authoritarian regimes where very little civil society existed.[31] Even in cases where states used violent repression against civil resist-ance campaigns, these campaigns still succeeded more than twice as often as armed insurgencies that faced repression. Indeed, as we saw in Chapters 2 and 4, it appears that widely publicized repressive episodes are sometimes precisely the sparks that trigger these mass uprisings, seemingly out of nowhere. Mobilization of the Egyptian population in 2011 over the killing of Khaled Said is a case in point. So was the rapid spread of protests in Sudan in December 2018 in response to the heavy-handed killings of Sudanese protesters who were objecting to high bread prices.

Third, inklings of people power are present in many places around the world, regardless of the use of smart repression tactics. In November 2020, Americans rejected Trump's bid for reelection with record voter turnout, and then protected the results through protests, demonstrations, rallies and street parties meant to deter violence and harassment against poll workers tallying votes. Organizers rallied behind local and state election officials in Michigan, Pennsylvania, Wisconsin, Arizona, and Georgia to resist Trump's heavy-handed bullying and certify Biden as the winner. Protests are still underway in Poland, India, Brazil, Thailand, Israel, and other countries where hope remains that popular pressure will likewise prevent far-right governments from further crackdowns on civil society and marginalized groups. The central government in China is openly concerned about the rise of localized protests throughout the country, including in Hong Kong. And even in Russia, visible opposition to Vladimir Putin has occurred from 2017 to 2020 at higher rates than it has during other periods of his tenure. Indeed, perhaps the greatest testimony to the effectiveness of civil resistance is the great lengths to which authoritarian leaders must go to prevent and subvert it.

Moreover, activists have begun to adapt to smart repression techniques in a number of ways. For instance, in Egypt in 2011, anti-Mubarak activists circulated a pamphlet called "How to Protest Intelligently," urging activists to circulate the document only through photocopy.[32] In the document, organizers stated the five demands of the Egyptian revolution. They named three "strategic goals of civil disobedience," which included taking over important government buildings, winning the army and police over to the side of the people, and protecting one another from state violence. Then organizers asked people to follow specific steps to carry out the plan, including assembling in neighborhoods as far away from security forces as possible, moving through alleyways and nearby neighborhoods while inviting friends and neighbors to join, assembling large crowds to overtake government buildings, and shouting peaceful and hopeful slogans along the way. The pamphlet encouraged people to bring cooking pot lids to use as shields from rubber bullets, spray paint to use to obscure riot police helmet visors and the windshields of armed cars and trucks, and flowers to signal the peaceful nature of the uprising. But it also asked people who received the pamphlet not to post it online and to only share it via paper to protect supporters from regime surveillance.

Activists have adapted other technologies to thwart high-tech surveillance as well. For example, in Hong Kong in 2019, when protesters began to rise up against the pro-Beijing government there, participants anticipated that they needed to protect their identities because of the ubiquity of security cameras and other surveillance devices, along with the advancement of facial recognition capabilities that could identify protesters based on their appearance. Movement participants responded by wearing face masks to evade facial recognition technology, and wielding umbrellas and traffic cones to protect people against pepper spray and tear gas. With the rise of the coronavirus pandemic, face masks later became commonplace all over the world as a way to contain the spread of the virus among large gatherings while thwarting facial recognition technology.

Regardless, with regimes threatening to drive nonviolent resistance movements underground, strategic planning and strategic thinking remain crucial elements to a successful nonviolent campaign.

What happens after nonviolent campaigns end?

Countries follow a number of paths after nonviolent campaigns end. One of the concerns expressed about nonviolent revolutions is that they bring to power governments that are even more repressive than those they replace. Or, if nonviolent campaigns fail, armed revolutionaries will take over the struggle, leading to civil war.

With historical precedent, these concerns are warranted. As we have seen in earlier chapters, the Egyptian Revolution of 2011 was overturned by a popular coup in 2013, which brought to power a brutal autocratic regime. In Libya and Syria in 2011, nascent nonviolent uprisings were overtaken by bloodshed, as security forces slaughtered unarmed civilians, armed groups organized to protect civilians from state violence, and international actors began to support armed groups trying to overthrow dictators Muammar Qaddafi and Bashar al-Assad, respectively.

But most research suggests that these cases are the exceptions rather than the rule. Numerous studies have shown that nonviolent resistance campaigns often lead to democratic transitions—and that such transitions tend to lead to full democratic consolidation.[33] The skills that animate nonviolent civic mobilizing tend to empower and accelerate the give-and-take, coalition-building dimensions of democratization.[34] Critically, even countries that experienced *failed* nonviolent campaigns were still about four times more likely to transition to democracy within five years of the conflict's end, compared with countries that experienced armed struggle.[35] This was true in Burma, for instance, whose "defeated" 2007 Saffron Revolution led to the empowering of reformers within the military regime, who began to initiate a transition to more political openness in the ensuing years. Of course, democracy is not the only aim for many movements, whose demands also include social, economic, and racial justice above and beyond democratic institutions like elections, checks and balances, and civil rights. But democracy is often a necessary—if insufficient—prerequisite for realizing these broader goals of social, economic, and racial justice.

In addition to transitions to democracy, other research has found that countries emerging from nonviolent resistance campaigns are less likely to experience a civil war in the following decade.[36] And countries that have had a nonviolent mass campaign emerge with higher life expectancies[37]—a proxy for better quality of life—with fewer conflict-related fatalities along the way.[38]

The bottom line is that societies emerge from nonviolent resistance campaigns far less devastated, and often with transformed power relationships within the society. Higher levels of political participation and civil society organizing are generally positive influences on longer-term levels of democracy, since civil resistance campaigns give people experience with using nonviolent methods to demand and create government accountability. Importantly, though, if mass uprisings turn into violent conflicts (like in Libya or Syria), then the prospects that democracy will spread are virtually nil.

Why does civil resistance sometimes result in authoritarian backsliding after the movement wins?

Post-revolutionary events typically fall short of the revolutionary expectations that develop during the periods of elation that follow the collapse of a brutal regime. In his book on the Arab uprisings, sociologist Asef Bayat wrote, "Nothing as much as revolution simultaneously demands hope, inspires hope, and betrays hope."[39]

There are many potential reasons why authoritarian backsliding might take place. The first explanation is rooted in the same reasons why nonviolent resistance campaigns succeed in the first place—namely, mass, broad-based participation. When widespread participation develops quickly, a movement can create a "negative coalition"—meaning a group of people who cooperate to overthrow a dictator—without necessarily overcoming their differences and creating political institutions that can help to build a new consensus.[40] Sometimes dictatorships collapse before civil society groups can organize themselves into viable contenders for power in the new system. For instance, they may not be able to agree to support a unity candidate who can clearly articulate a platform that appeals across constituencies, or compromises may not be supported by a wide range of the population.

In these contexts, the best-organized political groups are typically holdovers from the regime, religious institutions, or the military itself. In Egypt following the victory of the 2011 revolution, the Muslim Brotherhood won elections among widespread fragmentation among liberal and secular parties. The liberal opposition grew increasingly concerned with the Islamist leanings of the elected president, Mohammed Morsi. Seeing no attractive alternatives among other political parties, many of these groups threw their support behind the military's return to power through a popular coup in July 2013. Abdel Fattah al-Sisi became president and since cracked down on all members of the opposition—Muslim Brotherhood and liberals alike—to tighten his grip on power.

But even when an unarmed struggle is unable to achieve total victory, we shouldn't ignore major shifts, even though they fail to realize the campaign's vision of the future. To return to the Egypt example: what was at first a breathtaking victory quickly turned dire for human rights defenders and supporters of democracy. But we can remain hopeful for one major reason: Egyptians living inside and outside the country continue to speak about their views, their grievances, and their remaining conflicts. They steadfastly continue to unearth abuses committed by al-Sisi's regime and demand just resolutions. Moreover, there remain numerous resources for future organizing—including a cohort of experienced activists who have learned a great deal about how to remain resilient under severe repression. Even though the aspirations of many of Egypt's 2011 revolutionaries are still unfulfilled, Egyptians have broken the barrier of fear that kept them silent about their grievances for so many years. In a place where only twelve years ago, one could not speak openly against Mubarak's regime, even to friends, people have decided to not be afraid anymore. And that should continue to inspire hope.

How have movements prepared themselves for transitions after they successfully force a political breakthrough?

On their own, nonviolent mass uprisings rarely resolve systemic governance problems, like the lack of independent institutions, deep-seated corruption, and inadequate power-sharing mechanisms. As many have argued, democratic consolidation requires the development of new citizen habits, investment in independent institutions, separation of powers, reform of security forces, and a constitution that respects the rights of all citizens.[41]

The process of consolidation takes time—often at least a generation—but we should not minimize the importance of mass civic mobilization in removing the most immediate obstacles to progress, engaging large and diverse participants in critical conversation, enshrining norms of nonviolent conflict resolution, and putting systemic issues front and center in the national dialogue. Indeed, political scientist Jay Ulfelder argues that mass protests (again, only one method of civil resistance) are probably a necessary condition for countries to transition to political democracy. Contrary to the view that mass action destabilizes democratic transitions, mobilization typically accelerates and solidifies them.[42]

One way that revolutionary campaigns can maximize their chances at achieving more representative institutional alternatives is to develop parallel institutions as the struggle unfolds. We saw the power of these efforts in Chapters 1 and 4. The Polish Solidarity movement entailed two decades of public protests and underground activities that gradually eroded the communist authorities' grip on the population. The secret publication of samizdat newspapers, resistance theater, and mobilization in churches, followed by the famous 1980 Gdansk shipyard strike that brought workers en masse into the opposition camp, paved the way to negotiations between the Solidarity movement and the regime that first legalized trade unions, then led to first-ever elections that sent the autocratic government packing.

When Poland emerged from communist rule, it did so with a new set of electoral rules and practices that allowed for a much more durable and confident turn toward democracy. Although problems remained, Polish civil society remained fully mobilized to hold its new leaders accountable—including Solidarity leader Lech Walesa.

But even the best-prepared campaigns cannot guarantee that future generations will enjoy the fruits of their labor without sustained and robust civil society engagement in political life. Thirty years after Solidarity's victory, Poland has experienced a major democratic reversal. Soon after the right-wing Law and Justice (PiS) came to power in 2015, its leadership attempted to adopt extremely restrictive policies regarding women's reproductive health, debating a bill in 2016 that would have banned abortion in all cases except for those in which the life of the mother was directly threatened. Tens of thousands of women went on strike in the fall of 2016, leading the majority of parliamentarians to vote against the restrictive bill. This bought the movement time. But pro-democracy activists have had less luck since, as the PiS has tried to dismantle key checks and balances. The PiS has managed to implement a number of illiberal laws interfering with judicial independence, pressuring media, stacking public corporation boards with party members, and launching dehumanizing attacks on LGBTQ people. These acts put Poland at risk of becoming a democracy in name only—with the existence of elections the only remaining indicator of democratic governance. In 2020, PiS secured another electoral victory and finally pushed through its controversial law restricting women's access to abortions. As I write, hundreds of thousands of Poles have mobilized for months to resist the law, with uncertain prospects for reversing it.

Has civil resistance ever succeeded at achieving truly revolutionary goals?

As always, the question is: compared to what?

Compared to the status quo, nonviolent revolutions have indeed created major societal breakthroughs, pushing society forward to topple autocrats, adopt democratic reforms, and expand rights for women, minority groups, unions, and other groups that historically have been excluded from power. And as I discussed earlier, compared to armed revolution, nonviolent revolutions have a better track record at producing more immediate and less bloody results. Chapter 2 also details a number of ways in which civil resistance campaigns have helped to transform oppressive systems, like slavery and the legal subjugation of women, in most countries around the world.

And although total victory has not yet materialized in many ongoing struggles against oppressive systems, numerous smaller victories have certainly advanced these causes. One should not expect complete and immediate displacement of these systems, but should instead recognize when people have made real progress in areas that seemed hopeless—and in situations that had made them feel powerless.[43]

Progress is rarely linear. There are always setbacks, often produced by counter-movements that want to grab back power and return the country to the prerevolutionary context. This is what has happened in the United States, where white supremacist groups have reemerged to undermine progress on racial justice over the past decade. And it is what happened in Egypt in 2013, when millions of Egyptians backed a military coup to restore authoritarian rule in a nascent democracy governed by the Muslim Brotherhood.

How have civil resistance campaigns responded to the COVID pandemic?

There is no doubt that the coronavirus pandemic dealt an abrupt blow to dozens of movements ongoing around the world. During March and April of 2020, it became standard to see headlines in major newspapers announcing the end of protest as a result of social distancing mandates, as well as warnings about the expansion of emergency powers in countries like Hungary, Brazil, and the United States.[44]

But that does not mean that social movements disappeared. On the contrary, at the time of writing, their causes remain alive, and the global shutdown seemed to have provided movements with opportunities for important stock-taking, regrouping, and planning for the next phase of protracted struggles for democracy and rights. The future capacity to build people power from below depends partly on how movements invested their time and resources during the global shutdown.

There is reason for cautious optimism in this regard. First, the pandemic has provided opportunities for stark comparisons between the way that populists and autocrats respond to the crisis, compared with liberal or social democratic regimes. At least five of the top ten countries in terms of the number of reported coronavirus infections—the United States, Russia, Brazil, India, and the United Kingdom—were headed at the peak of the crisis by populist leaders whose pandemic decisions were disastrous. Instead of preventively preparing their publics for a protracted period of quarantine, making testing widely available, and prioritizing flattening the curve through timely and accurate information, leaders in all countries either denied or minimized the pandemic. Many devised conspiracy theories to deflect blame and stoked domestic political divisions, including calling for defiance against mayors and governors who advocated strict public health mandates. Although these missteps had both deadly consequences and sinister implications for the longer term, they also sharpened public awareness of the urgency of political change, as well as the ways that mismanaged crises affect people living in the country. For instance, in the United States, the pandemic's disproportionate death toll within Black and brown communities laid bare the ways that racism had created health vulnerabilities within these groups as well as unequal public health access across the country. Around the world, many movements quickly and effectively adjusted their frames to focus on the need for genuine democratic renewal, solutions to economic insecurity, resolution of social problems like racism or ethnocentrism, and accountability for political leadership. Because the pandemic has affected the lives of billions of people worldwide, such claims are likely to resonate with a broader base than before the crisis.

Second, the shutdowns caused by the pandemic have provided a much-needed pause for many activists and organizers who previously moved from one protest to the next, with little time for reflection, strategy development, or relationship-building. Because of the shutdown, movements could step away from planning large-scale events and focus on building resilient coalitions with a greater capacity for long-term transformation. Many movements around the world—including the pro-democracy movement in the United States—have spent time during lockdowns investing in planning, longer-term strategy sessions, building and deepening relationships among potential coalition partners, and developing plans and training modules for launching effective future challenges.

Finally, many of the measures that were activated by pro-democracy or progressive activists in response to the pandemic—the organization or amplification of mutual aid pods, strikes, stay-at-homes and sick-ins, online teach-ins, and various expressions of solidarity and collective support for frontline workers—were productive shifts in the movement landscape. For instance, in my home state of Massachusetts, organizers in numerous neighborhoods developed or channeled support to mutual aid groups to address community needs due to job loss or lack of access to food and medical supplies. Organizers crowdsourced food, personal protection equipment, transport, rent support, and emergency relief funds for people in need. Sewing circles popped up throughout the country and around the world to make handmade facemasks to respond to a global shortage of commercial medical masks. Although such measures rarely make for eye-catching photos the way mass demonstrations do, they represent a new phase of tactical innovation that replenishes the outdated activism playbook where movements overrelied on protest and underused methods of noncooperation or the development of alternative institutions.[45]

Of course, many protests have continued—either in outright defiance of social distancing measures or in spite of them. In the United States, mass protests erupted across the country in May and June 2020 to demand justice following the killings of Ahmaud Arbery, Breonna Taylor, and George Floyd—three unarmed Black people. Many protesters have worn facemasks, trying to observe suggested federal guidelines for containing the spread of the coronavirus. This seemed to have succeeded somewhat in preventing further spread of the virus in most cases; coronavirus hotspots that emerged in the wake of the protests were largely concentrated in places that had reopened prior to the protests, or where people had not observed mask-wearing or social distancing guidelines. Of course, police use of crowd control techniques such as kettling or corralling, the use of respiratory agents such as tear gas, and the lack of personal protective equipment (PPE) in jails and prisons have made large-scale street protests riskier. Yet the uprisings in defense of Black lives became the broadest mass mobilization in US history, with between 15 and 25 million Americans participating in racial justice protests nationwide.[46]

Also in May 2020, pro-democracy protesters in Hong Kong violated stay-at-home guidance to hit the streets again, objecting to the Chinese government's steps to undermine Hong Kong's autonomy in what many saw as a final battle to salvage the territory's semi-democratic system. Other activists began to experiment with socially distant protests (like a twelve-hundred-person socially distant protest against Israeli Prime Minister Netanyahu in Tel Aviv in April 2020); car caravans and rallies; work stoppages in the medical, grocery, tech, and meatpacking sectors; and other forms of noncooperation.

Thus, in spite of the recent setbacks for nonviolent campaigns around the world, 2020 did not necessarily represent the end of protest or the end of nonviolent resistance more generally. Instead, the pandemic may have served as a strategic reset and reorientation for many movements worldwide.

Since civil resistance has proven effective in so many instances, what keeps people from embracing it more fully?

It is hard to know why people remain attached to violent action instead of embracing the full range of civil resistance tactics, and the reasons probably vary by context. Although there has been growing awareness of the power of nonviolent resistance over time, most people still do not know that nonviolent resistance is a realistic alternative for creating social change. Daily life is full of countless stories, movies, myths, and other cultural desiderata glorifying violence. This constant glorification of violence also serves to erase the extraordinary human history of civil resistance, and the people power movements that have waged nonviolent struggle over the millennia.[47]

And even if people accepted the premise that civil resistance works, they may not have accurate information about how to effectively plan, execute, and participate in a nonviolent revolution. Part of the reason is that governments have gone to great pains to prevent people from learning about these techniques. In the antebellum South, slaveowners refused to allow enslaved people to learn to read and write, for fear that they would read the news and draw inspiration from slave revolts happening in the Caribbean and in other US states. More recently, governments facing nonviolent revolts in Egypt, Iran, Indian-occupied Kashmir, and Sudan have shut off the internet to prevent activists from communicating with and learning about nonviolent resistance from one another. The websites for the International Center on Nonviolent Conflict—and even an on-line bibliography of books and articles about people power called "civilresistance.info"[48]—are reportedly blocked in China.

Others may refuse to embrace nonviolent resistance because they are convinced that it does not work—or that it can't work without violence mixed in. Because of their own experience with, for example, a protest gone wrong, they may conclude that the entire technique of nonviolent resistance is futile. Or they may understand their adversaries to be so entrenched or so complex—or the movement's goals are so ambitious—that they believe that they cannot overcome the situation without resorting to dramatic and destructive measures.

Still others may be actively invested in the use of violence, for ideological, personal, or commercial reasons. For example, even though the texts of most religious denominations endorse peace and nonviolence, many interpretations of religious traditions also contain moral justifications for violence—from Christianity to Islam to Judaism and beyond.[49] These justifications include self-defense, defense of co-religionists, and heresy. And, of course, white supremacy, sexism, homophobia, transphobia, anti-Semitism, Islamophobia, and xenophobia are all ideological worldviews that explicitly or implicitly condone violence on the basis of the need to dominate or destroy people who are different from those in the ruling group. Some Marxist approaches to social change argue for the necessity of armed insurrection to separate the capitalist class from their wealth and property, redistribute it equitably, and create a new economic system of co-ownership among the masses. This interpretation has made many Marxists skeptical of the idea that nonviolent struggle could overcome entrenched economic inequality and bring about true economic justice. Others suggest that proponents of nonviolent resistance themselves are promoting a kind of dogma, preferring to leave all options on the table as a way to resist hierarchy and domination in all its forms.[50]

Recent studies have also uncovered strong personal motivations for supporting or engaging in violence. In particular, despite public attempts to defend violence on the basis of its efficacy, in private people tend to endorse or commit violence because of revenge. For example, in a quasi-experimental study of Americans' attitudes toward torture, researchers found that support for torture was largely motivated by an understanding that suspected terrorists should be punished for their crimes, regardless of whether they had useful information for interrogators.[51] Similarly, personal encounters of violence often generate feelings of personal humiliation, despair, and a desire for revenge.[52] Others turn to violence because of a personal desire for notoriety.[53]

Third, there are strong commercial reasons to maintain the myth that violence is the only way for people to wage conflict. The arms trade is one of the most lucrative industries in the world. There is no mystery here—it's just that powerful interests tend to reinforce messages that justify their existence. Arms manufacturers in the United States support the National Rifle Association and other groups that promote and lobby for gun safety over gun control, for example.

In sum, although we've seen a dramatic rise in the use of civil resistance among revolutionary movements over the past fifty years, many people around the world still have not yet been exposed to these ideas or remain more sympathetic to violent alternatives— and, as a result, default to apathy or violence as their only options.

How can civil resistance be made easy and accessible to the public?

First, we need to carefully debunk the myths about nonviolent resistance—that it is passive, weak, or ineffective, or requires the adversary to care about morality.

Second, people need to better understand why civil resistance has succeeded and failed in different contexts. Especially, activists employing methods of nonviolent action should not learn the wrong lessons from their contemporaries around the globe. For instance, one might be tempted to think, based on simplistic news coverage of the mass demonstrations and strikes in Tunisia during 2010–2011, that three weeks' worth of demonstrations unseated a dictator. Yet such understandings miss the fact that Tunisia had a unique recent history of robust organized labor activity, which lent its structured support to the uprising. Moreover, expansive general strikes threatened to devastate the Tunisian economy, such that economic and business elites began to withdraw their support from Ben Ali, as did security forces, who defied his order to strafe the demonstrators with bullets.

Instead, ordinary people should learn the right lessons from historical examples—that some basic patterns provide clear implications for contemporary movements. First, movements that involve careful planning, organization, training, and coalition-building prior to mass mobilization are more likely to draw a large and diverse following than movements that take to the streets before developing a political program and strategy. Second, movements that grow in size and diversity are more likely to succeed—particularly if they are able to maintain momentum. Third, movements that do not solely rely on protests, demonstrations, and digital activism, but also build power through parallel institutions, community organizing, and noncooperation techniques are more likely to build an effective and sustainable following. Fourth, movements that anticipate and develop a strategy for counteracting smart repression are more likely to succeed—this requires seeing and identifying repression tactics as they emerge and evolve. And finally, movements that develop tools and strategies for maintaining unity and discipline under pressure may fare better than movements that leave these developments to chance.

What are the five things that everyone should know about civil resistance?

By now, they should sound familiar:

1. Civil resistance is a realistic and more effective alternative to violent resistance in most settings. Civil resistance is not about being nice or civil, but refers to resistance grounded in community action. It is about fighting back and building new alternatives using methods that are more inclusive and effective than violence.
2. Civil resistance works not by melting the adversary's heart, but by creating defections from his support base.
3. Civil resistance involves much more than just protest—it includes methods of noncooperation, like strikes, and the creation of new alternatives, like mutual aid organizations, alternative economic systems, and alternative political groups, where people experience what life under a new system might look like.

4. Civil resistance has been far more effective over the past one hundred years than armed resistance, both in pushing forward major progressive change and democratization, and doing so without creating long-term humanitarian crises in the meantime.

5. Although nonviolent resistance does not always succeed, it works much more than its detractors want you to know.

Appendix

SELECTED RESOURCES

Websites
Albert Einstein Institution. https://www.aeinstein.org/
Beautiful Trouble: A Toolbox for Revolution. https://beautifultrouble.org/
BlackOUT Collective. https://blackoutcollective.org/
CivilResistance.info. https://civilresistance.info
Global Nonviolent Action Database. https://nvdatabase.swarthmore.edu/
The International Center on Nonviolent Conflict's Resource Library. https://www.
　　nonviolent-conflict.org
Training for Change. https://trainingforchange.org/
Waging Nonviolence. https://www.wagingnonviolence.org

Training Guides (*available for free PDF download online)
Abujbara, Juman, Andrew Boyd, Dave Mitchell, and Marcel Taminato, eds.
　　2017. *Beautiful Rising: Creative Resistance from the Global South*. Portland:
　　O/R Books.
*Bloch, Nadine, and Lisa Schirch. 2019. *Synergizing Nonviolent Action and
　　Peacebuilding (SNAP): An Action Guide*. Washington, DC: United States
　　Institute of Peace.
*Community of Democracies. 2011. *The Diplomat's Handbook for Democracy
　　Development and Support, 2nd edition.*
*Marović, Ivan. 2019. *The Path of Most Resistance: A Step-by-Step Guide to Planning
　　Nonviolent Campaigns*. Washington, DC: International Center on Nonviolent Conflict.
*Martin, Brian. *Backfire Manual: Tactics against Injustice*. Sparsnäs, Sweden: Irene
　　Publishing, 2012.
*Popović, Srdja, Slobodan Djinović, Andrej Miliojević, Hardy Merriman, and
　　Ivan Marović. 2007. *CANVAS Core Curriculum: A Guide to Effective Nonviolent
　　Struggle*. Belgrade: Centre for Applied Nonviolent Action and Strategies.
*Wanis-St. John, Anthony, and Noah Rosen. 2017. *Negotiating Civil Resistance*.
　　Peaceworks Special Report, Washington, DC: United States Institute of Peace.
*War Resisters' International. 2014. *Handbook for Nonviolent Campaigns, 2nd edition*.
　　Barcelona: WRI.

Documentary Films
A Force More Powerful (dir. Steve York, 2000)
Bringing Down a Dictator (dir. Steve York, 2005)

Budrus (dir. Julia Bacha, 2009)
Crip Camp: A Disability Revolution (dir. Nicole Newnham & James LeBrecht, 2020)
The Edge of Democracy (dir. Petra Costa, 2019)
Egypt: Revolution Interrupted? (dir. Steve York, 2015)
How to Survive a Plague (dir. David France, 2012)
Naila and the Uprising (dir. Julia Bacha, 2018)
Orange Revolution (dir. Steve York, 2005)
Pray the Devil Back to Hell (dir. Gini Reticker, 2008)
The Third Harmony (dir. Michael Nagler, 2020)

Essential Books

The following is a non-exhaustive list of accessible works I recommend for those interested in further overviews and applications of civil resistance.

Berry, Mary Frances. 2018. *History Teaches Us to Resist: How Progressive Movements Have Succeeded in Challenging Times*. Boston: Beacon Press.

Carter, April. 2011. *People Power and Political Change: Key Issues and Concepts*. New York: Routledge.

Engler, Mark, and Paul Engler. 2017. *This Is an Uprising: How Nonviolent Revolt Is Shaping the Twenty-First Century*. New York: Nation Books.

Fithian, Lisa. 2019. *Shut It Down: Stories from a Fierce, Loving Resistance*. White River Junction, VT: Chelsea Green.

Garza, Alicia. 2020. *How We Come Together When We Fall Apart*. New York: One World.

Gbowee, Leymah. 2011. *Mighty Be Our Powers: How Sisterhood, Prayer, and Sex Changed a Nation at War*. New York: Public Affairs.

Haga, Kazu. 2019. *Healing Resistance: A Radically Different Response to Harm*. Berkeley, CA: Parallax Press.

King, Martin Luther, Jr. 1963. Letter from a Birmingham Jail. http://www.africa. upenn.edu/Articles_Gen/Letter_Birmingham.html.

Kurlansky, Mark. 2006. *Nonviolence: The History of a Dangerous Idea*. New York: Modern Library.

Lewis, John, Andrew Aydin, and Nate Powell. *March: Vols. 1-3*. Marietta, GA: Top Shelf Productions.

Long, Michael G. 2019. *We the Resistance: Documenting a History of Nonviolent Protest in the United States*. San Francisco: City Lights.

Maathai, Wangari. 2007. *Unbowed: A Memoir*. New York: Anchor.

Nepstad, Sharon Erickson. 2015. *Nonviolent Struggle: Theories, Strategies, and Dynamics*. New York: Oxford University Press.

Schell, Jonathan. 2003. *The Unconquerable World: Power, Nonviolence, and the Will of the People*. New York: Metropolitan Books.

Shock, Kurt. 2015. *Civil Resistance Today*. London: Polity Press.

Sharp, Gene. 2005. *Waging Nonviolent Struggle: Twentieth-Century Practice and Twenty-First-Century Potential*. Boston: Porter Sargent.

Solnit, Rebecca. 2004. *Hope in the Dark: Untold Histories, Wild Possibilities*. Chicago: Haymarket.

LIST OF NONVIOLENT AND VIOLENT REVOLUTIONARY CAMPAIGNS, 1900–2019

Campaign	Location	Year Began	Year Ended	Outcome	Primary Method
Filipino nationalists	Philippines	1899	1902	failure	violent
Dervish resistance	Somalia	1899	1904	failure	violent
Boer separatists	South Africa	1899	1902	failure	violent
La Revolucion Libertador	Venezuela	1901	1903	failure	violent
Acre rebellion	Bolivia	1902	1903	failure	violent
VMRO Rebels (Macedonians) in Ilinden uprising	Ottoman Empire	1903	1903	failure	violent
South West African Revolt (Herrero Revolt)	Namibia/South West Africa	1904	1906	failure	violent
Blancos rebellion	Uruguay	1904	1904	failure	violent
Constitutional Revolution	Iran	1905	1906	success	nonviolent
Peasant/worker rebellion	Russia	1905	1906	partial success	violent
Maji Maji Revolt	Tanzania/German East Africa	1905	1906	failure	violent

(continued)

Campaign	Location	Year Began	Year Ended	Outcome	Primary Method
Zulu rebellion (Natal rebellion)	Natal	1906	1906	failure	violent
Fez Caids rebellion	Morocco	1907	1908	failure	violent
Peasant rebellion	Romania	1907	1907	failure	violent
Constitutionalists	Iran	1908	1909	success	violent
Liberals and Radicals rebellion	Mexico	1910	1920	success	violent
Republicans	China	1911	1913	failure	violent
Wars of Independence	Morocco	1911	1917	failure	violent
Anti-Dutch colonial struggle	West Papua	1911	1943	failure	nonviolent
First War of Independence	Tibet	1912	1913	partial success	violent
Burmese independence movement	Burma	1916	1938	failure	nonviolent
Yunnan rebellion	China	1916	1918	partial success	violent
Dominican insurgency	Dominican Republic	1916	1924	failure	violent
Urkun uprising	Russia	1916	1917	success	violent
Arab revolt	Turkey	1916	1918	partial success	violent
Anti-Bolsheviks	Russia	1917	1921	failure	violent
Russian Revolution	Russia	1917	1917	success	violent
Egyptian revolution for independence	Egypt	1918	1922	success	nonviolent
Communist rebels	Finland	1918	1918	failure	violent
Caco Revolt	Haiti	1918	1920	failure	violent
Third Anglo-Afghan War	Afghanistan	1919	1919	success	violent
May the Fourth Movement	China	1919	1919	partial success	nonviolent
Anti-Estrada Cabrera	Guatemala	1919	1920	success	nonviolent

Anti-communist movement (Whites)	Hungary	1919	1920	success	violent
Indian independence movement	India	1919	1947	partial success	nonviolent
Iraqi rebels	Iraq	1920	1920	partial success	violent
Italo-Libyan War (Sanusi)	Libya	1920	1931	failure	violent
Anti-British Mandate	Palestine	1920	1936	failure	nonviolent
Franco-Syrian War	Syria	1920	1920	failure	violent
Kockiri rebellion Kurdistan (KTC)	Turkey	1920	1922	failure	violent
Peasants in Ta (Tambov rebellion)	USSR	1920	1921	failure	violent
Moplah rebellion	India	1921	1922	failure	violent
Rifian rebellion	Morocco	1921	1926	failure	violent
Agrarian League movement	Bulgaria	1923	1923	failure	violent
Ruhrkampf resistance	Germany	1923	1924	success	nonviolent
Huerta-led rebels	Mexico	1923	1924	failure	violent
Anti-Reformist movement	Afghanistan	1924	1929	failure	violent
Conservative movement	Honduras	1924	1924	failure	violent
Sheikh Said insurgency	Turkey	1924	1927	failure	violent
Druze revolt	Lebanon	1925	1927	failure	violent
Nicaraguan guerrillas	Nicaragua	1925	1933	success	violent
Cristeros rebellion	Mexico	1926	1929	failure	violent
Chinese communist movement	China	1927	1949	success	violent
Escoban-led rebellion	Mexico	1929	1929	failure	violent
Ikhwan rebellion	Saudi Arabia	1929	1930	failure	violent
Saya San's rebellion	Burma	1930	1932	failure	violent

(continued)

Campaign	Location	Year Began	Year Ended	Outcome	Primary Method
Anti-Ibanez campaign	Chile	1931	1931	success	nonviolent
Manchurian guerrillas	China	1931	1941	success	violent
Paolistas	Brazil	1932	1932	failure	violent
Leftist rebellion	El Salvador	1932	1932	failure	violent
Aprista rebels	Peru	1932	1932	failure	violent
Socialists	Austria	1934	1934	failure	violent
Asturian miners	Spain	1934	1934	failure	violent
Central Asian rebels	USSR	1934	1934	failure	violent
Palestinian Arab revolt	Palestine	1936	1939	partial success	violent
Fascists	Spain	1936	1939	success	violent
Chinese rebels	China	1937	1945	failure	violent
Kenyan independence movement	Kenya	1938	1938	failure	violent
Danish resistance	Denmark	1940	1943	partial success	nonviolent
French resistance	France	1940	1944	partial success	violent
Norwegian resistance	Norway	1940	1945	partial success	nonviolent
Philippines Malayan insurgency	Philippines	1941	1945	failure	violent
Belarus resistance	USSR	1941	1945	failure	violent
Balkan resistance	Yugoslavia	1941	1945	partial success	violent
Greek resistance	Greece	1943	1944	failure	violent
Italian resistance	Italy	1943	1945	failure	violent
Anti Aguirre y Salinas	El Salvador	1944	1945	failure	nonviolent
Strike of Fallen Arms	El Salvador	1944	1944	success	nonviolent

October Revolutionaries	Guatemala	1944	1944	success	nonviolent
Honduran pro-democracy movement	Honduras	1944	1944	failure	nonviolent
Independent Liberal Party	Nicaragua	1944	1944	failure	nonviolent
Polish resistance	Poland	1944	1944	failure	violent
Shifta insurgency	Eritrea	1945	1952	failure	violent
Metsavennad (Forest Brothers, Estonian anti-occupation campaign)	Estonia	1945	1953	failure	violent
Indonesian revolt	Indonesia	1945	1949	success	violent
KDPI (First Separatist Movement)	Iran	1945	1946	failure	nonviolent
Meza Brali (Forest Brothers, Latvian anti-occupation campaign)	Latvia	1945	1950	failure	violent
Mikso Broliai (Forest Brothers, Lithuanian anti-occupation campaign)	Lithuania	1945	1956	failure	violent
Independence movement	Nigeria	1945	1950	partial success	nonviolent
Jewish resistance	Palestinian Territories	1945	1948	success	violent
Indochina revolt	Vietnam	1945	1954	success	violent
Popular revolutionary movement	Bolivia	1946	1946	success	violent
Cambodian independence movement	Cambodia	1946	1954	success	violent
Greek communist movement	Greece	1946	1949	failure	nonviolent
Greek civil war	Greece	1946	1949	failure	violent
Pro-democracy movement	Haiti	1946	1946	success	nonviolent
Punnapra-Vayalar uprising	India	1946	1946	failure	violent
Trieste strikes	Italy	1946	1946	partial success	nonviolent

(continued)

Campaign	Location	Year Began	Year Ended	Outcome	Primary Method
Laotian independence	Laos	1946	1949	success	violent
Hukbalahap rebellion	Philippines	1946	1954	failure	violent
Ukrainian rebellion	USSR	1946	1951	failure	violent
Taiwanese revolt	China	1947	1947	failure	violent
Anti-Picado	Costa Rica	1947	1947	partial success	nonviolent
Franco-Madagascan	Madagascar	1947	1948	failure	violent
leftist rebellion	Paraguay	1947	1947	failure	violent
Karens	Burma	1948	1994	failure	violent
Kachin rebels	Burma	1948	1994	failure	violent
La Violencia / Liberals of 1949	Colombia	1948	1958	failure	violent
National Union Party	Costa Rica	1948	1948	success	violent
Telangana People's Front	India	1948	1952	failure	violent
Hyderabad activists	India	1948	1948	failure	violent
Malayan emergency	Malaysia	1948	1960	partial success	violent
Yahya Family revolt	Yemen Arab Republic	1948	1948	success	violent
Sino-Tibetan War	China	1950	1951	failure	violent
Moluccans	Indonesia	1950	1950	failure	violent
First Pathet Lao	Laos	1950	1957	failure	violent
White Revolution	Lebanon	1951	1952	success	nonviolent
leftists	Bolivia	1952	1952	success	violent
Mau Mau rebellion	Kenya	1952	1956	failure	violent
First Defiance Campaign	South Africa	1952	1961	failure	nonviolent

Tunisian independence movement	Tunisia	1952	1954	success	violent
East German uprising	East Germany	1953	1953	failure	nonviolent
Darul Islam	Indonesia	1953	1953	failure	violent
Moroccan Independence War	Morocco	1953	1956	success	violent
Algerian Revolt / National Liberation Front	Algeria	1954	1962	success	violent
Ethniki Organosis Kyprios Agoniston	Cyprus	1954	1959	success	violent
Conservative movement	Guatemala	1954	1954	success	violent
Revolucion Libertadora	Argentina	1955	1955	success	violent
Anti-colonialist movement	Cameroon	1955	1960	success	violent
Convention People's Party movement	Ghana	1955	1957	success	nonviolent
Yemeni insurgency	Yemen	1955	1957	failure	violent
Hundred Flowers Movement	China	1956	1957	failure	nonviolent
Tibetan resistance	China	1956	1959	failure	violent
Anti-Magloire movement	Haiti	1956	1956	success	nonviolent
Hungarian anticommunist	Hungary	1956	1956	failure	nonviolent
Hungarian anti-Soviet	Hungary	1956	1956	failure	violent
Naga rebellion	India	1956	2019	failure	violent
Leftists	Indonesia	1956	1960	failure	violent
Naga insurgency	Myanmar	1956	2019	failure	violent
Poznan protests	Poland	1956	1956	partial success	nonviolent
Rwandan independence	Rwanda	1956	1962	success	violent
Georgian anti-Khrushchev protests	USSR	1956	1956	failure	nonviolent

(continued)

Campaign	Location	Year Began	Year Ended	Outcome	Primary Method
Anti-Rojas	Colombia	1957	1957	success	nonviolent
Ifni war	Morocco	1957	1958	failure	violent
Cuban Revolution	Cuba	1958	1959	success	violent
leftists (anti-Shamun)	Lebanon	1958	1958	failure	violent
Nyasaland African Congress	Malawi	1958	1959	partial success	nonviolent
Anti-Jimenez campaign	Venezuela	1958	1958	success	nonviolent
Congolese Independence Movement	Democratic Republic of Congo	1959	1960	partial success	nonviolent
Shammar Tribe and pro-Western officers	Iraq	1959	1959	failure	violent
Second Pathet Lao	Laos	1959	1975	success	violent
Cameroon anti-Ahidjo government movement	Cameroon	1960	1971	failure	violent
Anti-Lemus campaign	El Salvador	1960	1960	success	nonviolent
French Nationalists/SAO	France	1960	1962	failure	violent
Anti-Kishi Campaign	Japan	1960	1960	partial success	nonviolent
Student Revolution	South Korea	1960	1960	success	nonviolent
Students Lead Protest for Regime Change	Turkey	1960	1960	success	nonviolent
North Vietnam (National Liberation Front)	Vietnam	1960	1975	success	violent
Katanga-led leftists	Zaire/DRC	1960	1965	failure	violent

Popular Movement for the Liberation of Angola	Angola	1961	1974	success	violent
Anti-Balaguer strikes	Dominican Republic	1961	1962	success	nonviolent
Kurdish rebellion	Iraq	1961	1970	partial success	violent
North Vietnam (National Liberation Front) anti-occupation	Vietnam	1961	1975	success	violent
Zambian independence movement	Zambia	1961	1963	success	nonviolent
Former rebel leaders	Algeria	1962	1963	failure	violent
Brunei Revolt	Brunei	1962	1962	failure	violent
Anti-Ydigoras	Guatemala	1962	1962	failure	nonviolent
Front for the Liberation of Mozambique	Mozambique	1962	1975	success	violent
Popular Front for the Liberation of Oman and the Arab Gulf (PFLOAG)	Oman	1962	1976	partial success	violent
Second Balochistan separatist movement	Pakistan	1962	1969	failure	violent
Armed Forces for National Liberation (FALN)	Venezuela	1962	1965	failure	violent
Royalists	Yemen Arab Republic	1962	1969	partial success	violent
Benin antigovernment protests	Benin	1963	1963	success	nonviolent
PAIGC	Guinea-Bissau	1963	1974	success	violent
Watusi	Rwanda	1963	1964	failure	violent
1963 Buddhist Protests	South Vietnam	1963	1963	success	nonviolent

(continued)

Campaign	Location	Year Began	Year Ended	Outcome	Primary Method
Anya Nya	Sudan	1963	1972	partial success	violent
Tupamaros	Uruguay	1963	1972	failure	violent
FLOSY, NLF in Aden	Yemen	1963	1967	success	violent
Bolivian antigovernment protests	Bolivia	1964	1964	failure	nonviolent
Revolutionary Armed Forces of Colombia, National Liberation Army, M-19	Colombia	1964	2016	failure	violent
CNL	Democratic Republic of Congo	1964	1965	failure	violent
NFDLM secessionists	Kenya	1964	1968	failure	violent
1964 anti-Khanh protests	South Vietnam	1964	1964	success	nonviolent
Anti-Huong	South Vietnam	1964	1965	success	nonviolent
October Revolution	Sudan	1964	1964	success	nonviolent
Leftists	Dominican Republic	1965	1965	failure	violent
1965 anti-junta campaign	Ecuador	1965	1966	success	nonviolent
Greece premier protest	Greece	1965	1966	failure	nonviolent
Communist rebels	Thailand	1965	1982	failure	violent
West Papua rebels	West Papua	1965	1978	failure	violent
Frolinat	Chad	1966	1990	success	violent
Marxist rebels (URNG)	Guatemala	1966	1996	partial success	violent
Mizo revolt	India	1966	1986	partial success	violent
1966–1967 anti-Ky protests	South Vietnam	1966	1967	failure	nonviolent

Anti-military government	South Vietnam	1966	1966	failure	nonviolent
Buganda Tribe	Uganda	1966	1966	failure	violent
Cultural Revolution Red Guards	China	1967	1968	failure	violent
Naxalite insurgency	India	1967	1971	ongoing	violent
Biafrans	Nigeria	1967	1970	failure	violent
Czech uprising	Czechoslovakia	1968	1968	failure	nonviolent
IRA / Irish nationalists	Northern Ireland	1968	1998	partial success	violent
Anti-Khan campaign	Pakistan	1968	1969	partial success	nonviolent
Moro National Liberation Front	Philippines	1968	1987	failure	violent
Poland Anti-Communist I	Poland	1968	1968	failure	nonviolent
ETA	Spain	1968	2011	failure	violent
student protests	Yugoslavia	1968	1968	partial success	nonviolent
Khmer Rouge	Cambodia	1970	1975	success	violent
Naxalite rebellion	India	1970	1971	failure	violent
Palestinian activists	Jordan	1970	1970	failure	violent
Poland anticommunist II	Poland	1970	1970	partial success	nonviolent
Antigovernment protests	Turkey	1970	1971	success	nonviolent
Croatian nationalists	Yugoslavia	1970	1971	failure	nonviolent
Bengalis	Pakistan	1971	1971	success	violent
JVP	Sri Lanka	1971	1971	failure	violent
Hutu rebellion	Burundi	1972	1973	failure	violent
Anti-Tsiranana	Madagascar	1972	1972	success	nonviolent
New People's Army	Philippines	1972	1992	failure	violent

(continued)

Campaign	Location	Year Began	Year Ended	Outcome	Primary Method
Zimbabwe African People's Union	Zimbabwe	1972	1979	partial success	violent
ERP/Monteneros	Argentina	1973	1977	failure	violent
Pinochet-led rebels	Chile	1973	1973	success	violent
Oromiya self-determination	Ethiopia	1973	2018	partial success	violent
Greek anti-military	Greece	1973	1974	success	nonviolent
Third Balochistan separatist movement	Pakistan	1973	1977	failure	violent
Palestinian Liberation	Palestinian Territories	1973	2019	ongoing	violent
Carnation Revolution	Portugal	1973	1974	success	nonviolent
Student protests	Thailand	1973	1973	success	nonviolent
Eritrean-led rebels	Ethiopia	1974	1991	success	violent
1974–1975 anti-Thieu protests	South Vietnam	1974	1975	failure	nonviolent
UNITA	Angola	1975	2002	partial success	violent
Freitilin	East Timor	1975	1979	failure	violent
Anti-Indira Campaign	India	1975	1975	failure	nonviolent
GAM	Indonesia	1975	2005	partial success	violent
Leftists	Lebanon	1975	1990	failure	violent
Western Sahara Freedom Movement (POLISARIO)	Western Sahara	1975	1989	partial success	violent
Shanti Bahini	Bangladesh	1976	1997	failure	violent
Democracy Movement	China	1976	1979	failure	nonviolent
Somali rebels (Ogaden)	Ethiopia	1976	1980	failure	violent

(continued)

SWAPO	Namibia	1976	1988	success	violent
Warsaw Workers' uprising	Poland	1976	1976	partial success	nonviolent
Pro-democracy movement	Argentina	1977	1983	success	nonviolent
Pro-independence campaign	Aruba	1977	1977	failure	nonviolent
Bolivian anti-juntas	Bolivia	1977	1982	success	nonviolent
El Salvador anti-junta	El Salvador	1977	1980	failure	nonviolent
Anti-Indira Campaign (phase 3)	India	1977	1977	success	nonviolent
Iranian Revolution	Iran	1977	1979	success	nonviolent
Anti-Bhutto	Pakistan	1977	1977	success	nonviolent
FLNC	Zaire/DRC	1977	1978	failure	violent
Afghans	Afghanistan	1978	1979	success	violent
Kampuchean United Front for National Salvation	Cambodia	1978	1979	success	violent
Hundred-Day War	Lebanon	1978	1978	success	violent
Anti-Somoza strike	Nicaragua	1978	1978	failure	nonviolent
FSLN	Nicaragua	1978	1979	success	violent
Kurdish rebellion	Turkey	1978	1999	failure	violent
Second Khmer Rouge	Cambodia	1979	1997	failure	violent
Farabundo Marti National Liberation Front (FMLN)	El Salvador	1979	1991	partial success	violent
Manipur	India	1979	2019	ongoing	violent
KDPI	Iran	1979	1996	failure	violent
Renamo	Mozambique	1979	1992	failure	violent

Campaign	Location	Year Began	Year Ended	Outcome	Primary Method
South Korean anti-junta	South Korea	1979	1980	failure	nonviolent
Taiwan pro-democracy	Taiwan	1979	1985	success	nonviolent
West Papua self-determination struggle	West Papua	1979	2019	ongoing	nonviolent
NDF	Yemen	1979	1982	failure	violent
Anti-Soviet movement (3 Hut uprising)	Afghanistan	1980	1980	failure	nonviolent
Afghan resistance	Afghanistan	1980	1989	success	violent
Muslim fundamentalists	Nigeria	1980	1984	failure	violent
Senderista Insurgency (Sendero Luminoso) The Shining Path	Peru	1980	2012	failure	violent
Solidarity	Poland	1980	1989	success	nonviolent
Muslim Brotherhood	Syria	1980	1982	failure	violent
National Resistance Army	Uganda	1980	1986	success	violent
Mujahideen	Iran	1981	2001	failure	violent
Druze resistance	Israel	1981	1982	partial success	nonviolent
Contras	Nicaragua	1981	1990	success	violent
Kosovo Albanian nationalist movement	Yugoslavia	1981	1981	failure	nonviolent
Tigrean Liberation Front	Ethiopia	1982	1991	success	violent
Hizballah	Lebanon	1982	2000	success	violent
MFDC secessionist campaign	Senegal	1982	1983	failure	nonviolent
Casamance conflict	Senegal	1982	2014	failure	violent
Clan factions; SNM	Somalia	1982	1991	success	violent
Students' anti-Chun protest	South Korea	1982	1987	failure	nonviolent

Anti-Pinochet campaign	Chile	1983	1989	success	nonviolent
Pro-democracy movement	Pakistan	1983	1983	failure	nonviolent
People Power	Philippines	1983	1986	success	nonviolent
LTTE	Sri Lanka	1983	2009	failure	violent
SPLA-Garang faction	Sudan	1983	2005	partial success	violent
Anti-Bouterse	Suriname	1983	1984	failure	nonviolent
PF-ZAPU guerrillas	Zimbabwe	1983	1987	partial success	violent
Diretas ja	Brazil	1984	1985	success	nonviolent
Ogaden self-determination	Ethiopia	1984	2018	ongoing	violent
Sikh insurgency	India	1984	1994	failure	violent
South African Second Defiance Campaign	South Africa	1984	1994	success	nonviolent
Uruguay anti-military campaign	Uruguay	1984	1985	success	nonviolent
Anti-Siles Zuazo	Bolivia	1985	1985	partial success	nonviolent
Anti-Duvalier campaign	Haiti	1985	1986	success	nonviolent
Assam independence	India	1985	2019	ongoing	violent
Kurdish secession against Saddam	Iraq	1985	1991	failure	violent
Anti-Jaafar	Sudan	1985	1985	success	nonviolent
Bodoland independence campaign (secession)	India	1986	2019	ongoing	violent
Gurkha independence campaign	India	1986	1986	failure	nonviolent
1986–1987 Khalistan campaign	India	1986	1987	failure	nonviolent
Anti–Zia al-Haq	Pakistan	1986	1986	failure	nonviolent

(continued)

Campaign	Location	Year Began	Year Ended	Outcome	Primary Method
South Korean anti-military	South Korea	1986	1987	success	nonviolent
LRA	Uganda	1986	2017	failure	violent
Leftists	Yemen People's Republic	1986	1986	partial success	violent
Argentina anti-coup	Argentina	1987	1987	success	nonviolent
Anti-Ershad campaign	Bangladesh	1987	1990	success	nonviolent
Singing Revolution	Estonia	1987	1991	success	nonviolent
Indo-Fijian anti-coup campaign	Fiji	1987	1987	failure	nonviolent
Anti-coalition government campaign	Fiji	1987	1987	success	violent
Anti-National Governing Council (CNG)	Haiti	1987	1987	failure	nonviolent
Anti-PRI campaign	Mexico	1987	2000	success	nonviolent
First Intifada	Palestine	1987	1990	partial success	nonviolent
Anti-Noriega campaign	Panama	1987	1989	failure	nonviolent
Anti-Ceaucescu movement	Romania	1987	1989	failure	nonviolent
JVP II	Sri Lanka	1987	1990	failure	violent
Tibetan independence movement	Tibet	1987	1989	failure	nonviolent
UPA	Uganda	1987	1992	failure	violent
Belarus anticommunist	Belarus	1988	1991	success	nonviolent
Pro-democracy movement in Burma	Burma	1988	2019	ongoing	violent
Pro-democracy movement/Sajudis	Lithuania	1988	1991	success	nonviolent
Bougainville revolt	Papua New Guinea	1988	1998	failure	violent

Anti–Roh Tae Woo	South Korea	1988	1992	failure	nonviolent
Kosovo Albanian	Yugoslavia	1988	1998	failure	nonviolent
Benin anticommunist	Benin	1989	1990	success	nonviolent
Bulgarian anticommunist	Bulgaria	1989	1990	partial success	nonviolent
Tiananmen Square	China	1989	1989	failure	nonviolent
Velvet Revolution	Czechoslovakia	1989	1989	success	nonviolent
Pro-democracy movement	East Germany	1989	1989	partial success	nonviolent
Timorese resistance	East Timor	1989	1999	success	nonviolent
Pro-democracy movement	Hungary	1989	1989	success	nonviolent
Tripura	India	1989	2019	ongoing	violent
SCIRI	Iraq	1989	1996	failure	violent
Ivorian pro-democracy movement	Ivory Coast	1989	1990	success	nonviolent
Pro-democracy movement	Latvia	1989	1991	success	nonviolent
Anti-Doe rebels	Liberia	1989	1990	success	violent
Tuaregs	Mali	1989	1995	failure	violent
Mongolian anticommunist	Mongolia	1989	1990	success	nonviolent
Anti-Ceaucescu rebels	Romania	1989	1989	success	violent
Public Against Violence	Slovakia	1989	1992	success	nonviolent
Slovenia anticommunist	Slovenia	1989	1990	success	nonviolent
Donetsk miners' strike	Ukraine	1989	1991	partial success	nonviolent
Georgian anti-Soviet movement	USSR	1989	1991	partial success	nonviolent
Albanian anticommunist	Albania	1990	1991	success	nonviolent

(continued)

Campaign	Location	Year Began	Year Ended	Outcome	Primary Method
CCCN and Union pro-democracy movement	Central African Republic	1990	1993	success	nonviolent
Anti-Burnham/Hoyte campaign	Guyana	1990	1992	success	nonviolent
1990 Kashmir plebiscite protests	India	1990	1990	failure	nonviolent
Kashmiri Muslim separatists	India	1990	2005	failure	violent
Anti–Arap Moi	Kenya	1990	1991	success	nonviolent
Kyrgyzstan Democratic Movement	Kyrgyzstan	1990	1991	success	nonviolent
Mali anti-military	Mali	1990	1991	success	nonviolent
The Stir	Nepal	1990	1990	success	nonviolent
Niger anti-military	Niger	1990	1992	success	nonviolent
Ogoni movement	Nigeria	1990	1995	failure	nonviolent
1990 Anti-Government Protests	Romania	1990	1992	partial success	nonviolent
The Golaniad	Romania	1990	1993	failure	nonviolent
Pro-democracy movement	Russia	1990	1991	success	nonviolent
Tutsi rebels	Rwanda	1990	1993	success	violent
Slovenian independence	Slovenia	1990	1991	success	nonviolent
Students Union Protests	Ukraine	1990	1990	success	nonviolent
Zambia anti-single party rule	Zambia	1990	1991	success	nonviolent
Cabinda Conflict	Angola	1991	2019	ongoing	violent
Armenians in Nagorno-Karabakh	Azerbaijan	1991	1994	partial success	violent
Burundian Civil War	Burundi	1991	2008	failure	violent
Tutsi supremacists	Burundi	1991	1992	success	violent

Campaign	Location			Outcome	Type
NCCOP pro-democracy movement	Cameroon	1991	1991	success	nonviolent
Serbian Republic of Krajina (secession campaign)	Croatia	1991	1995	failure	violent
Afar insurgency	Djibouti	1991	1994	failure	violent
Southern Ossetian separatist campaign	Georgia	1991	1992	failure	violent
Anti-Saddam protests	Iraq	1991	1991	partial success	nonviolent
Shiite rebellion	Iraq	1991	1991	failure	violent
Active Voices	Madagascar	1991	1993	success	nonviolent
RUF	Sierra Leone	1991	1996	partial success	violent
Somali civil war	Somalia	1991	2000	failure	violent
1991 opposition protests	Tajikistan	1991	1991	partial success	nonviolent
Anti-Eyadema	Togo	1991	1991	partial success	nonviolent
Croats	Yugoslavia	1991	1992	success	violent
Sacred Union	Zaire/DRC	1991	1993	failure	violent
Taliban/antigovernment forces	Afghanistan	1992	1996	success	violent
Islamic Salvation Front	Algeria	1992	2002	failure	violent
Serb militias	Bosnia-Herzegovina	1992	1995	failure	violent
Anti-Collor protests	Brazil	1992	1992	success	nonviolent
Egyptian Insurgency-Jamaat Al Islamiyya	Egypt	1992	1999	failure	violent
Georgia-Abkhazia War	Georgia	1992	1994	failure	violent
NPFL & ULIMO	Liberia	1992	1995	partial success	violent

(continued)

Campaign	Location	Year Began	Year Ended	Outcome	Primary Method
Anti-Banda campaign	Malawi	1992	1994	success	nonviolent
Dniestr	Moldova	1992	1992	partial success	violent
Popular Democratic Army (UTO)	Tajikistan	1992	1997	partial success	violent
Tanzania pro-democracy	Tanzania	1992	1995	partial success	nonviolent
Pro-democracy movement	Thailand	1992	1992	success	nonviolent
Anti-Perez	Venezuela	1992	1992	failure	nonviolent
Military Forces of Hugo Chávez	Venezuela	1992	1992	failure	violent
Republic of Western Bosnia (secession)	Bosnia-Herzegovina	1993	1995	failure	violent
Anti-Serrano	Guatemala	1993	1993	success	nonviolent
Nigeria anti-military	Nigeria	1993	1999	success	nonviolent
Anti-Lissouba Campaign (Cocoyes, Ninjas, Cobras)	Republic of the Congo	1993	1997	success	violent
Anti-Yeltsin	Russia	1993	1993	failure	violent
Somalia militia insurgencies	Somalia	1993	1994	success	violent
1994–1996 Awami League Campaign	Bangladesh	1994	1996	success	nonviolent
Multiple factions	Central African Republic	1994	1997	success	violent
Rebels	Chad	1994	1998	failure	violent
Mohajir	Pakistan	1994	1999	failure	violent
Democratic Republic of Yemen Secessionist Movement	Republic of Yemen	1994	1994	failure	violent
Chechen separatists	Russia	1994	2009	failure	violent

Patriotic Front	Rwanda	1994	1994	success	violent
Students' Anti-Kim protest	South Korea	1995	1995	failure	nonviolent
Kabila-ADFL	Democratic Republic of Congo	1996	1997	success	violent
Kurdish civil conflict	Iraq	1996	1996	failure	violent
national patriotic forces	Liberia	1996	1996	failure	violent
Hutu nationalist insurgency	Rwanda	1996	2001	failure	violent
Anti-Milošević	Serbia	1996	2000	success	nonviolent
ADF Insurgency	Uganda	1996	2019	ongoing	violent
Anjouan Separatist Movement	Comoros	1997	2000	partial success	violent
Anti-Sassou-Nguessou Campaign (Cocoyes, Ninjas, Ntsiloulous)	Congo-Brazzaville (ROC)	1997	2003	failure	violent
Denis Sassou Nguesso campaign	Congo-Brazzaville (ROC)	1997	1999	success	violent
1997 anti-Bucaram Campaign	Ecuador	1997	1997	success	nonviolent
Anti-Suharto campaign	Indonesia	1997	1998	success	nonviolent
Fair election campaign	Lesotho	1997	2002	partial success	nonviolent
Anti–Hun Sen	Cambodia	1998	1998	failure	nonviolent
MDJT	Chad	1998	2003	failure	violent
Second Congo War	Democratic Republic of Congo	1998	2002	failure	violent
Military Junta for the Consolidation of Democracy, Peace and Justice	Guinea-Bissau	1998	1999	failure	violent

(continued)

Campaign	Location	Year Began	Year Ended	Outcome	Primary Method
Reformasi	Malaysia	1998	1999	failure	nonviolent
KLA	Serbia	1998	1999	partial success	violent
Croatian pro-democracy	Croatia	1999	2000	success	nonviolent
Student Protests (Anti-Habibie)	Indonesia	1999	1999	success	nonviolent
Tir 18 Riot for democracy	Iran	1999	1999	failure	nonviolent
LURD	Liberia	1999	2003	success	violent
Western Sahara independence movement	Morocco	1999	2005	failure	nonviolent
Anti-Cubas protests	Paraguay	1999	1999	success	nonviolent
Anti-Wijdenbosch	Suriname	1999	2000	success	nonviolent
2000 anti-Mahuad protests	Ecuador	2000	2000	success	nonviolent
Kefaya	Egypt	2000	2005	partial success	nonviolent
Anti-Chaudhry campaign	Fiji	2000	2000	success	nonviolent
Anti-Rawlings campaign	Ghana	2000	2000	success	nonviolent
RDFG	Guinea	2000	2001	failure	violent
Anti-Guei Protests	Ivory Coast	2000	2000	success	nonviolent
Anti-Fujimori campaign	Peru	2000	2000	success	nonviolent
Anti-Diouf campaign	Senegal	2000	2000	success	nonviolent
Orange Revolution	Ukraine	2000	2005	partial success	nonviolent
Taliban	Afghanistan	2001	2019	ongoing	violent
NLA insurgency	Macedonia	2001	2001	failure	violent
CPN-M/UPF	Nepal	2001	2006	partial success	violent

People Power II	Philippines	2001	2001	failure	nonviolent
Second People Power Movement	Philippines	2001	2001	success	nonviolent
Anti-Kumaratunga	Sri Lanka	2001	2001	failure	nonviolent
Economic Crisis Sparks Calls for Resignation	Turkey	2001	2001	failure	nonviolent
Anti-Chiluba campaign	Zambia	2001	2001	success	nonviolent
PMIC	Ivory Coast	2002	2005	failure	violent
Pro-democracy movement	Madagascar	2002	2002	success	nonviolent
Nepalese antigovernment	Nepal	2002	2006	success	nonviolent
2002 Anti-Chávez Campaign	Venezuela	2002	2004	failure	nonviolent
Anti-coup	Venezuela	2002	2002	success	nonviolent
Anti–Sanchez de Lozada Campaign	Bolivia	2003	2003	success	nonviolent
Seleka rebellion	Central African Republic	2003	2013	success	violent
Rose Revolution	Georgia	2003	2003	success	nonviolent
Anti-Aristide campaign 2004	Haiti	2003	2004	success	nonviolent
Anti-Gayoom campaign	Maldives	2003	2008	success	nonviolent
JEM/SLA	Sudan	2003	2012	failure	violent
Oust the Government campaign	Bangladesh	2004	2004	failure	nonviolent
Anti-Mesa campaign (phase 1)	Bolivia	2004	2004	failure	nonviolent
Iraqi insurgency (Sunni/AQI/ISIL)	Iraq	2004	2019	ongoing	violent
Fourth Balochistan separatist movement	Pakistan	2004	2019	ongoing	violent

(continued)

Campaign	Location	Year Began	Year Ended	Outcome	Primary Method
2004 Southern Thai insurrection	Thailand	2004	2019	ongoing	violent
Al-Houthi rebellion	Yemen	2004	2015	success	violent
Anti-Mesa campaign (phase 2)	Bolivia	2005	2005	success	nonviolent
Anti-Deby rebellion	Chad	2005	2009	failure	violent
Chadian civil war I	Chad	2005	2006	failure	violent
Rebellion of the Forajidos	Ecuador	2005	2005	success	nonviolent
Pro-Aristide campaign	Haiti	2005	2010	failure	nonviolent
PJAK	Iran	2005	2018	ongoing	violent
Tulip Revolution	Kyrgyzstan	2005	2005	success	nonviolent
Cedar Revolution	Lebanon	2005	2005	success	nonviolent
Anti-Thaksin campaign	Thailand	2005	2006	success	nonviolent
Togo Anti-Gnassingbe / coup crisis	Togo	2005	2005	success	nonviolent
Pro-democracy protests	Tonga	2005	2006	partial success	nonviolent
Awami League protests	Bangladesh	2006	2007	success	nonviolent
Denim revolution	Belarus	2006	2006	failure	nonviolent
Chadian civil war II	Chad	2006	2010	failure	violent
CNDP	Democratic Republic of Congo	2006	2008	failure	violent
Anti-Alkatiri	East Timor	2006	2006	success	nonviolent
2006 Lebanon war	Lebanon	2006	2006	failure	violent
Lebanon political crisis	Lebanon	2006	2008	success	nonviolent
Anti-Calderon campaign	Mexico	2006	2006	failure	nonviolent

Campaign	Location	Start	End	Outcome	
Islamist insurgency	Somalia	2006	2019	ongoing	violent
Armenian Opposition Protest / March 1st Movement	Armenia	2007	2009	partial success	nonviolent
Anti-Mubarak movement	Egypt	2007	2011	success	nonviolent
2007 anti-Saakashvili campaign	Georgia	2007	2007	partial success	nonviolent
Pro-democracy movement	Guinea	2007	2010	failure	nonviolent
Saffron Revolution	Myanmar	2007	2007	failure	nonviolent
Mahadeshi autonomy campaign	Nepal	2007	2007	partial success	nonviolent
Islamist insurgency	Pakistan	2007	2019	ongoing	violent
Anti-Musharraf campaign (Lawyers' Movement)	Pakistan	2007	2008	success	nonviolent
Caucasus Emirate	Russia	2007	2019	ongoing	violent
Dissenters' march	Russia	2007	2008	failure	nonviolent
Anti-military government campaign	Thailand	2007	2007	partial success	nonviolent
South Yemen secessionist movement	Yemen	2007	2014	partial success	nonviolent
Palipehutu-FNL	Burundi	2008	2008	failure	violent
Third South Ossetian campaign	Georgia	2008	2008	success	violent
Anti-MINUSTAH campaign	Haiti	2008	2008	failure	nonviolent
Cutlery Revolution (Kitchenware / Kitchen Implement Revolution)	Iceland	2008	2009	success	nonviolent
Sadars' anti-US occupation campaign	Iraq	2008	2009	failure	nonviolent
Red Shirt campaign	Thailand	2008	2010	failure	nonviolent

(continued)

Campaign	Location	Year Began	Year Ended	Outcome	Primary Method
People's Alliance for Democracy Campaign	Thailand	2008	2008	success	nonviolent
Anti-socialist demonstrations	Bulgaria	2009	2009	failure	nonviolent
2009 Anti-Saakashvili campaign	Georgia	2009	2009	failure	nonviolent
Frente Nacional de Resistencia Popular (FNRP)	Honduras	2009	2009	failure	nonviolent
Green Revolution and Day of Rage	Iran	2009	2013	partial success	nonviolent
Anti-Rajoelina movement	Madagascar	2009	2014	partial success	nonviolent
Anti-Ravalomanana movement	Madagascar	2009	2009	success	nonviolent
Moldovan "Grapevine" Revolution	Moldova	2009	2009	success	nonviolent
Anti-Zardari campaign	Pakistan	2009	2009	failure	nonviolent
Al Qaeda in the Arabian Peninsula	Yemen	2009	2019	ongoing	violent
Anti-Abdelaziz Bouteflika campaign	Algeria	2010	2012	partial success	nonviolent
Pro-Ouattara campaign	Ivory Coast	2010	2011	success	nonviolent
Anti-interim government	Kyrgyzstan	2010	2010	failure	nonviolent
Second Revolution	Kyrgyzstan	2010	2010	success	nonviolent
Maoist antigovernment protests	Nepal	2010	2010	success	nonviolent
Snow Revolution	Russia	2010	2019	ongoing	nonviolent
Anti–Ben Ali campaign (Jasmine Revolution)	Tunisia	2010	2011	success	nonviolent
Renewed Western Sahara independence protests	Western Sahara	2010	2019	ongoing	nonviolent
Anti-King Hamad campaign	Bahrain	2011	2019	ongoing	nonviolent

Djibouti Arab Spring	Djibouti	2011	failure	nonviolent
Day of Rage protests	Iraq	2011	partial success	nonviolent
Protest for Constitutional Reform	Jordan	2013	partial success	nonviolent
Libyan civil war	Libya	2011	success	violent
Anti-Mutharika	Malawi	2012	success	nonviolent
Anti-Aziz protests	Mauritania	2014	failure	nonviolent
Boko Haram	Nigeria	2011	ongoing	violent
SPLM/A	South Sudan	2011	ongoing	violent
South Kordofan and Blue Nile conflict	Sudan	2011	ongoing	violent
Anti-al-Bashir government	Sudan	2011	failure	nonviolent
Swaziland anti-monarchy protests	Swaziland	2011	failure	nonviolent
Syrian civil war	Syria	2011	ongoing	violent
Syrian uprising	Syria	2011	failure	nonviolent
Anti-Museveni	Uganda	2011	failure	nonviolent
Anti Ali Adduallah Saleh campaign	Yemen	2011	success	nonviolent
Kirti Monastery protests	China	2012	failure	nonviolent
M23	Democratic Republic of Congo	2012	failure	violent
Anti-Shiite government protests	Iraq	2014	partial success	nonviolent
Nasheed supporters	Maldives	2013	failure	nonviolent
Anti-Nasheed campaign	Maldives	2012	success	nonviolent
Northern Mali conflict	Mali	2015	partial success	violent
Anti-Maoist campaign	Nepal	2012	success	nonviolent

(continued)

Campaign	Location	Year Began	Year Ended	Outcome	Primary Method
2012 antigovernment protests	Romania	2012	2012	success	nonviolent
Anti-Wade June 23 Movement	Senegal	2012	2012	success	nonviolent
Let's Save Togo (anti-Gnassingbe)	Togo	2012	2013	failure	nonviolent
Dance with Me campaign	Bulgaria	2013	2014	success	nonviolent
2013 Cambodian election protests	Cambodia	2013	2014	failure	nonviolent
Jama'atu Ahlis Sunna Lidda'awati wal-Jihad (Boko Haram affiliate)	Cameroon	2013	2019	ongoing	violent
Anti-Balaka	Central African Republic	2013	2014	success	violent
Sinai insurgency	Egypt	2013	2019	ongoing	violent
Pro-Morsi protests	Egypt	2013	2014	failure	nonviolent
Anti-Morsi protests	Egypt	2013	2013	success	nonviolent
Islamic State	Syria	2013	2019	ongoing	violent
Civil Movement for Democracy	Thailand	2013	2014	success	nonviolent
Protests Against the Crisis Talks	Tunisia	2013	2013	success	nonviolent
Anti-Islamist government protests	Tunisia	2013	2014	success	nonviolent
Anti-Erdogan	Turkey	2013	2015	partial success	nonviolent
Euromaidan	Ukraine	2013	2014	success	nonviolent
UDAR	Bosnia-Herzegovina	2014	2014	failure	nonviolent
Anti-Compaore campaign	Burkina Faso	2014	2014	success	nonviolent
Hong Kong pro-democracy (Umbrella Movement)	China	2014	2019	ongoing	nonviolent
Anti-Martelly campaign	Haiti	2014	2016	success	nonviolent

Campaign	Country	Start	End	Outcome	Type
Islamist militia factions (second Libyan civil war)	Libya	2014	2019	ongoing	violent
2014 Mexican anti-corruption campaign	Mexico	2014	2015	failure	nonviolent
2014 anti-Sharif campaign	Pakistan	2014	2014	failure	nonviolent
New Democracy Movement	Thailand	2014	2019	ongoing	nonviolent
Rebels in East Ukraine (Ukrainian civil war)	Ukraine	2014	2019	ongoing	violent
Ultras "United Ukraine" Campaign	Ukraine	2014	2014	failure	nonviolent
Anti-Maduro	Venezuela	2014	2019	ongoing	nonviolent
ISIS-Afghanistan	Afghanistan	2015	2019	ongoing	violent
Anti-Rousseff	Brazil	2015	2016	success	nonviolent
Anti-Nkurunziza campaign	Burundi	2015	2015	failure	nonviolent
Out Correa campaign	Ecuador	2015	2017	partial success	nonviolent
Guatemala uprising	Guatemala	2015	2015	success	nonviolent
Honduran *indignados*	Honduras	2015	2015	failure	nonviolent
Western Southeast Asia Front	India	2015	2019	ongoing	violent
Kenyan Al-Shabaab insurgency	Kenya	2015	2019	ongoing	violent
Kosovo Anti-Government Protests	Kosovo	2015	2019	ongoing	nonviolent
Colorful Revolution	Macedonia	2015	2017	success	nonviolent
Anti-Yameen	Maldives	2015	2019	success	nonviolent
Moldovan antigovernment protest	Moldova	2015	2016	partial success	nonviolent
Montenegrin opposition protest	Montenegro	2015	2015	failure	nonviolent

(continued)

Campaign	Location	Year Began	Year Ended	Outcome	Primary Method
Western Southeast Asia Front	Myanmar	2015	2019	ongoing	violent
Colectiv Revolution	Romania	2015	2015	success	nonviolent
Anti-Park protests	South Korea	2015	2017	success	nonviolent
Renewed Kurdistan Workers' Party (PKK)	Turkey	2015	2019	ongoing	violent
Anti-Houthi movement	Yemen	2015	2019	ongoing	nonviolent
Panama Papers antigovernment protest	Iceland	2016	2016	partial success	nonviolent
Kashmir anti-India protests	India	2016	2019	ongoing	nonviolent
Anti–prime minister protest	Papua New Guinea	2016	2016	failure	nonviolent
Anti–right wing government	Poland	2016	2019	ongoing	nonviolent
Catalan separatist protest	Spain	2016	2019	ongoing	nonviolent
Anti-Mugabe	Zimbabwe	2016	2017	success	nonviolent
Anglophone crisis / Ambazonia independence	Cameroon	2017	2019	ongoing	violent
Ambazonia independence	Cameroon	2017	2018	failure	nonviolent
Anti-Kabila campaign	Democratic Republic of Congo	2017	2018	success	nonviolent
Anti-Morales protests	Guatemala	2017	2019	ongoing	nonviolent
Anti-Hernandez	Honduras	2017	2019	ongoing	nonviolent
Anti-Orban	Hungary	2017	2019	ongoing	nonviolent
2017 Iran antigovernment protests	Iran	2017	2018	failure	nonviolent
Romania antigovernment protest	Romania	2017	2019	ongoing	nonviolent
Anti-Vucic	Serbia	2017	2019	ongoing	nonviolent

Campaign	Country				
Anti-Zuma	South Africa	2017	2018	success	nonviolent
2017 anti-Gnassingbe	Togo	2017	2019	ongoing	nonviolent
Anti-Erdogan II	Turkey	2017	2019	ongoing	nonviolent
Anti-Trump resistance	United States	2017	2019	ongoing	nonviolent
2018 antigovernment protests	Armenia	2018	2018	success	nonviolent
Yellow Vests	France	2018	2019	ongoing	nonviolent
Anti-Jovenel Moise protests	Haiti	2018	2019	ongoing	nonviolent
Anti-Ortega protests	Nicaragua	2018	2019	ongoing	nonviolent
Sudan uprising	Sudan	2018	2019	success	nonviolent
Albanian anti-corruption	Albania	2019	2019	ongoing	nonviolent
Smile Revolution	Algeria	2019	2019	success	nonviolent
Anti-Macri protests	Argentina	2019	2019	success	nonviolent
Anti-Áñez protests	Bolivia	2019	2019	ongoing	nonviolent
Anti-Morales protests	Bolivia	2019	2019	success	nonviolent
Anti-Pinera	Chile	2019	2019	ongoing	nonviolent
Anti-Duque movement	Colombia	2019	2019	ongoing	nonviolent
Anti-Moreno	Ecuador	2019	2019	partial success	nonviolent
Anti-al-Sisi protests	Egypt	2019	2019	failure	nonviolent
2019 Georgian protests	Georgia	2019	2019	partial success	nonviolent
Hernández Must Go campaign	Honduras	2019	2019	failure	nonviolent
2019 Iranian protests	Iran	2019	2019	ongoing	nonviolent
Anti-Mahdi movement	Iraq	2019	2019	success	nonviolent
October Revolution	Lebanon	2019	2019	success	nonviolent
97000 Resist campaign	Montenegro	2019	2019	failure	nonviolent

NOTES

Prelims
1 This summary is adapted from a blog post I wrote about the origins of my interest in nonviolent conflict in 2014.
2 Chenoweth & Stephan 2011.
3 Chenoweth 2020a.
4 Chenoweth, et al. 2019.

Introduction
1 Foot 2016, p. 5.
2 Global Nonviolent Action Database.
3 Kurlansky 2006.
4 Scalmer 2011.
5 Desai and Vahed 2015.
6 Bartkowski 2013; Presbey 2013.
7 Khawaja 1993; King 2007; Pearlman 2011; Rigby 1991; Schiff and Ya'ari 1989; Stephan 2005.
8 Boserup and Mack 1974; Liddell Hart 1954; Roberts 1969; Schell 2003; Scalmer 2011; Schelling 1969.
9 See, for instance, Deming 1971.
10 Sharp 1990; 2003.
11 See, for instance, Abujbara, et al. 2017.
12 Ackerman and Kruegler 1994; Zunes 2009b.
13 Stephan & Chenoweth 2008; Chenoweth & Stephan 2011.
14 Conser, et al. 1986; Conser 2013.
15 Adams 1856, Vol. 10, p. 172.
16 Presbey 2013, p. 51.
17 Beitler 2004; Clark 2010.
18 Sémelin 1993; Stephan & Mundy 2006.
19 Hamann, et al. 2013.
20 Barrell 1993; Wink 1987; Zunes 1999b.
21 Buchanon, Bui, & Patel 2020.
22 Dorff 2015.
23 Beyerle 2014, pp. 115–135.
24 Piven and Cloward 1977.

25   Rasler 1996; Kurzman 1996, 2004; Zunes 2009a.
26   Bennhold 2018.

Chapter 1
1   Schock 2003; 2015a.
2   Smithey 2013.
3   Sharp calls this a "monolithic" theory of power (1973).
4   Fanon 1961.
5   Gene Sharp refers to this as a "pluralistic" theory of power (1973).
6   Throughout the text, I capitalize "Black" to recognize Black political identity and history in the US context. I note, however, that in South Africa, the politics of capitalization is reversed. The lower-case term "invokes black consciousness and can be used to describe people of African, Indian, and mixed heritage and descent." I intend my use of "Black" to capture the common cause in how these terms are used in the US, across Africa, and throughout the Diaspora (Kessi, Marks, & Ramugondo 2020, pp. 280–281).
7   Bueno de Mesquita & Smith 2011.
8   Looney 2012, pp. 431–434.
9   Chapter 4 explores these dynamics in more detail.
10   Author correspondence with Mary Elizabeth King, September 18, 2020.
11   Sharp 2005.
12   Burrowes 1996; Schock 2005.
13   Schock 2005; Stephan & Gallagher 2019.
14   Quoted in Barnard 2015.
15   Quoted at Tea After Twelve, http://www.tea-after-twelve.com/all-issues/issue-01/issue-01-overview/chapter2/art-revolution/.
16   King 2011.
17   Popovic, quoted in *Bringing Down a Dictator*, 2005.
18   Dave 2020.
19   Filkins 2020.
20   Sombatpoonsiri 2015.
21   Schell 2003.
22   Herzog 2011.
23   Kishtainy 2010, p. 62.
24   Kishtainy 2010, p. 54.
25   Cochran 2019.
26   Presbey 2013.
27   Nagler 2014.
28   Havel 1986, p. 89.
29   Case 2018.
30   Wasow 2020.
31   Huet-Vaughn 2017.
32   Chenoweth & Belgioioso 2019.
33   Rothman 2015.
34   Rothman 2015.
35   Chenoweth & Pressman 2020.
36   See, for instance, Abaraonye 1998. Thanks to Zoe Marks for bringing this example to my attention.
37   Kurlansky 2006, 78.
38   Quoted in Australian Broadcasting Company 2013.

39 Klein 1998.
40 Newman 2019.
41 Potter 2015, pp. 2–3.
42 Bray 2017.
43 Gandhi, *Young India,* June 16, 1927.
44 The King Center, n.d.
45 Bartkowski 2017.
46 Quoted in Guha 2018, p. 78.
47 Quoted in Guha 2018, pp. 77–78.
48 Hellmeier & Weidmann 2019.
49 Gandhi, *Harijan,* October 27, 1946, pp. 369–70.
50 Brown 1984, pp. 22–23.
51 Rossdale 2019.
52 Quoted in Hoyte 2016.
53 The author thanks Matt Meyer for conveying this point during correspondence in 2017.

Chapter 2

1   "The low road" from *THE HUNGER MOON: NEW AND SELECTED POEMS, 1980–2010* by Marge Piercy, copyright © 2011 by Middlemarsh, Inc. Used by permission of Alfred A. Knopf, an imprint of the Knopf Doubleday Publishing Group, a division of Penguin Random House LLC. All rights reserved.
2   See Chenoweth & Stephan 2014; Nepstad 2015; Roberts 2015; Robertson 2011.
3   See also Schock 2015a; Sharp 2005.
4   Chenoweth & Stephan 2011; 2016.
5   Chenoweth & Stephan 2011.
6   Binnendijk & Marović 2006.
7   Schock 2005; Zunes 1994.
8   Thurber 2015; 2019.
9   Swarthmore Nonviolent Action Database.
10 See Chapters 3 and 4 for more specifics.
11 Lee 2009; Martin 2015; Martin, Varney, & Vickers 2001.
12 Author correspondence with Ivan Marović, 2014.
13 Author correspondence with Mary Elizabeth King, 2015.
14 McAdam 1999.
15 McAdam 1996a; 1996b.
16 See McAdam, Tarrow, & Tilly 2001; Schock 2015a; Tarrow 1998.
17 Chenoweth & Ulfelder 2017.
18 Chenoweth & Ulfelder 2017.
19 Dahlum 2019; Dahlum & Wig 2019.
20 Chenoweth & Ulfelder 2017.
21 Butcher, Gray, & Mitchell 2018.
22 Butcher & Svensson 2014; Dahlum & Wig 2019; Wittels 2017.
23 Piot 2011; Author correspondence with Mary Elizabeth King, April 2011.
24 Chenoweth & Ulfelder 2017.
25 Pearlman 2013.
26 Braithwaite, Braithwaite, & Kucik 2015; Finkel 2015.
27 Chenoweth & Ulfelder 2017.
28 Gleditsch & Rivera 2017; Weyland 2014; Beissinger 2007.
29 Chenoweth & Ulfelder 2017.

30 Chenoweth & Ulfelder 2017.
31 DeNardo 1985; Lichbach 1994a; Lichbach 1994b; Marwell & Oliver 1993.
32 Chenoweth & Belgioioso 2019.
33 Ackerman & Merriman 2014.
34 Chenoweth & Stephan 2011; Marks & Chenoweth 2019.
35 Bartkowski & Polyakova 2015; see also Dorff 2015.
36 Principe 2017.
37 Marks & Chenoweth 2019.
38 Marks & Chenoweth 2019.
39 Barbash & Wax 2004.
40 Abonga et al. 2019.
41 This section is adapted from Chenoweth 2013.
42 Chenoweth & Stephan 2011.
43 Butcher, Gray, & Mitchell 2018.
44 Sharp 2005; Helvey 2004.
45 Grewal 2019; Makara 2013.
46 Binnendijk & Marović 2004.
47 Swarthmore Nonviolent Action Database.
48 This section is adapted from Chenoweth 2013.
49 Author correspondence with Ivan Marović, 2015.
50 Johnson 1987; Lee 2009; Schock 2005; Zunes 1999a.
51 Johnson & Thyne 2018.
52 King 2015.
53 Hamann et al., 2013.
54 Sharp 2005; Ackerman & Kruegler 1994; Schock 2005.
55 Chenoweth, et al. 2020.
56 Gladwell & Shirky 2011.
57 Howard 2010.
58 Howard 2010; for applications and cases of digital activism, see the websites
    for the Meta-Activism Project (http://www.meta-activism.org/) and
    iRevolutions (https://irevolutions.org/).
59 King 2013.
60 Tufekci 2017.
61 Morozov 2010.
62 Gohdes 2020.
63 Gunitsky 2015.
64 Meier 2011.
65 Madrigal 2011.
66 The next several sections draw from Chenoweth 2020b.
67 Lichbach 1994a.
68 Chenoweth & Belgioioso 2019.
69 Chenoweth & Shay 2019.
70 Chenoweth 2020b.
71 According to Chenoweth & Shay 2019; see also Chenoweth 2020b.
72 Chenoweth and Pressman 2017.
73 Mazumder 2018; Wasow 2020.
74 Johnstad 2012.
75 Beissinger 2013.
76 Jamal 2005; King 2007; Pearlman 2011.

77 Chenoweth, et al. 2019.
78 Freeman 1970.
79 Freeman 1970.
80 Freeman 1970.
81 Stephan & Gallagher 2019.
82 Woodly 2020.
83 Svensson & Lindgren 2010.
84 Tarrow 1989.
85 Stephan 2010; Zunes, Kurtz, & Asher 1999.
86 Marks, Chenoweth, & Okeke 2019.
87 Stephan 2010.
88 Kurlansky 2006.
89 Nepstad 2011.
90 Bartkowski & Kahf 2013.
91 Chenoweth & Olsen 2015.
92 Gause 2020; Gillion 2020.
93 Beyerle 2014.
94 Quoted in Fisher 2009, p. 1.
95 Lakey 2018.
96 Thurber 2015; 2019.
97 Lakey 2018.
98 Lakey 2018.
99 Gleditsch & Rivera 2017; Bunce & Wolchik 2011; Weyland 2014.
100 Weyland 2009.
101 Weyland 2014.
102 Chenoweth & Stephan 2011.
103 Murdie & Bhaisin 2011.
104 Chenoweth & Stephan 2021.
105 Gallo-Cruz 2012; Keck & Sikkink 1998.
106 Fazal 2018.
107 Clark 2010; Stephan 2005; Stephan & Mundy 2006; Summy 1994.
108 Chenoweth & Stephan 2021; Keck & Sikkink 1998; Kinsman & Bassuener 2016.
109 Kuran 1989; Kuran 1991.
110 Chenoweth & Ulfelder 2017.
111 Chenoweth & Lewis 2013.
112 Ackerman 2007.
113 Koren 2014; Sémelin, Andrieu, & Gensburger 2014; Stephan 2016.
114 Koren 2014; Perkoski & Chenoweth 2018.

Chapter 3

1 Kauffman 2017.
2 Belgioioso, Costalli, & Gleditsch 2019.
3 Edwards & Arnon 2019.
4 Other forms of violence are more difficult to observe across space and time. For example, many people might point to psychological or emotional violence, which might harm a person in ways that are difficult to detect from distant observation. Other categories of violence, such as structural violence, involve systemic deprivations of basic human needs and dignities

such as access to food, water, shelter, healthcare, and education, often in a way that discriminates against particular groups. Many people therefore see acts of exclusion and silencing of marginalized groups or communities as acts of violence.

5 Bjork-James 2020; Kadivar & Ketchley 2018; Pressman 2017.
6 Bray 2017.
7 Pressman 2017.
8 Chenoweth & Kang 2020.
9 Tarrow 1989.
10 White 1989.
11 Chenoweth & Shay 2019.
12 Chenoweth & Shay 2019.
13 Chenoweth, Kang, & Moore 2021.
14 Chenoweth & Pressman 2020.
15 Chenoweth & Shay 2019.
16 Haines 1984.
17 Stockman 2017.
18 Kadivar & Ketchley 2018.
19 Bjork-James 2020.
20 Bray 2017.
21 Stockman 2017.
22 Cobb 2014.
23 Rossdale 2019.
24 Kydd & Walter 2006.
25 Thaler 2019.
26 Enos et al. 2019.
27 Enos et al. 2019.
28 Mazumder 2018; Wasow 2020.
29 Isaac, et al. 2006.
30 Barrell 1993.
31 Haines 1984; McCammon, Bergner, & Arch 2015; Belgioioso, Costalli, & Gleditsch 2019.
32 Graeber 2012.
33 Carey 2010; Chenoweth, Pinckney, & Lewis 2018; Steinert-Threlkeld, Joo, & Chan 2019.
34 Chenoweth & Stephan 2019.
35 Abrahms 2006.
36 Chenoweth & Schock 2015.
37 Thompkins 2015.
38 Steinert-Threlkeld, Joo, & Chan 2019.
39 Grossman 1995.
40 Chenoweth 2019.
41 Chenoweth 2019.
42 Author correspondence with Stephan Zunes, 2016.
43 Thomas & Louis 2014.
44 Orazani & Leidner 2019.
45 Adelman, Leidner, & Orazani 2017.
46 Selvanathan & Lickel 2019.

47 Simpson, Willer, & Feinberg 2018.
48 Wasow 2020; Mazumder 2018.
49 Huet-Vaughn 2017.
50 Chenoweth & Schock 2015.
51 Thompkins 2015.
52 Carey 2010.
53 Steinert-Threlkeld, Joo, & Chan 2019.
54 Lupu & Wallace 2019.
55 Conrad & Moore 2010.
56 Chenoweth & Stephan 2019.
57 Sharp 1973; Pearlman 2011.
58 Chenoweth & Stephan 2011; Chenoweth & Schock 2015.
59 Davenport, Soule, & Armstrong 2011.
60 Mitts & Manekin 2019.
61 Adelman, Leidner, & Orazani 2017; Muñoz & Anduiza 2019; Selvanathan & Lickel 2019; Thomas & Louis 2014.
62 Chenoweth & Stephan 2011.
63 Chenoweth & Stephan 2011; Wantchekon & García-Ponce 2017.
64 Marx 2012.
65 Marx 2012.
66 Davenport 2015.
67 Marx 2012.
68 Parham 2017.
69 Chase 2017a; 2017b.
70 Pinckney 2016.
71 Walzer 2001.
72 Pearlman 2011.
73 Pinckney 2016.
74 Pinckney 2016; Cunningham 2014.
75 Pinckney 2016, p. 74.
76 Pinckney 2016.
77 Sharp 2005, p. 200.
78 L'Obs 2019.
79 Author correspondence with Tom Hastings, 2015.
80 Pinckney 2016, p. 74.
81 Edwards & Arnon 2019.
82 Nagler 2019.
83 Dudouet 2013.
84 Braithwaite 2014a; 2014b.
85 Adler 2019.
86 Chenoweth & Stephan 2011.

Chapter 4

1 Ritter & Conrad 2016.
2 Chenoweth & Ulfelder 2017.
3 Klein & Regan 2018.
4 Davenport 2007.
5 Chenoweth & Ulfelder 2017.
6 Pearlman 2011.

7   Pearlman 2011.
8   Pearlman 2011, p. 106; see also Pressman 2017.
9   Chenoweth & Stephan 2011.
10 Bloom 2005.
11 Pearlman 2011.
12 Bloom 2005.
13 Sutton, Butcher, & Svensson 2014.
14 Bob & Nepstad 2007.
15 Sullivan 2016.
16 Valentino 2004.
17 Perkoski & Chenoweth 2018.
18 Martin 2007; Smithey & Kurtz 2018.
19 Foot 2016; Sémelin 1993; Sharp 1973; Sharp 2005; Summy 1994.
20 Stephan 2006.
21 Author correspondence with Mary Elizabeth King, 2014.
22 Chenoweth & Shay 2019.
23 Mazumder 2018.
24 Perkoski & Chenoweth 2018.
25 Ackerman & DuVall 2000.
26 Barrell 1993.
27 Sullivan 2017.
28 Sutton, Butcher, & Svensson 2014.
29 Quoted in Guha 2016, pp. 80–81.
30 Kurlansky 2006.
31 Liddell-Hart 1968, p. 205.
32 Quoted in Sharp 1973, p. 43.
33 Quoted in Summy 1994, p. 133.
34 Reck-Malleczewen 2000, entry from August 1943, pp. 194–95.
35 Stoltzfus 1996; Summy 1994.
36 Valentino 2004.
37 Foot 2016; Kurlansky 2006.
38 Perkoski & Chenoweth 2018.
39 Telegraph Staff 2009.
40 Foot 2016, p. 62.
41 Sémelin 1996.
42 Sémelin, et al. 2004.
43 Kaplan 2013a.
44 Kaplan 2013b.
45 Kaplan 2017.
46 Svensson, Hall, Krause, & Skoog 2019.
47 Stephan 2016.
48 Hess & Martin 2006.
49 Stephan & Chenoweth 2008.
50 Hess & Martin 2006; Martin 2007.
51 King 2013.
52 Snowden 2019.
53 Hsiao & Lim 2016, pp. 21–22.
54 Perkoski & Chenoweth 2018.

55 Robinson 2009.
56 Chenoweth & Stephan 2011; Schock 2005; Zunes 1999a.
57 Coy 2012.
58 Coy 2012.
59 Chenoweth & Stephan 2011.

Chapter 5
1   This chapter is adapted from Chenoweth 2020a and contains some similar verbiage and ideas.
2   Pinker 2011.
3   Bartkowski 2013.
4   Gallo-Cruz 2019.
5   Repucci 2020.
6   Chenoweth & Pressman 2020; Marantz 2020.
7   Chenoweth 2017; 2018; 2019.
8   Ritter 2015.
9   Chenoweth & Stephan 2011.
10 Hamann, et al. 2013.
11 Wasow 2020; Chenoweth & Schock 2015.
12 This section is adapted from Chenoweth 2014b; 2017; 2018; and 2019. See also Smithey & Kurtz 2018.
13 Martin 2007.
14 Spector 2006, p. 1.
15 Herszenhorn 2014.
16 Heydemann 2007; Spector 2006.
17 Frantz & Kendall-Taylor 2014.
18 Bueno de Mesquita & Smith 2011, pp. 198–200.
19 Ross 2012.
20 Spector 2006; Carothers & Brechenmacher 2014.
21 Spector & Krickovic 2008, p. 9.
22 Hellmeier & Weidmann 2019.
23 Marx 2012.
24 Dobson 2012.
25 Author correspondence with Patrick Meier, 2011.
26 Spector & Krickovic 2008, p. 6.
27 Spector & Krickovic 2008, p. 7.
28 Spector & Krickovic 2008, p. 11.
29 Spector & Krickovic 2008, p. 7.
30 Chenoweth 2018.
31 Chenoweth & Stephan 2011.
32 Madrigal 2011.
33 Bayer et al. 2016; Chenoweth & Stephan 2011; Rivera and Gleditsch 2013; Pinckney 2020; Ulfelder 2010; Wantchekon & García-Ponce 2017.
34 Beissinger 2013.
35 Chenoweth & Stephan 2011.
36 Chenoweth & Stephan 2011.
37 Stoddard 2013.
38 Chenoweth & Shay 2019.
39 Bayat 2017, p. 219.

40   Beissinger 2013.
41   Pinckney 2018; 2020.
42   Tarrow 1989; Ulfelder 2010.
43   Taylor 2016.
44   Gertsmann 2020.
45   Chenoweth, et al. 2020.
46   Buchanan, Bui, & Patel 2020; Chenoweth & Pressman 2020.
47   Ackerman & DuVall 2000; Kurlansky 2006; Smithey 2013.
48   Carter, Clark, & Randle 2006.
49   Kurlansky 2006.
50   Rossdale 2019.
51   Carlsmith & Sood 2009.
52   Iqbal 2015, pp. 95–120; Richardson 2006.
53   Richardson 2006.

REFERENCES

Abaraonye, Felicia Ihuoma. 1998. "The Women's War of 1929 in South-Eastern Nigeria," in M. J. Diamond, ed. *Women and Revolution: Global Expressions*, 109–132. Springer.

Abonga, Francis, Raphael Kerali, Holly Porter, and Rebecca Tapscott. 2019. "Naked Bodies and Collective Action: Repertoires of Protest in Uganda's Militarised, Authoritarian Regime." *Civil Wars*, November 12, 2019, pp.1–26.

Abrahms, Max. 2006. "Why Terrorism Does Not Work." *International Security* 31(2): 42–78.

Abujbara, Juman, Andrew Boyd, Dave Mitchell, and Marcel Taminato, eds. 2017. *Beautiful Rising: Creative Resistance from the Global South*. Portland: O/R Books.

Ackerman, Peter. 2007. "Skills or Conditions: What Key Factors Shape the Success or Failure of Civil Resistance?" International Center for Nonviolent Conflict; paper delivered at the Conference on Civil Resistance and Power Politics, St. Antony's College, March 15–18, University of Oxford.

Ackerman, Peter, and Jack DuVall. 2000. *A Force More Powerful: A Century of Nonviolent Conflict*. London: St. Martin's Press / Palgrave Macmillan.

Ackerman, Peter, and Christopher Kruegler. 1994. *Strategic Nonviolent Conflict: The Dynamics of People Power in the Twentieth Century*. Westport, CT: Praeger.

Ackerman, Peter, and Hardy Merriman. 2014. "The Checklist for Ending Tyranny," in Maria J. Stephan and Mat Burows, eds., *Is Authoritarianism Staging a Comeback?* 63–80. Washington, DC: Atlantic Council.

Adams, John. 1856. *The Works of John Adams, vol. 10*. Boston: Little Brown.

Adelman, Levi, Bernhard Leidner, and Seyed Nima Orazani. 2017. "Psychological Contributions to Philosophy: The Cases of Just War Theory and Nonviolence." *In* Florian Demont-Biaggi, ed. *The Nature of Peace and the Morality of Armed Conflict*, 267–291. London: Palgrave Macmillan.

Adler, Paul. 2019, November 29. "What the 'Battle of Seattle' Can Teach Today's Progressives," *Washington Post*, https://www.washingtonpost.com/outlook/2019/11/29/what-battle-seattle-can-teach-todays-progressives/.

Australian Broadcasting Company (ABC). 2013, June 13. *7.30 News Program*. "ABC's 7.30 Interviews His Holiness the Dalai Lama in Sydney." ABC News, https://www.youtube.com/watch?v=mEvftYpmRAs.

Barbash, Fred, and Emily Wax. 2004, October 8. "Wangari Maathai, the Kenyan F . . ." *Washington Post,* https://www.washingtonpost.com/archive/business/technology/2004/10/08/wangari-maathai-the-kenyan-f/98bc5690-0a8e-4ea0-82e8-0f27c14a324f/.

Barnard, Anne. 2015, June 7. "Brides of Syria Were Joined in Opposition to Violence." *New York Times,* https://www.nytimes.com/2015/06/10/world/middleeast/syria-trials-of-spring.html.

Barrell, Howard. 1993. *Conscripts to Their Age: African National Congress Operational Strategy, 1976–1986.* Ph.D. dissertation, St. Antony's College, Oxford University.

Bartkowski, Maciej, ed. 2013. *Recovering Nonviolent History: Civil Resistance in Liberation Struggles.* Boulder, CO: Lynne Rienner.

Bartkowski, Maciej. 2017, April 1. "Popular Uprising against Democratically Elected Leaders: What Makes It Legitimate?" *Huffington Post,* https://www.huffpost.com/entry/popular-uprising-against-_b_9567604.

Bartkowski, Maciej, and Mohja Kahf. 2013. Syria: A tale of two struggles. Updated September 23, 2013. Retrieved August 13, 2015 (https://www.opendemocracy.net/civilresistance/maciej-bartkowski-mohja-kahf/syrian-resistance-tale-of-two-struggles)

Bartkowski, Maciej, and Alina Polyakova. 2015, October 12. "To Kill or Not to Kill?: Ukrainians Opt for Nonviolent Civil Resistance." *Political Violence at a Glance,* https://politicalviolenceataglance.org/2015/10/12/to-kill-or-not-to-kill-ukrainians-opt-for-nonviolent-civil-resistance/.

Bayer, Markus, Felix S. Bethke, & Daniel Lambach. 2016. "The Democratic Dividend of Nonviolent Resistance." *Journal of Peace Research* 53(6): 758–771.

Bayat, Asef. 2017. *Revolution without Revolutionaries: Making Sense of the Arab Spring.* Palo Alto, CA: Stanford University Press.

Beissinger, Mark R. 2007. "Structure and Example in Modular Political Phenomena: The Diffusion of Bulldozer/Rose/Orange/Tulip Revolutions." *Perspectives on Politics* 5(02): 259–276.

Beissinger, Mark R. 2013. "The Semblance of Democratic Revolution: Coalitions in Ukraine's Orange Revolution." *American Political Science Review* 107(3): 574-592.

Beitler, Ruth. 2004. *The Path to Mass Rebellion: An Analysis of Two Intifadas.* New York: Lexington Books.

Belgioioso, Margherita, Stefano Costalli, and Kristian Skrede Gleditsch. 2019, March 11. "Better the Devil You Know?: How Fringe Terrorism Can Induce an Advantage for Moderate Nonviolent Campaigns." *Terrorism and Political Violence*: 1–20.

Bennhold, Katrin. 2018, December 27. "Germany's far right rebrands: friendlier face, same doctrine." *The New York Times,* https://www.nytimes.com/2018/12/27/world/europe/germany-far-right-generation-identity.html.

Beyerle, Shaazka. 2014. *Curtailing Corruption: People Power for Accountability and Justice.* Boulder, CO: Lynne Rienner.

Binnendijk, Anika Locke, and Ivan Marovic. 2006. "Power and Persuasion: Nonviolent Strategies to Influence State Security Forces in Serbia (2000) and Ukraine (2004)." *Communist and Post-Communist Studies* 39(3) (September): 411–429.

Bjork-James, Carwil. 2020. "Unarmed Militancy: Tactical Victories, Subjectivity, and Legitimacy in Bolivian Street Protest." *American Anthropologist* 122, no. 3: 514–527.

Bloom, Mia. 2005. *Dying to Kill: The Allure of Suicide Terror*. New York: Columbia University Press.

Bob, Clifford, and Sharon Erickson Nepstad. 2007. "Kill a Leader, Murder a Movement? Leadership and Assassination in Social Movements." *American Behavioral Scientist* 50 (10) (June): 1370–1394.

Boserup, Anders, and Andrew Mack. 1974. *War without Weapons: Non-Violence in National Defence*. London: Frances Pinter.

Braithwaite, John. 2014a. "Limits on Violence; Limits on Responsive Regulatory Theory." *Law & Policy* 36(4): 431–456.

Braithwaite, John. 2014b. "Rethinking Radical Flank Theory: South Africa." RegNet Research Paper No. 2014/23. Canberra: Australian National University.

Braithwaite, Alex, Jessica Maves Braithwaite, and Jeffrey Kucik, 2015. "The Conditioning Effect of Protest History on the Emulation of Nonviolent Conflict." *Journal of Peace Research* 52(6): 697–711.

Bray, Mark. 2017. *Antifa: The Anti-Fascist Handbook*. Brooklyn, NY: Melville House.

Brown, Wilmette. 1984. *Black Women and the Peace Movement*. Bristol: Falling Wall Press.

Buchanan, Larry, Quoctrung Bui, and Jugal K. Patel. 2020, July 3. "Black Lives Matter May Be the Largest Movement in U.S. History." *New York Times*, https://www.nytimes.com/interactive/2020/07/03/us/george-floyd-protests-crowd-size.html.

Bueno de Mesquita, Bruce, and Alastair Smith. 2011. *The Dictator's Handbook: Why Bad Behavior Is Almost Always Good Politics*. New York: Public Affairs.

Bunce, Valerie, and Sharon Wolchik. 2011. *Defeating Authoritarian Leaders in Post-Communist Countries*. New York: Cambridge University Press.

Burrowes, R. J. 1996. *The Strategy of Nonviolent Defense: A Gandhian Approach*. Albany: State University of New York Press.

Butcher, Charles, John Laidlaw Gray, and Liesel Mitchell. 2018. "Striking It Free? Organized Labor and the Outcomes of Civil Resistance." *Journal of Global Security Studies* 3(3): 302–321.

Carey, Sabine C. 2010. "The Use of Repression as a Response to Domestic Dissent." *Political Studies* 58(1): 167–186.

Carothers, Thomas, and Saskia Brechenmacher. 2014. "Closing Space: Democracy and Human Rights Support Under Fire." Washington, DC: Carnegie Endowment for International Peace.

Carlsmith, Kevin, and Avani Mehta Sood. 2009. "The Fine Line Between Interrogation and Retribution." *Journal of Experimental Social Psychology* 45(1): 191–196.

Carter, April. 2011. *People Power and Political Change: Key Issues and Concepts*. New York: Routledge.

Carter, April, Howard Clark, and Michael Randle. 2006. *People Power and Protest since 1945: A Bibliography of Nonviolent Action*. London: Housmans.

Case, Benjamin. 2018. "Riots as Civil Resistance Rethinking the Dynamics of 'Nonviolent' Struggle." *Journal of Resistance Studies* 4(1): 9.

Chase, Steve. 2017a, July 18. "Let's Get Real: Facing Up to the Agent Provocateur Problem." Minds of the Movement Blog, International Center on Nonviolent Conflict, https://www.nonviolent-conflict.org/blog_post/lets-get-real-facing-agent-provocateur-problem/.

Chase, Steve. 2017b, June 20. "Let's Get Strategic: Why Moving 'Beyond Violence and Nonviolence' Is Flawed." Minds of the Movement Blog, International Center on Nonviolent Conflict, https://www.nonviolent-conflict.org/blog_post/lets-get-strategic-moving-beyond-violence-nonviolence-flawed/.

Clements, Kevin P. 2015. "Principled Nonviolence: An Imperative, Not an Optional Extra." *Asian Journal of Peacebuilding* 3(1): 1–17.

Chenoweth, Erica. 2013, July 31. "Changing Sides Doesn't Always Make for Transformation — Just Look at Egypt." openDemocracy, https://www.opendemocracy.net/en/transformation/changing-sides-doesnt-always-make-for-transformation-just-look-at-e/.

Chenoweth, Erica. 2014a. "Civil Resistance: Reflections on an Idea Whose Time Has Come." *Global Governance: A Review of Multilateralism and International Organizations* 20(3): 351–358.

Chenoweth, Erica. 2014b. "Trends in Civil Resistance and Authoritarian Responses." In Maria J. Stephan and Mat Burrows, eds., *Is Authoritarianism Staging a Comeback?* 53–62. Washington, DC: Atlantic Council.

Chenoweth, Erica. 2017. "Trends in Nonviolent Resistance and State Response: Is Violence toward Civilian-Based Movements on the Rise?" *Global Responsibility to Protect* 9(1): 86–100.

Chenoweth, Erica. 2018. "The Trump Administration's Adoption of the Anti-Revolutionary Toolkit." *PS: Political Science and Politics* 51(1) (January): 17–25.

Chenoweth, Erica. 2019. "Women's Participation and the Fate of Nonviolent Resistance Campaigns." One Earth Future report, https://oefresearch.org/sites/default/files/documents/publications/Womens_Participation_Nonviolent_Campaigns_Digital_0.pdf.

Chenoweth, Erica. 2020a. "The Future of Nonviolent Resistance" *Journal of Democracy* 31(3): 69–84.

Chenoweth, Erica. 2020b. "Questions, Answers, and Some Cautionary Updates Regarding the 3.5% Rule." *Carr Center Discussion Paper Series* 2020-005. Kennedy School of Government, Harvard University.

Chenoweth, Erica, and Margherita Belgioioso. 2019. "The Physics of Dissent and the Effects of Movement Momentum." *Nature Human Behaviour* 3(10): 1088–1095.

Chenoweth, Erica, Austin Choi-Fitzpatrick, Jeremy Pressman, Felipe G. Santos, and Jay Ulfelder. 2020, April 20. "The Global Pandemic Has Spawned New Forms of Activism—and They're Flourishing." *The Guardian*, https://www.theguardian.com/commentisfree/2020/apr/20/the-global-pandemic-has-spawned-new-forms-of-activism-and-theyre-flourishing.

Chenoweth, Erica, Sirianne Dahlum, Sooyeon Kang, Zoe Marks, Christopher Shay, and Tore Wig. 2019, November 16. "This May Be the Largest Wave of Nonviolent Mass Movements in World History. What Comes Next?" *Washington Post*, https://www.washingtonpost.com/politics/2019/11/16/this-may-be-largest-wave-nonviolent-mass-movements-world-history-what-comes-next/.

Chenoweth, Erica, Sooyeon Kang, and Pauline Moore. 2021. Major Episodes of Contention Dataset. Harvard Dataverse.

Chenoweth, Erica, and Orion A. Lewis. 2013. "Unpacking Nonviolent Campaigns: Introducing the NAVCO 2.0 Dataset." *Journal of Peace Research* 50(3) (May): 415–442.

Chenoweth, Erica, and Tricia Olsen. 2015. "Civil Resistance and Corporate Behavior: Mapping Trends and Assessing Impact." Democracy, Human Rights, and Governance Research and Innovation Grant Report, USAID, August.

Chenoweth, Erica, Jonathan Pinckney, and Orion A. Lewis. 2018. "Days of Rage: Introducing the NAVCO 3.0 Dataset." *Journal of Peace Research* 55(4) (July): 524–534.

Chenoweth, Erica, and Jeremy Pressman. 2017, February 7. "This Is What We Learned by Counting the Women's Marches." *Washington Post*, Monkey Cage, https://www.washingtonpost.com/news/monkey-cage/wp/2017/02/07/this-is-what-we-learned-by-counting-the-womens-marches/.

Chenoweth, Erica, and Jeremy Pressman. 2020, October 17. "This Summer's Black Lives Matter Protesters Were Overwhelmingly Peaceful, Our Research Finds," *The Washington Post*, https://www.washingtonpost.com/politics/2020/10/16/this-summers-black-lives-matter-protesters-were-overwhelming-peaceful-our-research-finds/.

Chenoweth, Erica, and Kurt Schock. 2015. "Do Contemporaneous Armed Challenges Affect the Outcomes of Mass Nonviolent Campaigns?" *Mobilization: An International Quarterly* 20(4): 427–451.

Chenoweth, Erica, and Christopher W. Shay. 2019. NAVCO 2.1 Dataset. Harvard Dataverse.

Chenoweth, Erica, and Maria J. Stephan. 2011. *Why Civil Resistance Works: The Strategic Logic of Nonviolent Conflict*. New York: Columbia University Press.

Chenoweth, Erica, and Maria J. Stephan. 2014. "Drop Your Weapons: When and Why Civil Resistance Works." *Foreign Affairs* 93(4) (July/August): 94–106.

Chenoweth, Erica, and Maria J. Stephan. 2016, January 18. "How the World Is Proving Martin Luther King Right about Nonviolence" *Washington Post*, Monkey Cage, https://www.washingtonpost.com/news/monkey-cage/wp/2016/01/18/how-the-world-is-proving-mlk-right-about-nonviolence/.

Chenoweth, Erica, and Maria J. Stephan. 2019, December 18. "Violence Is a Dangerous Route for Protesters." *Foreign Policy Magazine*, https://foreignpolicy.com/2019/12/18/violent-resistance-protests-nonviolence/.

Chenoweth, Erica, and Maria J. Stephan. 2021. *The Role of External Support in Nonviolent Campaigns: Poisoned Chalice or Holy Grail?* Washington, DC: International Center on Nonviolent Conflict.

Chenoweth, Erica, and Jay Ulfelder. 2017. "Can Structural Conditions Explain the Onset of Nonviolent Uprisings?" *Journal of Conflict Resolution* 61(2) (February): 298–324.

Clark, Howard. 2010. "The Limits of Prudence: Civil Resistance in Kosovo, 1990–1998." In Adam Roberts and Timothy Garton Ash, eds., *Civil Resistance and Power Politics: The Experience of Non-Violent Action from Gandhi to the Present*, 277–294. Oxford: Oxford University Press.

Cobb, Raymond. 2014. *This Nonviolent Stuff'll Get You Killed: How Guns Made the Civil Rights Movement Possible*. New York: Basic Books.

Cochran, David. 2019. "The Irish Revolution's Overlooked History of Nonviolent Resistance." *Waging Nonviolence*, January, https://wagingnonviolence.org/2019/01/irish-revolution-overlooked-history-nonviolent-resistance/.

Conrad, Courtenay Ryals, and Will H. Moore. 2010. "What Stops the Torture?" *American Journal of Political Science* 54(2) (April): 459–476.

Conser, Walter H., Ronald McCarthy, David Toscano, and Gene Sharp, eds. 1986. *Resistance, Politics, and the American Struggle for Independence, 1765–1775.* Boulder, CO: Lynne Rienner Publishers.

Conser, Walter. 2013. "Cuba: Nonviolent Strategies for Autonomy and Independence, 1810s–1902," in Maciej Bartkowski, *Recovering Nonviolent History: Civil Resistance in Liberation Struggles*, 299–318. Boulder, CO: Lynne Rienner Publishers.

Coy, Patrick G. 2012. "Nonpartisanship, Interventionism and Legality in Accompaniment: Comparative Analyses of Peace Brigades International, Christian Peacemaker Teams, and the International Solidarity Movement." *International Journal of Human Rights* 16(7) (October): 963–981.

Cunningham, Kathleen. 2014. *Inside the Politics of Self-Determination.* New York: Oxford University Press.

Dahlum, Sirianne. 2019. "Students in the Streets: Education and Nonviolent Protest." *Comparative Political Studies* 52(2): 277–309.

Dahlum, Sirianne, and Tore Wig. 2019. "Who Revolts? Empirically Revisiting the Social Origins of Democracy." *The Journal of Politics* 81(4): 1494–1499.

Dave, Nomi. 2020. *The Revolution's Echoes: Music, Politics, and Pleasure in Guinea.* Chicago: University of Chicago Press.

Davenport, Christian. 2007. "State Repression and Political Order." *Annual Review of Political Science* 10: 1–23.

Davenport, Christian. 2015. *How Social Movements Die: Repression and Demobilization of the Republic of New Africa.* New York: Cambridge University Press.

Davenport, Christian, Sarah A. Soule, and David Armstrong. 2011. "Protesting While Black?: The Differential Policing of American Activism, 1960 to 1990." *American Sociological Review* 76(1) (February): 152–178.

Deming, Barbara. 1971. *Revolution and Equilibrium.* Chicago: Grossman.

DeNardo, James. 1985. *Power in Numbers: The Political Strategy of Protest and Rebellion.* Princeton, NJ: Princeton University Press.

Desai, Ashwin, and Goolam Vahed. 2015. *The South African Gandhi: Stretcher-Bearer of Empire.* Palo Alto, CA: Stanford University Press.

Dobson, William J. 2012. *The Dictator's Learning Curve: Inside the Global Battle for Democracy.* New York: Doubleday.

Dorff, Cassy. 2015. "Civilian Survival in Armed Conflict: Perceptions on the Efficacy of Nonviolent and Violent Strategies, Evidence from Mexico." Unpublished manuscript, University of Denver.

Dudouet, Véronique. 2013. "Dynamics and Factors of Transition from Armed Struggle to Nonviolent Resistance." *Journal of Peace Research* 50(3) (May): 401–413.

Edelman, Marek [obituary]. 2009, October 4. *The Telegraph*, https://www.telegraph.co.uk/news/obituaries/politics-obituaries/6259900/Marek-Edelman.html.

Edwards, Pearce, and Daniel Arnon. 2019, December 12. "Violence on Many Sides: Framing Effects on Protest and Support for Repression." *British Journal of Political Science*: 1–19.

Enos, Ryan, Aaron Kaufman, and Melissa Sands. 2019. "Can Violent Protest Change Local Policy Support? Evidence from the Aftermath of the 1992 Los Angeles Riot." *American Political Science Review* 113(4): 1012–1028.

Fanon, Frantz. 1961. *The Wretched of the Earth*. New York: Grove Press.

Fazal, Tanisha M. 2018. "Go Your Own Way: Why Rising Separatism May Lead to More Conflict." *Foreign Affairs* (July/August): 113–123.

Filkins, Dexter. 2020, May 25. "Twilight of the Iranian Revolution." *New Yorker*.

Finkel, Yevgeny. 2015. "The Phoenix Effect of State Repression: Jewish Resistance during the Holocaust." *American Political Science Review* 109(2): 339–353.

Fisher, Mark. 2009. *Capitalist Realism: Is There No Alternative?* London: Zero.

Foot, M. R. D. 2016. *Resistance: European Resistance to the Nazis, 1940–1945*. London: Biteback Publishing.

Francisco, Ronald. 2004. "After the Massacre: Mobilization in the Wake of Harsh Repression." *Mobilization: An International Journal* 9(2) (June): 107–126.

Frantz, Erica, and Andrea Kendall-Taylor. 2014. "A Dictator's Toolkit: Understanding How Co-optation Affects Repression in Autocracies." *Journal of Peace Research* 51(3) (May): 332–346.

Freeman, Jo. 1970. "The Tyranny of Structurelessness," https://www.jofreeman.com/joreen/tyranny.htm, last accessed November 21, 2020.

Gallo-Cruz, Selina. 2012. "Organizing Global Nonviolence: The Growth and Spread of Nonviolent INGOs, 1948–2003." *Research in Social Movements, Conflicts, and Change* 34: 213–256.

Gallo-Cruz, Selina. 2019. "Nonviolence beyond the State: International NGOs and Local Nonviolent Mobilization." *International Sociology* 34(6): 655–674.

Gamson, William A. 1990. *The Strategy of Social Protest*. 2nd edition. Belmont, CA: Wadsworth.

Gertsmann, Evan. 2020, April 12. "How the COVID-19 Crisis Is Threatening Freedom and Democracy across the Globe," *Forbes.com*.

Gillion, Daniel. 2013. *The Political Power of Protest: Minority Activism and Shifts in Public Policy*. New York: Cambridge University Press.

Gillion, Daniel. 2020. *The Loud Minority: Why Protests Matter in American Democracy*. Princeton, NJ: Princeton University Press.

Gladwell, Malcolm, and Clay Shirky. 2011. "From Innovation to Revolution: Do Social Media Make Protests Possible?" *Foreign Affairs* 90(2): 153–154.

Gleditsch, Kristian S., and Mauricio Rivera. 2017. "The Diffusion of Nonviolent Campaigns." *Journal of Conflict Resolution* 61(5): 1120–1145.

Global Nonviolent Action Database. Retrieved November 21, 2020, https://nvdatabase.swarthmore.edu/.

Gohdes, Anita. 2020. "Repression Technology: Internet Accessibility and State Violence." *American Journal of Political Science* (2020): 1–16.

Graeber, David. 2012, February 9. "Concerning the Violent Peace-Police: An Open Letter to Chris Hedges." *n+1 Magazine Online*, http://nplusonemag.com/concerning-the-violent-peace-police.

Grewal, Sharan. 2019. "Military Defection during Localized Protests: The Case of Tataouine." *International Studies Quarterly* 63(2): 259–269.

Grossman, Dave. 1995. *On Killing: The Psychological Cost of Learning to Kill in War and Society*. Boston: Little, Brown.

Guha, Ramachandra. 2018. *Gandhi: The Years That Changed the World, 1914–1948*. New York: Alfred A. Knopf.

Guntisky, Seva. 2015. "Corrupting the Cyber-Commons: Social Media as a Tool of Autocratic Stability." *Perspectives on Politics* 13(1) (March): 42–54.

Haines, Herbert. 1984. "Black Radicalization and the Funding of Civil Rights: 1957–1970." *Social Problems* 32(1) (October): 31–43.

Haines, Herbert. 1988. *Black Radicals and the Civil rights Mainstream*. Knoxville: University of Tennessee Press.

Hamann, Kerstin, Alison Johnston, and John Kelly. 2004. "Striking Concessions from Governments: Explaining the Success of General Strikes in Western Europe, 1980–2009." *Comparative Politics* 46(1): 23–41.

Hassanpour, Navid. 2014. "Media Disruption and Revolutionary Unrest: Evidence from Mubarak's Quasi-Experiment." *Political Communication* 31(1) (January): 1–24.

Havel, Václav. 1986. *Václav Havel, or, Living in Truth: Twenty-Two Essays Published on the Occasion of the Award of the Erasmus Prize to Václav Havel*, ed. Jan Vladislav. London: Faber & Faber.

Hellmeier, Sebastian, and Nils B. Weidmann. 2019. "Pulling the Strings? The Strategic Use of Pro-Government Mobilization in Authoritarian Settings." *Comparative Political Studies* 53(1): 71–108.

Helvey, Robert. 2004. *On Strategic Nonviolent Conflict: Thinking about Fundamentals*. Boston: Albert Einstein Institute.

Herszenhorn, David M. 2014, April 13. "Xenophobic Chill Descends on Moscow." *New York Times*.

Herzog, Rudolph. 2011. *Dead Funny: Humor in Hitler's Germany*. New York: Melville House.

Hess, David, and Brian Martin. 2006. "Repression, Backfire, and the Theory of Transformative Events." *Mobilization: An International Journal* 11(2) (June): 249–267.

Heydemann, Steven. 2007. "Upgrading Authoritarianism in the Arab World." Saban Center Analysis Paper Series 13, *Brookings Institution*. October.

Howard, Philip N. 2010. *The Digital Origins of Dictatorship and Democracy: Information Technology and Political Islam*. Oxford: Oxford University Press.

Hoyte, Harry. 2016, June 30. "Ella Baker and the Politics of Hope—Lessons from the Civil Rights Movement." *Huffington Post*, https://www.huffpost.com/entry/ella-baker-and-the-politi_b_7702936.

Hsiao, Andrew, and Audrea Lim, eds. 2016. *The Verso Book of Dissent: Revolutionary Words from Three Millennia of Rebellion and Resistance*. London: Verso.

Huet-Vaughn, Emiliano. 2017. Quiet Riot: The Causal Effect of Protest Violence. Unpublished manuscript, UCLA, https://papers.ssrn.com/sol3/papers.cfm?abstract_id=2331520.

Iqbal, Khuram. 2015. *The Making of Pakistani Human Bombs*. Lanham, MD: Lexington Books.

Interfax. 2007, February 19. "Putin against using human rights as instrument of political influence."

International Center on Nonviolent Conflict. 2005. *Bringing Down a Dictator*, https://www.nonviolent-conflict.org/bringing-dictator-english/.

Isaac, Larry W., Steve McDonald, and Greg Lukasik. 2006. "Takin' It from the Streets: How the Sixties Breathed Life into the Labor Movement." *American Journal of Sociology* 112(1) (July): 46–96.

Jamal, Amal. 2005. *The Palestinian National Movement: Politics of Contention, 1967–2005*. Bloomington: Indiana University Press.

Johnson, Bryan. 1987. *The Four Days of Courage: The Untold Story of the People Who Brought Marcos Down*. New York: Free Press.

Johnson, Jaclyn, and Clayton L. Thyne. 2018. "Squeaky Wheels and Troop Loyalty: How Domestic Protests Influence Coups d'État, 1951–2005." *Journal of Conflict Resolution* 62(3) (March): 597–625.

Johnstad, Petter Grahl. 2012. "When the Time Is Right: Regime Legitimacy as a Predictor of Nonviolent Protest Outcome." *Peace & Change* 37(4) (October): 516–543.

Kadivar, Mohammad Ali, and Neil Ketchley. 2018. "Sticks, Stones, and Molotov Cocktails: Unarmed Collective Violence and Democratization." *Socius* 4 (May 31).

Kaplan, Oliver. 2013a. "Nudging Armed Groups: How Civilians Transmit Norms of Protection." *Stability: International Journal of Security and Development* 2(3) (December): 62.

Kaplan, Oliver. 2013b. "Protecting Civilians in War: The Institution of the ATCC in Colombia." *Journal of Peace Research* 50(3) (May): 351–367.

Kaplan, Oliver. 2017. *Resisting War: How Communities Protect Themselves*. Cambridge and New York: Cambridge University Press.

Kauffman, L.A. 2017. *Direct Action: Protest and the Reinvention of American Radicalism*. London: Verso.

Keck, Margaret E., and Kathryn Sikkink. 1998. *Activists Beyond Borders: Advocacy Networks in International Relations*. Ithaca, NY: Cornell University Press.

Kessi, Shose, Zoe Marks, and Elelwani Ramugondo. 2020. "Decolonizing African Studies." *Critical African Studies* 12(3) (October): 271–282.

Khawaja, Marwan. 1993. "Repression and Popular Collective Action: Evidence from the West Bank." *Sociological Forum* 8(1): 47–71.

Kishtainy, Khalid. 2010. "Humor and Resistance in the Arab World and Greater Middle East." In Maria J. Stephan, ed., *Civilian Jihad: Nonviolent Struggle, Democratization, and Governance in the Middle East*, 53–64. New York: Palgrave Macmillan.

King, Mary E. 2007. *A Quiet Revolution: The First Palestinian Intifada and Nonviolent Resistance*. New York: Nation Books.

King, Mary. 2011. "The Power of Song, from Selma to Syria." Waging Nonviolence, July 23, https://wagingnonviolence.org/2011/07/the-power-of-song-from-selma-to-syria/.

King, Mary Elizabeth. 2013. " 'A Single Garment of Destiny': Martin Luther King Jr and Our World." Remarks at the Martin Luther King, Jr., Foundation, The Hague, Netherlands. May 24.

King, Mary. 2015. *Gandhian Nonviolent Struggle and Untouchability in South India: The 1924–25 Vykom Satyagraha and Mechanisms of Change*. New Delhi: Oxford University Press.

The King Center. n.d. "The King Philosophy," accessed November 2, 2020, from https://thekingcenter.org/king-philosophy/.

Kinsman, Jeremy, and Kurt Bassuener, eds. 2016. *A Diplomat's Handbook for Democracy Development Support*. Montreal, Quebec: McGill-Queen's University Press.

Klein, Graig R., and Patrick Regan. 2018. "Dynamics of Political Protests." *International Organization* 72(2): 485–521.

Klein, Naomi. 1998, July 23. "Computer Hacking New Tool of Political Activism." *Toronto Star*.

Koren, Ore. 2014. "Military Structure, Civil Disobedience, and Military Violence." *Terrorism and Political Violence* 26(4): 688–712.

Kuran, Timur. 1989. "Sparks and Prairie Fires: A Theory of Unanticipated Political Revolution." *Public Choice* 61(1) (April): 41–74.

Kuran, Timur. 1991. "Now Out of Never: The Element of Surprise in the East European Revolution of 1989." *World Politics* 44(1) (October 1): 7–48.

Kurlansky, Mark. 2006. *Nonviolence: Twenty-Five Lessons from the History of a Dangerous Idea*. New York: Modern Library.

Kurtz, Lester, and Lee Smithey. 2018. *The Paradox of Repression and Nonviolent Movements*. Syracuse, NY: Syracuse University Press.

Kurzman, Charles. 1996. "Structural Opportunity and Perceived Opportunity in Social-Movement Theory: The Iranian Revolution of 1979." *American Sociological Review* 61(1) (February): 153–170.

Kurzman, Charles. 2004. *The Unthinkable Revolution in Iran*. Cambridge, MA: Harvard University Press.

Kydd, Andrew, and Barbara Walter. 2006. "The Strategies of Terrorism." *International Security* 31(1): 49–80.

Lakey, George. 2018. *How We Win: A Guide to Nonviolent Direct Action Campaigning*. Brooklyn, NY: Melville House.

Lee, Terence. 2009. "The Armed Forces and Transitions from Authoritarian Rule: Explaining the Role of the Military in 1986 Philippines and 1998 Indonesia." *Comparative Political Studies* 42(5) (May): 640–669.

Lichbach, Mark Irving. 1994a. *The Rebel's Dilemma*. Ann Arbor: University of Michigan Press.

Lichbach, Mark. 1994b. "Rethinking Rationality and Rebellion: Theories of Collective Action and Problems of Collective Dissent." *Rationality and Society* 6(1) (January): 8–39.

Liddell Hart, Basil Henry. 1954. *Strategy: The Indirect Approach*. London: Faber and Faber.

Liddell Hart, Basil Henry. 1968. "The Second World War." *The New Cambridge Modern History*. Cambridge: Cambridge University Press.

L'Obs with AFP. 2019, March 8. "Les '18 commandements' du manifestant en Algérie," https://www.nouvelobs.com/monde/20190308.OBS1418/les-18-commandements-du-manifestant-en-algerie.html.

Long, Michael G. 2019. *We the Resistance: Documenting a History of Nonviolent Protest in the United States*. San Francisco: City Lights.

Looney, J. Jefferson, ed. 2012. *The Papers of Thomas Jefferson, Retirement Series, vol. 9, September 1815 to April 1816*. Princeton: Princeton University Press.

Lupu, Yonatan, and Geoffrey P. R. Wallace. 2019. "Violence, Nonviolence, and the Effects of International Human Rights Law." *American Journal of Political Science* 63(2) (April): 411–426.

Macleod, Jason. 2015. "Building Resilience to Repression in Nonviolent Resistance Struggles." *Journal of Resistance Studies* 1(1): 77–118.

Madrigal, Alexis. 2011. "Egyptian Activists' Action Plan: Translated." *The Atlantic*. January, https://www.theatlantic.com/international/archive/2011/01/egyptian-activists-action-plan-translated/70388/.

Makara, Michael. 2013. "Coup-Proofing, Military Defection, and the Arab Spring." *Democracy and Security* 9(4) (September): 334–359.

Marantz, Andrew. 2020, November 23. "The Anti-Coup." *The New Yorker*.

Marks, Zoe, and Erica Chenoweth. 2019. "Empowerment or Backlash? How Women's Participation in Mass Uprisings Provides a Rising Tide." Presentation at Global International Studies Association Meeting, University of Ghana, August 1–3.

Marks, Zoe, Jide Okeke, and Erica Chenoweth. 2019, April 25. "People Power Is Rising in Africa," *Foreign Affairs*, https://www.foreignaffairs.com/articles/africa/2019-04-25/people-power-rising-africa.

Martin, Brian. 2007. *Justice Ignited: The Dynamics of Backfire*. Lanham, MD: Rowman & Littlefield.

Martin, Brian. 2015. "From Political Jiu-Jitsu to the Backfire Dynamic: How Repression Can Promote Mobilization." In Kurt Schock, ed., *Civil Resistance: Comparative Perspectives on Nonviolent Struggle*, 145–167. Minneapolis and London: University of Minnesota Press.

Martin, Brian, Wendy Varney, and Adrian Vickers. 2001. "Political Jiu-Jitsu against Indonesian Repression: Studying Lower-Profile Nonviolent Resistance." *Pacifica Review: Peace, Security & Global Change* 13(2) (June): 143–156.

Marwell, Gerald, and Pamela Oliver. 1993. *The Critical Mass in Collective Action: A Micro-Social Theory*. Cambridge: Cambridge University Press.

Marx, Gary. 2012. "Agents Provocateurs as a Type of Faux Activist." In D. Snow, D. Della Porta, B. Klandermans, and D. McAdam, eds., *Encyclopedia of Social and Political Movements*. London: Blackwell.

Mazumder, Soumyajit. 2018. "The Persistent Effect of U.S. Civil Rights Protests on Political Attitudes." *American Journal of Political Science* 62(4): 922–935.

McAdam, Doug. 1996a. "The Framing Function of Movement Tactics: Strategic Dramaturgy in the American Civil Rights Movement." In Doug McAdam, John D. McCarthy, and Mayer N. Zald, eds., *Comparative Perspectives on Social Movements: Political Opportunities, Mobilizing Structures, and Cultural Framings*, 338–354. New York: Cambridge University Press.

McAdam, Doug. 1996b. "Political Opportunities: Conceptual Origins, Current Problems, Future Directions." In Doug McAdam, John D. McCarthy, and Mayer N. Zald, eds., *Comparative Perspectives on Social Movements: Political Opportunities, Mobilizing Structures, and Cultural Framings*, 23–40. New York: Cambridge University Press.

McAdam, Doug. 1999. *Political Process and the Development of Black Insurgency, 1930–1970*. Second ed. Chicago: University of Chicago Press.

McAdam, Doug, Sidney Tarrow, and Charles Tilly. 2001. *Dynamics of Contention*. New York: Cambridge University Press.

McCammon, Holly J., Erin M. Bergner, and Sandra C. Arch. 2015. "Are You One of Those Women? Within-Movement Conflict, Radical Flank Effects, and Social Movement Political Outcomes." *Mobilization* 20(2) (June): 157–178.

Meier, Patrick. 2011, February 10. "How to Use Facebook If You Are a Repressive Regime." *iRevolutions* blog, https://irevolutions.org/2011/02/10/facebook-for-repressive-regimes/.

Mitts, Tamar, and Devorah Manekin. 2019. "Ethnicity, Identity, and the Efficacy of Nonviolent Resistance." Paper presented at the American Political Science Association Annual Meeting, Washington, DC, August 29–September 1.

Morozov, Evgeny. 2010. *The Net Delusion: The Dark Side of Internet Freedom.* New York: PublicAffairs.

Muñoz, Jordi, and Eva Anduiza. 2019. " 'If a Fight Starts, Watch the Crowd': The Effect of Violence on Popular Support for Social Movements." *Journal of Peace Research* 56(4) (July): 485–498.

Murdie, Amanda, and Tavishi Bhaisin. 2011. "Aiding and Abetting: Human Rights INGOs and Domestic Protest." *Journal of Conflict Resolution* 55(2) (April): 163–191.

Nagler, Michael. 2014. *The Nonviolence Handbook: A Guide for Practical Action.* San Francisco: Berrett-Koehler Publishers.

Nagler, Michael. 2019. "Commonly Posed Objections." Metta Center for Nonviolence. Accessed November 2, 2020, https://mettacenter.org/nonviolence/commonly-posed-objections/.

Nepstad, Sharon Erickson. 2011. *Nonviolent Revolutions: Civil Resistance in the Late 20th Century.* New York: Oxford University Press.

Nepstad, Sharon Erickson. 2015. *Nonviolent Struggle: Theories, Strategies, and Dynamics.* New York: Oxford University Press.

Newman, Lily Hay. 2019, May 2. "Hacktivists Are on the Rise—but Less Effective Than Ever." Wired, https://www.wired.com/story/hacktivism-sudan-ddos-protest/.

Orazani, Seyed Nima, and Bernhard Leidner. 2019. "The Power of Nonviolence: Confirming and Explaining the Success of Nonviolent (Rather Than Violent) Political Movements." *European Journal of Social Psychology* 49(4) (June): 688–704.

Parham, Jason. 2017, October 18. "Russians Posing as Black Activists on Facebook Is More Than Fake News." Wired, https://www.wired.com/story/russian-black-activist-facebook-accounts/.

Pearlman, Wendy. 2011. *Violence, Nonviolence, and the Palestinian National Movement.* Cambridge: Cambridge University Press.

Pearlman, Wendy. 2013. "Emotions and the Microfoundations of the Arab Uprisings." *Perspectives on Politics* 11(2) (June): 387–409.

Perkoski, Evan, and Erica Chenoweth. 2018. *Nonviolent Resistance and Prevention of Mass Killings during Popular Uprisings.* Washington, DC: International Center on Nonviolent Conflict.

Piercy, Marge. 1980. *The Moon Is Always Female.* New York: Knopf.

Pinckney, Jonathan. 2016. *Making or Breaking Nonviolent Discipline in Civil Resistance Movements.* Washington, DC: International Center on Nonviolent Conflict.

Pinckney, Jonathan. 2018. *When Civil Resistance Succeeds: Building Democracy after Popular Nonviolent Uprisings.* Washington, DC: International Center on Nonviolent Conflict.

Pinckney, Jonathan. 2020. *From Dissent to Democracy: The Promise and Perils of Civil Resistance Transitions*. New York: Oxford University Press.

Pinker, Steven. 2011. *The Better Angels of Our Nature: Why Violence Has Declined*. New York: Viking.

Piot, Olivier. 2011, February 4-5. "Tunisia: Diary of a Revolution," trans. Krystyna Horko, *Le Monde Diplomatique*, https://mondediplo.com/2011/02/04tunisia.

Piven, Frances Fox, and Richard A. Cloward. 1977. *Poor People's Movements: Why They Succeed, How They Fail*. New York: Pantheon Books.

Potter, Garry. 2015. "Anonymous: A Political Ontology of Hope." *Theory in Action* 8(1) (January): 1–22.

Presbey, Gail. 2013. "Zambia: Nonviolent Strategies against Colonialism, 1900s–1960s." In Maciej Bartkowski, ed., *Recovering Nonviolent History: Civil Resistance in Liberation Struggles*, 51–70. Boulder, CO: Lynne Rienner Publishers.

Pressman, Jeremy. 2017. "Throwing Stones in Social Science: Non-Violence, Unarmed Violence, and the First Intifada." *Cooperation and Conflict* 52(4): 519–536.

Principe, Marie. 2017. "Women in Nonviolent Movements." United States Institute of Peace Special Report, no. 399. Washington, DC.

Rasler, Karen. 1996. "Concessions, Repression, and Political Protest in the Iranian Revolution." *American Sociological Review* 61(1) (February): 132–152.

Reck-Malleczewen, Friederich. 2000. *Diary of a Man in Despair: A Non-Fiction Masterpiece about the Comprehension of Evil*, trans. Paul Rubens. London: Duckworth Books.

Repucci, Sarah. 2020. *A Leaderless Struggle for Democracy: 2020 Freedom in the World Report*. Washington, DC: Freedom House.

Richardson, Louise. 2006. *What Terrorists Want: Understanding the Enemy, Containing the Threat*. New York: Random House.

Rigby, Andrew. 1991. *Living the Intifada*. London and New Jersey: Zed Books.

Ritter, Daniel. 2015. *The Iron Cage of Liberalism*. New York: Oxford University Press.

Ritter, Emily H., and Courtenay R. Conrad. 2016. "Preventing and Responding to Dissent: The Observational Challenges of Explaining Strategic Repression." *American Political Science Review* 110(1): 85–99.

Rivera Celestino, Mauricio, and Kristian Skrede Gleditsch. 2013. "Fresh Carnations or All Thorn, No Rose? Nonviolent Campaigns and Transitions in Autocracies." *Journal of Peace Research* 50(3): 385–400.

Roberts, Adam, ed. 1969. *Civilian Resistance as a National Defence: Non-Violent Action against Aggression*. New York: Penguin Books.

Roberts, Adam. 2015. "Civil Resistance and the Fate of the Arab Spring." In Adam Roberts, Michael J. Willis, Rory McCarthy, and Timothy Garton Ash, eds., *Civil Resistance in the Arab Spring: Triumphs and Disasters*, 270–326. Oxford: Oxford University Press.

Roberts, Adam, and Timothy Garton Ash, eds. 2009. *Civil Resistance and Power Politics: The Experience of Non-Violent Action from Gandhi to the Present*. Oxford: Oxford University Press.

Roberston, Graeme. 2011. *The Politics of Protest in Hybrid Regimes: Managing Dissent in Post-Communist Russia*. New York: Cambridge University Press.

Robinson, Geoffrey. 2009. *"If You Leave Us Here, We Will Die:" How Genocide Was Stopped in East Timor*. Princeton, NJ: Princeton University Press.

Ross, Michael. 2012. *The Oil Curse: How Petroleum Wealth Shapes the Development of Nations*. Princeton, NJ: Princeton University Press.

Rossdale, Chris. 2019. *Resisting Militarism: Direct Action and the Politics of Subversion*. Edinburgh: Edinburgh University Press.

Rothman, Lily. 2015, April 25. "What Martin Luther King Jr. Really Thought about Riots." *Time*, https://time.com/3838515/baltimore-riots-language-unheard-quote/.

Scalmer, Sean. 2011. *Gandhi in the West: The Mahatma and the Rise of Radical Protest*. Cambridge: Cambridge University Press.

Schell, Jonathan. 2003. *The Unconquerable World: Power, Nonviolence, and the Will of the People*. New York: Metropolitan Books.

Schelling, Thomas C. 1969. "Some Questions on Civilian Defence." In Adam Roberts, ed., *Civilian Resistance as a National Defence: Nonviolent Action against Aggression*, 351–52. New York: Penguin Books.

Schiff, Ze'ev, and Ehud Ya'ari. 1989. *Intifada: The Palestinian Uprising—Israel's Third Front*, ed. Ina Friedman, trans. Ina Friedman. New York: Simon and Schuster.

Schock, Kurt. 2003. "Nonviolent Action and Its Misconceptions: Insights for Social Scientists." *Political Science and Politics* 36(4) (October): 705–712.

Schock, Kurt. 2005. *Unarmed Insurrections: People Power Movements in Nondemocracies*. Minneapolis: University of Minnesota Press.

Schock, Kurt. 2015a. *Civil Resistance Today*. London: Polity Press.

Schock, Kurt, ed. 2015b. *Civil Resistance: Comparative Perspectives on Nonviolent Struggle*. Minneapolis and London: University of Minnesota Press.

Selvanathan, Hema Preya, and Brian Lickel. 2019. "Empowerment and Threat in Response to Mass Protest Shape Public Support for a Social Movement and Social Change: A Panel Study in the Context of the Bersih Movement in Malaysia." *European Journal of Social Psychology* 49(2) (March): 230–243.

Semelin, Jacques. 1993. *Unarmed against Hitler: Civilian Resistance in Europe, 1939–1943*. Westport, CT: Praeger.

Sémelin, Jacques, Claire Andrieu, and Sarah Gensburger. 2014. *Resisting Genocide: The Multiple Forms of Rescue*. Oxford: Oxford University Press.

Sharp, Gene. 1973. *The Politics of Nonviolent Action*. Vols. 1–3. Boston: Porter Sargent.

Sharp, Gene. 1990. *Civilian-Based Defense: A Post-Military Weapons System*. Princeton, NJ: Princeton University Press.

Sharp, Gene. 1999. "Nonviolent Action." In Lester Kurtz and Jennifer E. Turpin, eds., *Encyclopedia of Violence, Peace, and Conflict*, Vol. 2, 567–74. New York: Academic Press.

Sharp, Gene. 2003. *There Are Realistic Alternatives*. Boston: Albert Einstein Institution.

Sharp, Gene, ed. 2005. *Waging Nonviolent Struggle: 20th-Century Practice and 21st-Century Potential*. Boston: Porter Sargent.

Simpson, Brent, Robb Willer, and Matthew Feinberg. 2018. "Does Violent Protest Backfire? Testing a Theory of Public Reactions to Activist Violence." *Socius* 4 (October). https://journals.sagepub.com/doi/10.1177/2378023118803189.

Smithey, Lee. 2013. "Identity Formation in Nonviolent Struggles." In Maciej Bartkowski, ed., *Recovering Nonviolent History: Civil Resistance in Liberation Struggles*, 31–50. Boulder, CO: Lynne Rienner Publishers

Smithey, Lee, and Lester R. Kurtz. 2018. "'Smart' Repression," in Lester R. Kurtz and Lee Smithey, eds. *The Paradox of Repression and Nonviolent Movements*. 185–214. Syracuse: Syracuse University Press.

Sombatpoonsiri, Janjira. 2015. *Humor and Nonviolent Struggle in Serbia*. Syracuse, NY: Syracuse University Press.

Snowden, Frank. 2019. *Epidemics and Society: From the Black Death to the Present*. New Haven, CT: Yale University Press.

Spector, Regine. 2006. "The Anti-Revolutionary Toolkit." *Central Asia-Caucasus Institute Analyst*, December 13.

Spector, Regine, and Andrej Krickovic. 2008. "Authoritarianism 2.0: "Non-Democratic Regimes Are Upgrading and Integrating Globally." Paper presented at the 49th Annual International Studies Association Conference, San Francisco, CA, March 26.

Steinert-Threlkeld, Zachary, Jungseock Joo, and Alexander Chan. 2019. "How Violence Affects Protests." APSA Preprints, doi: 10.33774/apsa-2019-bv6zd.

Stephan, Maria J. 2005. "Nonviolent Insurgency: The Role of Civilian-Based Resistance in the East Timorese, Palestinian, and Kosovo Albanian Self-Determination Movements." Ph.D. dissertation, Tufts University.

Stephan, Maria J. 2006. "Fighting for Statehood: The Role of Civilian-Based Resistance in the East Timorese, Palestinian, and Kosovo Albanian Self-Determination Struggles." *Fletcher Forum on World Affairs* 30(2) (Summer): 57–80.

Stephan, Maria J., ed. 2010. *Civilian Jihad: Nonviolent Struggle, Democratization, and Governance in the Middle East*. New York: Palgrave Macmillan.

Stephan, Maria. 2016. "Civil Resistance vs. ISIS." *Journal of Resistance Studies* 1(2): 127–150.

Stephan, Maria J., and Erica Chenoweth. 2008. "Why Civil Resistance Works: The Strategic Logic of Nonviolent Conflict." *International Security* 33(1) (Summer): 7–44.

Stephan, Maria J., and Adam Gallagher. 2019, December 13. "Five Myths about Protest Movements." *Washington Post*, https://www.washingtonpost.com/outlook/five-myths/five-myths-about-protest-movements/2019/12/12/700a8afc-1d1d-11ea-87f7-f2e91143c60d_story.html.

Stephan, Maria J., and Jacob Mundy. 2006. "A Battlefield Transformed: From Guerilla Resistance to Mass Nonviolent Struggle in the Western Sahara." *Journal of Military and Strategic Studies* 8(3) (April) https://jmss.org/article/view/57717.

Stockman, Sarah. 2017, February 2. "Anarchists Respond to Trump's Inauguration, By Any Means Necessary." *New York Times*, https://www.nytimes.com/2017/02/02/us/anarchists-respond-to-trumps-inauguration-by-any-means-necessary.html.

Stoddard, Judith. 2013. "How Do Major, Violent and Nonviolent Opposition Campaigns Impact Predicted Life Expectancy at Birth?" *Stability: International Journal of Security and Development* 2(2) (August). https://www.stabilityjournal.org/articles/10.5334/sta.bx/.

Stoltzfus, Nathan. 1996. *Resistance of the Heart: Intermarriage and the Rosenstrasse Protest in Nazi Germany*. New York: W. W. Norton & Co.

Suhru, Tridip. 2019, September 25. " 'You Are Today the One Person in the World Who Can Prevent a War.' Read Gandhi's Letters to Hitler." *Time*. September. https://time.com/5685122/gandhi-hitler-letter/.

Sullivan, Christopher. 2016. "Undermining Resistance: Mobilization, Repression, and the Enforcement of Political Order." *Journal of Conflict Resolution* 60(7) (October): 1163–1190.

Summy, Ralph. 1994. "Nonviolence and the Case of the Extremely Ruthless Opponent." *Pacifica Review: Peace, Security & Global Change* 6(1) (May): 1–29.

Sutton, Jonathan, Charles Butcher, and Isak Svensson. 2014. "Explaining Political Jiu-Jitsu: Institution-Building and the Outcomes of Regime Violence against Unarmed Protests." *Journal of Peace Research* 51(5) (September): 559–573.

Svensson, Isak, Jonathan Hall, Dino Krause, and Eric Skoog. 2019, March 22. "How Ordinary Iraqis Resisted the Islamic State." *Washington Post*, https://www.washingtonpost.com/politics/2019/03/22/civil-resistance-against-islamic-state-was-much-more-common-than-many-think.

Svennson, Isak, and Mathilda Lindgren. 2010. "Community and Consent: Unarmed Insurrections in Nondemocracies." *European Journal of International Relations* 17(1) (March): 97–120.

Tarrow, Sidney. 1989. *Democracy and Disorder: Protest and Politics in Italy, 1965–1975*. Oxford: Clarendon.

Tarrow, Sidney. 1998. *Power in Movement*. UK: Cambridge University Press.

Taylor, Keeanga-Yamahtta. 2016. *From #BlackLivesMatter to Black Liberation*. Chicago: Haymarket Books.

Telegraph Staff. 2009, October 9. "Obituary–Marek Edelman." *The Telegraph*, https://www.telegraph.co.uk/news/obituaries/politics-obituaries/6259900/Marek-Edelman.html.

Thaler, Kai. 2019. "Violence Is Sometimes the Answer." *Foreign Policy*, December 5, https://foreignpolicy.com/2019/12/05/hong-kong-protests-chile-bolivia-egypt-force-police-violence-is-sometimes-the-answer.

Thomas, Emma, and Winnifred Louis. 2014. "When Will Collective Action Be Effective? Violent and Non-Violent Protests Differentially Influence Perceptions of Legitimacy and Efficacy Among Sympathizers." *Personality and Social Psychology Bulletin* 40(2) (February): 263–276.

Thompkins, Elizabeth. 2015. "A Quantitative Reevaluation of Radical Flank Effects within Nonviolent Campaigns." *Research in Social Movements, Conflicts, and Change* 38: 2013–2135.

Thurber, Ches. 2015. "Between Mao and Gandhi: Strategies of Violence and Nonviolence in Revolutionary Movements." Ph.D. dissertation, Fletcher School of Law and Diplomacy, Tufts University.

Thurber, Ches. 2019. "Social Ties and the Strategy of Civil Resistance." *International Studies Quarterly* 63(4): 974–986.

Tufekci, Zeynep. 2017. *Twitter and Tear Gas: The Power and Fragility of Networked Protest*. New Haven, CT: Yale University Press.

Valentino, Benjamin. 2004. *Final Solutions: Mass Killing and Genocide in the 20th Century*. Ithaca, NY, and London: Cornell University Press.

Walzer, Michael. 2001. "Excusing Terror." *American Prospect*, November 2, https://prospect.org/features/excusing-terror/.

Wantchekon, Leonard, and Omar Garcia-Ponce. 2013. "Critical Junctures: Independence Movements and Democracy in Africa." IDEAS Working Paper Series from RePEc.https://ideas.repec.org/p/cge/wacage/173.html.

Wasow, Omar. 2020. "Agenda Seeding: How 1960s Black Protests Moved Elites, Public Opinion, and Voting." *American Political Science Review* 114(3): 638–659.

Wehr, Paul, Heidi Burgess, and Guy Burgess, eds. 1994. *Justice without Violence*. Boulder, CO: Lynne Reiner Publishers.

Weidmann, Nils, and Espen Geelmuyden Rød. 2019. *The Internet and Political Protest in Autocracies*. New York: Oxford University Press.

Weyland, Kurt. 2009. "The Diffusion of Revolution: '1848' in Europe and Latin America." *International Organization* 63(3): 391–423.

Weyland, Kurt. 2014. *Making Waves: Democratic Contention in Europe and Latin America since the Revolutions of 1848*. New York: Cambridge University Press.

White, Robert. 1989. "From Peaceful Protest to Guerrilla War: Micromobilization of the Provisional Irish Republican Army." *American Journal of Sociology* 94(6) (May): 1277–1302.

Wink, Walter. 1987. *Violence and Nonviolence in South Africa*. Philadelphia: New Society Publishers.

Wittels, Stephen. 2017. "Understanding the Outcomes and Aftermaths of Nonviolent Resistance." PhD Dissertation, Massachusetts Institute of Technology.

Woodly, Deva. 2020. Remarks given during Webinar on Protests in Perspective: Civil Disobedience & Activism Today. Carnegie Council for Ethics in International Affairs, New York, New York. November 13. https://www.carnegiecouncil.org/studio/multimedia/20201116-protests-perspective-civil-disobedience-activism-erica-chenoweth-deva-woodly.

Ulfelder, Jay. 2010. *Dilemmas of Democratic Consolidation: A Game Theory Approach*. Boulder, CO: Lynne Rienner Publishers.

Zunes, Stephen. 1994. "Unarmed Insurrections against Authoritarian Governments in the Third World: A New Kind of Revolution." *Third World Quarterly* 15(3) (September): 403–426.

Zunes, Stephen. 1999a. "The Origins of People Power in the Philippines." In Stephen Zunes, Lester Kurtz, and Sarah Beth Asher, eds., *Nonviolent Social Movements: A Geographical Perspective*, 129–57. Malden, MA: Blackwell Publishing.

Zunes, Stephen. 1999b. "The Role of Nonviolence in the Downfall of Apartheid." In Stephen Zunes, Lester Kurtz, and Sarah Beth Asher, eds., *Nonviolent Social Movements: A Geographical Perspective*, 203–230. Malden, MA: Blackwell Publishing.

Zunes, Stephen. 2009a, June 20. "Iran's History of Civil Insurrections." *Huffington Post*, https://www.huffpost.com/entry/irans-history-of-civil-in_b_217998.

Zunes, Stephen. 2009b. "Weapons of Mass Democracy: Nonviolent Resistance Is the Most Powerful Tactic against Oppressive Regimes." *Yes! Magazine*, September 16, https://www.yesmagazine.org/issue/learn/opinion/2009/09/17/weapons-of-mass-democracy.

Zunes, Stephen, Lester Kurtz, and Sarah Beth Asher, eds. 1999. *Nonviolent Social Movements: A Geographical Perspective*. Cambridge, MA: Blackwell Publishers.

INDEX